A Student's Guide to Education Studies

A Student's Guide to Education Studies is a much needed resource for any undergraduate making their first explorations into the fascinating world of education. The first publication of this book in 2004 helped to define the nature of the subject, introducing topics into the field which had not been previously considered. This new edition brings the subject up to date with the latest thinking and research on policy, globalisation, learning and knowledge, offering an accessible and wide-ranging introduction to a diverse selection of topics and issues in education.

Now fully updated to reflect rapid and significant changes in the field, this third edition considers topical issues including:

- the political dimension of education,
- the national debate about schooling and poverty,
- the marketisation of education,
- the end of Every Child Matters,
- the Coalition Government's policies for academies and free schools.

Organised around three enduring themes – 'Policies and politics', 'Global and environmental education', and 'Learning, knowledge and the curriculum' – each chapter contains summary points, questions for discussion, and annotated suggestions for further reading.

With a distinctive international and global focus, *A Student's Guide to Education Studies* is an essential resource for all students of Education Studies.

Stephen Ward was, until 2012, Dean of the School of Education at Bath Spa University, UK, where he led the pioneering Education Studies programme and Teacher Education degree. His research has traced the development of Education Studies as a university degree subject and he was a founder member of the British Education Studies Association (BESA), an academic network for tutors and students.

A Student's Guide to Education Studies

Third edition

Edited by Stephen Ward

Routledge
Taylor & Francis Group

LONDON AND NEW YORK

Third edition published 2013
by Routledge
2 Park Square, Milton Park, Abingdon, Oxon OX14 4RN

Simultaneously published in the USA and Canada
by Routledge
711 Third Avenue, New York, NY 10017

Routledge is an imprint of the Taylor & Francis Group, an informa business

First edition published by Routledge 2004
Second edition published by Routledge 2008

British Library Cataloguing in Publication Data
A catalogue record for this book is available from the British Library

Library of Congress Cataloging in Publication Data
A student's guide to education studies / edited by Stephen Ward. – 3rd ed.
p. cm.
I. Ward, Stephen, 1947-
LB1025.3.E334 2012
370.71'1–dc23   2012025042

ISBN: 978-0-415-80967-2 (hbk)
ISBN: 978-0-415-80968-9 (pbk)
ISBN: 978-0-203-13489-4 (ebk)

Typeset in Bembo
by Cenveo Publisher Services, Bengaluru, INDIA

MIX
Paper from
responsible sources
FSC® C004839
www.fsc.org

Printed and bound in Great Britain by
TJ International Ltd, Padstow, Cornwall

Contents

Acknowledgements

The ideas in these chapters were developed with Education Studies students at Bath Spa University. We learned from their enthusiastic and critical responses and they were the inspiration for this book.

Illustrations

Figures

Tables

Abbreviations

The following abbreviations are used in the text:

AIDS	Acquired immune deficiency syndrome
ALSPAC	Avon Longitudinal Study of Parents and Children
ASN	Additional support needs
BCS	British Cohort Study
BIS	(Government Department for) Business, Innovation and Skills
BME	black and minority ethnic
CLA	Cultural Learning Alliance
CPAG	Child Poverty Action Group
CSO	Civil Service Organisations
CWDC	Children's Workforce Development Council
DAC	Development Assistance Committee
DCMS	Department for Culture, Media and Sport
DCSF	Department for Children, Schools and Families
DEA	Development Education Association
DES	Department of Education and Science
DfEE	Department for Education and Employment
DfES	Department for Education and Skills
DfID	Department for International Development
DIUS	Department of Innovation, Universities and Skills
DWP	Department of Work and Pensions
EBac	English Baccalaureate
ECM	Every Child Matters
EFA	Education for All
EfS	Education for sustainability
EYPS	Early years professional status
FSM	Free school meals
GM	Genetically modified
HESA	Higher Education Statistics Agency
HIV	Human immunodeficiency virus
HMG	Her Majesty's Government
HMI	Her Majesty's Inspectorate
HMSO	Her Majesty's Stationery Office
ILEA	Inner London Education Authority

IMF	International Monetary Fund
JRF	Joseph Rowntree Foundation
KS	Key Stage
LA	Local Authority
LEA	Local Education Authority
LMS	Local management of schools
MCS	Millennium Cohort Study
MDG	Millennium development goals
NGO	Non-government Organisations
NHS	National Health Service
NLS	National Literacy Strategy
NNS	National Numeracy Strategy
NPM	New Public Management
Ofsted	Office for Standards in Education
PFI	Private Finance Initiative
PNS	Primary National Survey
PRU	pupil referral unit
PSHE	Personal, Social and Health Education
QCA	Qualifications and Curriculum Authority
QTS	Qualified Teacher Status
REC	Religious Education Council of England and Wales
SACRE	Standing Council on Religious Education
SCAA	Schools Curriculum and Assessment Authority
SEN	special educational needs
SMSC	Spiritual, moral, social and cultural
SpLD	Specific learning difficulty
TA	Teaching Agency
TDA	Training and Development Agency for Schools
TSO	third sector organisations
TTA	Teacher Training Agency
UNESCO	United Nations Educational, Scientific and Cultural Organization
UPIAS	Union of Physically Impaired People against Segregation
USAID	United States Agency for International Development

Introduction
The study of education

Stephen Ward

Introduction

Education Studies is now a popular and exciting university subject. It is concerned with understanding how people develop and learn throughout their lives, the nature of knowledge and critical engagement with ways of knowing. It offers intellectually rigorous analysis of educational processes and their cultural, social, political and historical contexts. We live in a time of rapid change in the world, and education is about both how we make change and manage change. So Education Studies includes perspectives on international education, economic relationships, globalisation, ecological issues and human rights. It also deals with beliefs, values and principles in education and the way that they change over time.

There is always discussion about what Education Studies should include, and the first two editions of this book have contributed to the thinking and development of the subject. This third edition continues the debate with analysis of the ways education has moved on in recent years. This introduction explains how the subject has developed and gives a taste of some of its topics through a summary of the chapters.

The growth of education studies

Education Studies has now become a fully fledged university subject in its own right. It began during the 1960s and 1970s as the theory for teacher training when teaching became an all-graduate profession and Bachelor of Education (BEd) degrees were introduced. The universities awarding BEd degrees were suspicious that teacher training was simply 'tips for teachers' and so degree courses were to be made more theoretical and 'academic'. Psychology, sociology, philosophy and the history of education were introduced as the theory for professional practice. Crook (2002) gives an interesting account of how educational theory came into being.

Education theory in this form had an unhappy start: students often found their studies of psychology, sociology and philosophy *too* theoretical and unrelated to their practice in school. Similarly, practising teachers distrusted their training, saying, 'you only learn to teach when you get into school'. Simon (1994) explains that these problems occurred because the academic theory in BEd degrees failed to relate theory to students' and teachers' practice. The result was the progressive discrediting of theory in teacher training.

This led to government intervention in teacher training and the formation in 1966 of the Teacher Training Agency (TTA), later the Training and Development Agency (TDA) and now the Teaching Agency (TA). The government took control of teacher training away from universities to make it practical and less theoretical. Universities were made to comply with a set of requirements and national 'standards' (TTA, 1998; TDA, 2007) and courses were rigorously inspected by Ofsted.

The 'de-theorising' of teacher training left many university staff dissatisfied with the courses they were teaching and there were moves to create non-teacher training Education Studies, free from the control of the government agency and from Ofsted inspection. At the same time there was increasing interest from students in studying education as an academic subject at university, but not as teacher training. Education Studies has become a subject of interest to a whole range of students with different career intentions. Some intend to be teachers, going on to take a PGCE course. It gives them a critical analysis of the policy and practice going on in schools which they are not likely to get in their teacher training course. Other graduates work in the new posts in schools and children's centres as teaching assistants, family link workers or advisers. Some work in education and training in art galleries and libraries and in commercial industry. Finally, Education Studies can simply be a subject of study for those who are interested in education as a feature of human activity and experience.

The new education studies

The Universities of York and Lancaster had Education Studies courses from the 1960s. However, for most universities it is in recent years that the academic community has created the 'new Education Studies'. The present author (Ward, 2006, 2008) researched the way the subject has been formed by interviewing course leaders in universities and found a wide range of content and origins. Some had based the subject on teacher training, with practical work in the school curriculum. But usually course leaders had been determined to make the subject distinctly different from teacher training and found new areas of study which defined Education Studies as a subject in its own right.

As noted on page xi, first attempts at theory in the old teacher training courses had been to import the 'foundation' disciplines of psychology, sociology, philosophy and history and to apply these to education. So Education Studies might simply be modules called 'Psychology' or 'Sociology of Education'. But the course leaders said that they wanted to see a subject with its own distinctive identity, rather than being a collection of the old disciplines. They also wanted to open up the political analysis of education as well as ecological and global perspectives, not possible within the constraints of regulated courses. They all said that Education Studies should provide a critical analysis of policy and practice in education.

Most courses have been drawn up by a group of academics in a university deciding what they consider to be important content for the subject. It is interesting that there was relatively little interaction between the academics in different institutions, and most courses have been derived from the particular knowledge and interests of the staff involved. The academic network for tutors and students in Education Studies is the British Education Studies Association (BESA) www.educationstudies.org.uk. There is an e-journal and an annual conference that share academic practice and research in Education Studies.

Critical analysis in education studies

We all know about education because we have had some kind of education or schooling and experienced discussions about education in the media and among family and friends. Discussion of education can be uninformed 'chat' about pet theories and opinions. Education Studies challenges everyday thinking and assumptions about education. It deconstructs taken-for-granted ideas and asks us to analyse what is really known and what is just belief or assumption. The theme that runs through this book is the 'critical analysis' of policy and practice in education.

This does not mean 'critical' in the sense of being negative; it is easy to grumble about the government, schools, teachers, parents and pupil behaviour. Critical analysis in a university means asking questions, such as: Why have we got the schools and the curriculum we have? What is education for? Is it about training children to become skilled workers in industry and consumers, or is it helping them to become autonomous citizens who can effect change in society and the world? A critical analysis of education is to have ideas about what alternatives there are for education in the future: to know what education *is*, but also what education *could be*, and *might be*. To answer the questions we need to look at conflicting theories about the subject. This means making an analysis of where ideas and thinking have come from and how they have been shaped by different philosophical and political viewpoints.

And this is where the disciplines come in. Asking the questions is a philosophical activity. A critical analysis of learning, teaching and schooling needs the theoretical perspectives and hard research evidence from psychology and sociology. Education systems need political theory and global economics. Education is worldwide and a critical understanding is to compare and contrast education in different countries and cultures. This requires an understanding of the world in which we live as well as global issues such as poverty, human rights and environmental sustainability. So Education Studies includes historical, economic and ecological perspectives. These are the broad theoretical perspectives used by authors in this book.

Structure of the book

The curriculum in a school or university course is a tiny selection of the vast range of topics that exist on the supermarket shelves of human knowledge. This book is written by tutors on the Education Studies programme at Bath Spa University and reflects the selection which they made in creating the subject. The topics have been chosen to give the reader a sample of current thinking. Chapters are designed to introduce the reader to the breadth of knowledge and understanding that Education Studies offers. They are starting points, and further readings give directions for study. In order to help with critical analysis, each chapter presents a set of questions which can be asked about the topic.

While the chapters in the book present the background information, research evidence and analysis, each author takes a particular line and makes an argument or a case for a position. You might find yourself agreeing or disagreeing, and that's fine: it's in the nature of education studies that we find ourselves on different sides of the argument.

There are three sections: *(1) Policies and politics; (2) Global and environmental education; (3) Knowledge, learning and the curriculum.* Each chapter draws on the different disciplines, knowledge and skills in Education Studies.

1 Policies and politics

Section 1 is about education in society, the policy, practice and political thinking behind education. Education used to be a social service determined by teachers in schools. Chapter 1 shows the ways in which governments have taken more and more control over schools and the curriculum to skill young people to compete in the global economy. It has 'marketised' education by making schools compete with each other to sell education as a 'commodity'. The chapter takes a historical approach to explaining education policy and some of the economic theories that have influenced politicians. Recently education has become part of the government's overall social policy for health and welfare with the Every Child Matters agenda. Chapter 2 analyses the policy and political theories about childhood, families and communities.

British politicians like to argue that education helps social mobility. Chapter 3 examines this idea and argues that what schools can achieve is limited in a society which has such high levels of economic inequality. Chapter 4 takes up the inequality issue and explains the effects of poverty on children's attainment in schools.

Chapters 4 and 5 continue the discussion of inequality through issues of race and gender in the education system. It is argued that while girls achieve well in schools, they are still denied success in the labour market, and that racism should be actively countered by schools. Cultural and religious diversity is a major issue for society and politicians and Chapter 7 examines how education responds to diversity, examining the role that religion has played in the development of the education system; it considers the controversial role of faith schools and the current political support for them. Inequality of opportunity continues in Chapter 8 which is concerned with special educational needs and social inclusion, arguing that the education system should be structured to remove barriers that prevent some children from realising their full potential.

The National Curriculum of the 1988 Education Act left pupils learning nothing about politics and society. The citizenship curriculum introduced in 2000 is discussed in Chapter 9 and questions are raised about the political assumptions that lie behind it and the role of education for democracy. It takes further the political and economic ideas in Chapter 1.

2 Global and environmental education

Education is a global phenomenon, but can vary in different contexts. It is easy to imagine that the education we know, or were brought up in, is the only one possible. A problem discussed in Section 1 is that strong government policy tends to lead to a single vision of what education is about. Section 2 is intended to make us aware of what happens in the rest of the world and to be able to hold alternative visions of education. It emphasises the crucial role of education in creating a sustainable future for the planet through environmental studies and by helping children to understand their democratic role as citizens of the future.

Chapter 10 introduces the idea of globalisation in education and the trend across the world to use formal schooling to service the 'knowledge economy'. It warns that international achievement tests are frequently used to justify government policy and beliefs about education and society. International differences in education mean that some children – particularly girls – are simply not educated. Chapter 11 looks at education in the so-called 'developing countries', drawing attention to the effects of global poverty. There are attempts to redress this with the United Nations Education for All by 2015 campaign, but education in some African countries still follows the old colonial pattern of nineteenth-century British or French curriculum and teaching methods.

Another aspect of global education is the divergence between education in different countries and cultures. Europe, while geographically a small area of the world, has a long cultural history of conflicts and differences between its member states. Chapter 12 examines the contrasts between the educational systems of European countries and attempts to forge convergence in the European Union.

The idea of the knowledge economy is taken up in Chapter 13, which shows the way the language about government policy on the information technology curriculum has been used to convey government assumptions about society and capitalism. This is an example of the way in which Education Studies deconstructs assumptions and ideas that are taken for granted.

Education must be about the future. Chapters 14 and 15 together explore the implications of education for a sustainable future for the planet. They examine the ways in which schools can educate children to be aware of their role as citizens in the future and what they can do to affect change, not just be passive recipients of change.

3 Learning, knowledge and the curriculum

There are many books for teachers about how to teach the curriculum. Education Studies deals not with 'how to teach', but with 'epistemology': what knowledge *is*, arguments about what counts as knowledge and how the curriculum is selected for children and students to learn. There is a long history of debate about how people learn and the third section of the book explores the nature of knowledge and learning.

Chapter 16 argues that knowledge is not simply inert 'stuff' that we load into children's heads, but is controversial and contested. Using science as an example, it looks at debates about the curriculum and what should be taught in schools. These political arguments surfaced at the time of the development of the National Curriculum and it is shown that we should not take for granted what is in the school curriculum.

Just as knowledge itself is contested, so is the way it is learned and taught. The next chapters explore the latest thinking about the nature of learning. Chapter 17 looks at the distinctive qualities of learning in young children and some of the theories that help us to understand the nature of early learning and the importance of play. Knowledge is not just about facts and ideas: it is about feelings and emotions – the 'affective' nature of learning. Chapter 18 argues for 'affective teaching' and 'emotion coaching' which help children to regulate their emotions for learning.

The study of learning has been an essentially psychological discipline, but Chapter 19 goes beyond the psychological to show the importance of cultural contexts in learning and how the individual can take control of his or her learning in different situations. One of the intriguing things about Education Studies is that we *learn* about *learning*, and the chapter gives us ways in an Education Studies degree to reflect on and analyse our own learning.

Chapter 20 challenges the traditional school curriculum as too narrow, with an overemphasis on language and mathematics. It shows how arts education incorporates strategies to address wider holistic educational agendas in relation to the needs of contemporary society and argues for different ways of thinking about learning and knowledge.

All the authors in the book refer to research findings. The final chapter discusses the role of educational research. It argues that an understanding of the nature of research, and the ability to carry out research, is an essential part of an Education Studies curriculum. There are examples of the ways in which Education Studies students can carry out collaborative research projects with schools in order to understand children's learning and to improve their educational experiences.

Summary points

- Education Studies is a new university subject in its own right which has grown from its origins in teacher training.
- Research shows that courses have developed differently in various universities.
- The foundation disciplines of psychology, sociology, philosophy and history play an important role in the academic rigour of the subject.
- There are new global, international, economic and ecological perspectives which inform the 'New Education Studies'.
- Education Studies is about understanding the nature of education in its broadest sense and about using critical analysis to challenge taken-for-granted assumptions.

Questions for discussion

- Why did you choose Education Studies?
- What are your career plans?
- Does Education Studies have to include the foundation disciplines of psychology, sociology, philosophy and history?
- What do you think about the new perspectives: global, international, ecological and economic?

References

Crook, D. (2002) Education Studies and Teacher Education. *British Journal of Education Studies* 50(1): 55–75.

Simon, B. (1994) The Study of Education. In: *The State and Educational Change: Essays in the history of education and pedagogy.* London: Lawrence and Wishart.

Training and Development Agency (TDA) (2007) *QTS Standards and ITT Requirements.* London: TDA.

Teacher Training Agency (TTA) (1998) *Teaching: High status, high standards. Standards for the award of qualified teacher status.* London: DfEE.

Ward, S. (2006) Undergraduate Education Studies as an Emerging Subject in Higher Education: The construction and definition of university knowledge. Unpublished PhD thesis, Bath: Bath Spa University.

Ward, S. (2008) Education Studies and Teacher Education. *EducationalFutures* 1(1). Available online at http://www.educationstudies.org.uk/materials/ward2.pdf (accessed 24 May 2012).

Section 1

Policies and politics

Chapter 1

Education policy and the marketisation of education

Stephen Ward

Introduction

This chapter explains the political and economic influences on education in England. While there have been similar developments in Scotland, Wales and Northern Ireland, and across many industrial nations, it is England that has experienced the extreme effects of educational politics. Over a century, education policy has swung between benign indifference, micromanagement and free-market economics. The chapter introduces:

- trends in government policy in England since 1870;
- political theories and their effects on education policy;
- the links between education and the economy;
- the development of market forces in education.

The beginnings of education policy

We are now so used to government education policy dictating the nature of schooling and education that we tend to take it for granted. But political control varies in different countries and it has changed over time in England. In the 1830s and 1840s some schooling for factory and workhouse children was provided by church foundations (see Chapter 6), but education was mainly for the rich in independent schools. Only in 1870, later than in other countries in Europe, the Forster Education Act introduced compulsory state elementary schooling for all.

In the nineteenth century the Industrial Revolution and its colonial powers made the British economy the envy of the world. The secret of its success was what economists call 'liberal economics': no state interference in production, with employers free to charge as much as possible for their products and pay as little as they need to their workers. Providers compete with each other, become more efficient, and the economy grows. However, liberal economics creates wide differentials between rich and poor, and by 1870 after years of unfettered free markets, British society was close to breakdown. It was time for government to intervene, and the 1870 Education Act was one of a series of reforms to protect the welfare of the poor (Gray, 1998).

When a government provides education, it wants to make the service 'accountable' to ensure that the taxpayer is getting 'value for money'. The first attempt at education policy was simple: children were taught a basic curriculum of reading, writing and arithmetic and given moral and religious instruction. To ensure that children were taught the curriculum Her Majesty's Inspectors (HMI) tested them to determine the level of teachers' pay: the so-called 'payment by results scheme'.

The 'political consensus' on education

The 1902 Balfour Education Act saw the abolition of payment by results, handing control of schooling and the curriculum to the teaching profession. It was an implicit statement of faith in teachers and, for the greater part of the century, left England with no national curriculum and no structure for monitoring education. Midway through the century the 1944 Butler Education Act introduced compulsory secondary education, but again did not stipulate a curriculum, except for religious education. In setting up compulsory secondary education, a tripartite system of selective and non-selective schools was constructed: grammar schools for the 'academically able', technical schools for the 'technologically able' and secondary modern schools for those destined for a non-academic and non-technical future. The system was based upon the psychological theory that intelligence testing at age ten could sort the child population into these categories.

The two main political rivals in the UK are the Conservative and Labour parties. The *right-wing* Conservative Party has been committed to 'freedom' in the liberal economic tradition, whereas the *left-wing* Labour Party has been inclined to state intervention: publicly-funded services – schools, hospitals, social workers – to protect the welfare of all. Traditionally, the Labour Party would have higher taxation to fund welfare services, whereas the Conservative Party would charge lower taxes to leave people with personal wealth to spend on services as they wish. Conservatives have criticised Labour for intervening in people's lives.

During the twentieth century the economic theories of J.M. Keynes became dominant. Keynes argued that the state should be an employer, and that the economy would be successful in a more equal society in which the population was supported by social services, health and education. From the end of World War II this became the direction of social policy in Britain with the creation of the National Health Service, social services and free education for all. Political interest in education lay mainly in debates about types of schools, social class and access to schooling. Conservatives argued for selective grammar schools to preserve high standards for an elite, usually middle-class, group. Labour campaigned for equal access for all, regardless of social class, and from 1965 tried to introduce secondary comprehensive schools open to all pupils regardless of income or ability. However, schools were controlled by Local Education Authorities (LEAs) and some Conservative authorities chose to retain selective grammar schools. The Labour Party always wanted to get rid of independent fee-paying schools as bastions of privilege, but of course they continued.

During this long debate about access and social class, central government took little or no interest in the curriculum, in teaching or in the running of schools. The administration and monitoring of education was left to the local authorities and a small number of HMIs. The tacit agreement not to interfere with schools Lawton (1992) calls a 'political consensus' on education. Economics, again, are important in understanding this 'hands-off' approach. During the twentieth century the British economy continued to be strong, and so, for politicians, there was no need to worry about the education system: it could be left to local authorities and teachers.

Education and the global economy

The oil crisis of the 1970s brought indifference to an end. Conflict in the Middle East and the loss of Britain's colonial control led to increasing oil prices which hit production in all the European economies. At the same time, there were concerns about rising crime, lower moral standards and the breakdown of traditional moral codes. Politicians looked for the culprits and in 1976 Jim Callaghan, Labour Prime Minister, accused schools of failing to equip young people for industry: falling school standards was the cause of the nation's economic and social ills (Callaghan, 1976).

By the 1980s the effects of the global economy were being realised, with the Asian 'tiger' economies of Japan, South Korea and Taiwan producing better industrial goods more cheaply and sucking away customers from Britain. Their education systems appeared to benefit from teaching basic skills through traditional methods. Multinationals, such as the Ford Motor Company, invest in Britain by establishing manufacturing plants and providing jobs. But they threaten to go elsewhere if the workforce is not suitably skilled. Making the curriculum suited to industrial production was seen as one of the means of enabling Britain to compete and the government began to treat education as the principal means of training industry for competition in the world by becoming more vocationally oriented.

The new right: Neoliberal economics and the marketisation of education

The 1979 general election saw the Conservative Government elected under Margaret Thatcher. She criticised Keynesian economics and social policy for creating a 'nanny state' in which people cease to be independent, functioning human beings. Her plan was to reduce taxation, 'roll back the state' and allow people greater personal control over their lives. This was the so-called 'New Right' politics, derived from nineteenth-century liberalism and so known as 'neo(new)liberalism'. Its ideas are based on the social philosopher Friedrich von Hayek (1899–1992) who argued in his book *The Road to Serfdom* (1991) that the welfare state disables creative energy and that individual freedom, while appearing self-serving and greedy, actually brings public good. For education, neoliberal economics means introducing the competition which made private businesses successful. Neoliberals want a 'free market' in education: education becomes a commodity which is bought and sold; schools are the providers and parents and children the consumers, or 'customers'.

It took Thatcher into her third election win, and 12 years after Callaghan's warning speech, for neoliberal politics to arrive with the Education 'Reform' Act of 1988. The Act is well known for introducing a national curriculum and standardised testing, but it also introduced local management of schools (LMS). This took financial control away from the local authorities by delegating the spending budget to schools. Schools were to use the money as they wished: to appoint teaching staff or non-teaching assistants, purchase more computers or repair the roof. Such decisions were now to be taken by the head teacher and the governing body of the school, not by local authority officials. LMS made schools into business corporations competing for pupils. The role of school governors was strengthened to get rid of 'provider capture': education is determined by the 'customers', not the providers, the education professionals.

The principle was consumer choice, with education accountable to its 'customers'. But schools are not open with their goods on display as are shops in the high street. So the machinery of a national curriculum, testing, league tables and Ofsted inspection was to bring education into the market. It was intended to change education from a public 'good' – a service provided by professionals to everyone for the benefit of everyone – to education as a commodity that may be purchased. Sometimes referred to as 'Thatcherism' it is part of a broader political movement taking place in many parts of the world (see Chapter 10).

LMS seems contradictory. On the one hand, the government had taken central control of the curriculum and national testing, but had *de*-centralised spending and management. So while the 1988 Act appears to devolve power from government to schools, it actually increased the power of central government by disempowering the local authorities. Legislation in 1992 introduced the Office for Standards in Education (Ofsted) with powers to inspect every school in the state system every four years. The Ofsted Framework for Inspection gives the most detailed list of every possible dimension of a school's work and it can be seen as part of a general trend in society towards increased accountability and surveillance. It is difficult to convey the magnitude and complexity of the systems that were put in place for education by the legislation of the late 1980s and early 1990s. They generated prodigious amounts of consultative documents and a variety of government agencies. They also led to furious debate among professionals and politicians, particularly in setting up the content of the National Curriculum (see Chapter 16). The logic under-pinning the 1988 Act was to make education accountable to the rest of society and to put it into the marketplace with freedom of choice for consumers.

The 1988 Act brought enormous changes to education in England. While the National Curriculum was the most public element, the introduction of the marketisation of educa-tion was the major reason for the Act and these could be seen as contradictory: if the idea is for 'customers' to choose their school, they ought to be able to choose their curriculum. So why have a uniform curriculum for all? Chitty (2004) notes from his interview with one of Thatcher's advisers, Stuart Sexton, that he saw the National Curriculum as 'a quite separate and unnecessary piece of legislation serving mainly to divert attention from the free market objectives' (Chitty, 2004: 53). So why was Thatcher, a neoliberal politician who talked of 'rolling back government' introducing this welter of legislation designed to control and regulate education? Gray (1998) explains that free-market economics cannot actually happen without government intervention:

> encumbered markets are the norm in every society, whereas free markets are a product of artifice, design and political coercion. *Laissez-faire* must be centrally planned: regulated markets just happen. The free market is not, as New Right thinkers have imagined or claimed, a gift of social evolution. It is an end-product of social engineering and unyielding political will.
>
> (Gray, 1998: 17).

So there was no contradiction in the paraphernalia of education legislation in 1988 and the early 1990s. The free market needed customers to be able to choose between schools, and government controls were to create a free market. The idea of neoliberals, that free markets do everything and no government is needed, is just too simple.

New Labour and the 'modernisers'

In 1997 the Labour Party under Tony Blair won the election. This did not mean a return to Keynesian economics, because this was 'New Labour' with a strong commitment to market forces. The politics of New Labour were not identical with the Conservative New Right. Blair did not see market forces as a philosophical doctrine as did the neoliberal Conservatives, but simply as the way to make the system work through competition. The political philosophy was different, but the effect was much the same. Blair's 'modernisation' meant that commitment to equality of opportunity through comprehensive education ended with the refusal to abolish independent and grammar schools, and the plan to get rid of 'bog-standard' comprehensive schools. The 2002 Education Act encouraged diversity, with specialist schools allowed to select pupils. Blair claimed this made sense 'because it works': increasing quality and standards to create an education system which provides the educated workforce for industry in globally competitive markets. Even if this created inequalities, it was worth it.

Contradictions in 'the Conservative mind' (Lawton, 1992), where neoliberals believe in the free market with as little government as possible, did not exist for New Labour. Blair's modernising meant 'intervention' and the political will to take on big issues such as child poverty, inequality and underachievement through a mixture of legislation, funding and persuasion. New Labour proved to be an even more enthusiastic proponent of market forces and privatisation than the Conservatives. Assessment and school league tables were strengthened with the setting of targets at all levels: national government targets for literacy and numeracy, as well as targets for LEAs, for schools and for individual pupils. Performance-related pay for teachers was introduced, failing local education authorities were taken over by private companies and school building was financed by profit-making organisations in the Private Finance Initiative (PFI). The privatisation of school meals, cleaning and other services begun by the Conservatives continued. All were designed to bring capital and private enterprise into the system.

Labour took up the Conservative government's desire to prescribe teaching methods and introduced the National Literacy and Numeracy Strategies. These required primary teachers to take a one-hour daily lesson in each subject, with a high proportion of interactive class teaching: the 'three-part' lesson. It is interesting that the profession should have allowed such an invasion into professional practice, and indicates the extent to which the government was prepared to 'micromanage' education. The same appetite for direction was shown in the government demand for the use of synthetic phonics in the teaching of reading, as recommended by the Rose Report (2006).

Education for the economy and the standards agenda

Old Labour policy had been to reduce inequalities by providing high levels of resources to schools. But Labour governments in the past had not succeeded in actually producing the finances. Blair's policy was to ensure that the economy was successful by maintaining neoliberal economics. New Labour abandoned its commitment to the egalitarian comprehensive school movement. Priorities were to be 'standards' of achievement, not the 'structures' of schools. New Labour's enthusiasm for privatisation and the market produced the policy for Academies: state-funded schools owned by private individuals or organisations. Academies set their own curriculum and are free from other constraints of state schools. As with privatising the railways, the assumption is that a school run by a private enterprise will be more efficient and more effective than one run by a state body. The theory of markets is that diversity provides customer choice and so it was government policy to increase the diversity of schools. The 2005 Education Act encouraged the expansion of faith schools to add to diversification (see Chapter 7).

In ten years Blair had shifted Labour policy onto the centre ground and away from the old Labour socialist 'tax-and-spend' image. The New Labour governments enjoyed a period of economic growth with one of the most efficient economies in Europe. The years saw increases in teachers' salaries, numbers of teaching assistants, better provision for early years, improved resources, and a commitment to rebuilding all secondary schools by 2015 with the Building Schools for the Future (BSF) programme. In 2007 the new Labour Prime Minister, Gordon Brown, argued for an end to the conflict between education as a market and as a social service:

> We need both strong public services and we need a dynamic market economy to have a fair and prosperous society. Arguments about the size of the state and the funding of public services mark important dividing lines in politics, investment in public services in my view is absolutely critical ... Each, markets and government, have their place.
>
> (Brown, 2007)

Economic disaster and the Coalition

But 2008 brought world economies to the brink of disaster with the banking crisis sparked by the collapse of Lehman Brothers Bank in the United States. Stiglitz (2010) explains that bankers across the world had made unsecured loans to make short-term profits and bonuses. The culture of reckless lending meant that British banks had to be 'recapitalised' by government loans, bringing government debt in 2010 to a total of some £160bn. As British Prime Minister, Gordon Brown had led the world in the global policy to support the banks with government funding to prevent the collapse of international capitalism. However, when it came to the general election of May 2010 his global success was not enough to save the Labour Government from defeat.

The Conservative Party did not win sufficient parliamentary seats to form a government, and was forced to join the Liberal Democrats in the first Coalition Government since World War II. A principle of the coalition agreement was that the government would pay off government debt by the end of the parliament in 2015. This meant massive cuts in government spending on social services, health and education. It allowed the new government to legitimate the Conservative political ideology of reducing the role of state in society and the economy. While this was essentially a return to Thatcher's mission to 'roll back the state', the Prime Minister, David Cameron, depicted it as 'the Big Society': instead of government bureaucracy managing and funding everything, control is handed to private enterprise and voluntary bodies, and decisions are taken locally by the people whose interests are served (see Chapter 2).

In education policy, economic principles were translated into immediate action by the new Secretary of State, Michael Gove. BSF was dramatically scrapped as part of the spending reductions, and the schools promised new buildings under the scheme were disappointed. The Labour Government's academies programme had been to revitalise education for working-class pupils in failing inner-city schools. Gove's concept of academies was to free schools from the control of local authorities. The hurried Academies Bill (DfE, 2010) permitted any school, including primary schools, to apply for academy status and to be self-governed. Known as 'converted' academies, such schools had to demonstrate that they were of sufficiently high quality to gain the status, as against Labour's 'sponsored' academies, which were formerly 'failing' schools. Gove forced failing schools to become academies.

The Gove academy, free of bureaucratic control, is a contribution to Cameron's Big Society vision. Another is the 'free school', which can be set up by any interested community of parents or teachers, as with an independent school, but receiving state funding. Free schools were intended to enable the provision of schooling suitable for local clients, and where special interest groups wished to provide a particular form of education not offered in an existing school. In its attempts to improve schooling by marketising education, Sweden had set up free schools; Gove was impressed with a concept that fitted neatly into his ideology. However, the evidence from Sweden is that free schools have not raised standards and have increased inequality (Mulready-Jones, 2011). Another concern about free schools is that they allow fundamentalist religious groups to teach creationism instead of evolution in the science curriculum.

The coalition's academies programme was intended to remove local authority control from the education system. As schools move out of local authority administration to become academies, funding to the authorities diminishes and they become reduced in size. The result is not only that LA control is reduced, but that their role becomes diffuse and eventually they cease to exist. During 2012 many secondary schools were rushing to academy status, while primary schools, often sympathetic to the remains of their LAs, wondered what to do. This made a context of indecision and uncertainty, which might be seen as government policy failure. Really, though, the intended outcome of Conservative policy is a volatile and fluid situation in which a market can operate and commercial and voluntary organisations can thrive. A recent debate, also originating in Sweden, is whether state schools should be allowed to operate on a for-profit basis, with shareholders taking part of the profits from financially successful schools. Again, if private for-profit companies do so well at manufacturing motor cars, why shouldn't for-profit companies run successful schools?

In 2007 Gordon Brown had changed the government Department for Education and Skills (DfES) to the Department for Children, Schools and Families (DCSF), indicating a broadening of state concerns beyond the school to the welfare of the whole child and its family with the Every Child Matters agenda (see Chapter 2). Michael Gove, on taking office, changed its title back to the Department for Education (DfE), as a sign of removing state interference in the family; the Every Child Matters material was dropped from the DfE website and the Children's Plan was scrapped. As a sign of traditionalism, the bright multicoloured décor of the department building was repainted in magnolia. The first White Paper, *The Importance of Teaching* (DfE, 2010b), signalled further 'traditional' Conservative Party policies: because highly knowledgeable people make good teachers, get the best graduates into teaching; because teaching is a craft, move teacher training from universities into schools; set up teaching schools to be responsible for initial teacher training and the professional development of teachers; improve behaviour in schools with 'troops to teaching', recruiting retired members of the armed forces.

Gove's Conservative politics led him to a traditional version of the curriculum, teaching and assessment. Another early decision was to scrap the Labour Government's review of the primary curriculum which had recommended a more combined subject approach (Rose, 2009). A traditional subject curriculum is what he sought to return to with the introduction of the English Baccalaureate (e-bac) requiring the study of English, Mathematics, Science, a Modern Language and History or Geography. Other 'newer' subjects, such as Citizenship, are left out of the list and given lower priority by schools. That Religious Education was left out was criticised by the Church of England. Also dismissed were the Labour Government's newly introduced Diplomas, which were intended to provide a high status qualification for vocational subjects such as 'Hair and Beauty' and 'Construction'. The Wolf Report (2011), accepted by Gove, criticised existing vocational education for failing to provide young people with the skills and knowledge required for employment.

Conclusion

Government policies have been to employ market forces to introduce efficiency in education and to equip the labour market for a global economy. The assumption is that a vocationally educated workforce will improve the economy and the economy will provide a good education system in a virtuous circle. New Labour policy was to equip the population for work in a global economy: to reduce child poverty and to promote social cohesion through 'joined-up' government with coordinated health, welfare and education policies (see Chapter 3). The Sure Start Scheme was introduced to coordinate the physical, intellectual and social development of young children. Every Child Matters (ECM) was the Labour government's attempt to do this (see Chapter 2). However, the Enquiry into Primary Education (Alexander, 2010) showed the limited impact on children's learning of government policy on teaching strategies and revealed anxieties among parents about over-assessment in schools. Chang (2011) shows that there is no evidence of a link between education and a successful economy.

Since 2010 the coalition government has strengthened marketisation and reduced the role of the state and local authorities by encouraging (and forcing) schools to become academies. It has taken government out of involvement in the family by scrapping the ECM agenda, reducing spending to cut the national deficit and returning to Conservative party models of education with a traditional subjects curriculum. With all the changes noted here, one constant feature is the way that the education of children is dictated by political whim, currently the economic theory that free markets and customer choice are the key to success in all human activity.

Summary points

- After three quarters of a century of political consensus and little state control of education, 1988 legislation brought stronger controls than in any other country in the world.
- Market forces were introduced to make education more efficient. Legislation was needed to enable customer choice.
- New Labour increased the controls of education beyond the curriculum, testing and inspection to include control of teaching methods.
- New Labour policies continued the neoliberal marketisation process and extended it to the privatisation of education services and privately owned academies.
- The Labour Government under Gordon Brown tried to use educational reform as a part of overall social policy with the Every Child Matters agenda.
- The 2010 UK coalition government pushed the privatisation of education further with more academies, free schools, 'for-profit' schools and the return to a traditional subject curriculum.

Questions for discussion

- How far should governments be involved in education?
- Is the principal role of education to help people to get jobs and to serve the economy?
- Should education be a public service, or be left to market forces?
- Should state schools be allowed to operate on a 'for-profit' basis?
- Do free schools offer better opportunities for the education of socially disadvantaged children and young people?

Recommended reading

Ball, S.J. (2008) *The Education Debate*. Bristol: Policy Press.
A strong critique of government policy.

Benn, M. (2011) *School Wars: The battle for Britain's education*. London: Verso.
Benn gives a well referenced and readable account of the recent debates about the marketisation of schooling.

Chang, H-J. (2011) *23 Things They Don't Tell You about Capitalism*. London: Allen Lane.
See 'Thing 17'. Chang gives a critique of the traditional assumptions about marketisation.

Chitty, C. (2009) *Education Policy in Britain* (2nd edn). Basingstoke: Palgrave Macmillan.
A thorough and detailed account of education policy.

Ward, S. and Eden, C. (2009) *Key Issues in Education Policy*. London: Sage.
Introduces a range of different aspects of education policy.

Whitty, G. (2002) *Making Sense of Education Policy*. London: Paul Chapman.
Outlines the tensions between pupils as consumers and as citizens (Chapter 5) and explains New Labour policy (Chapter 8).

References

Alexander, R. (2010) *Primary Review: Children, their world, their education*. Cambridge: Esmee Fairburn Foundation, University of Cambridge.

Brown, G. (2007) [Speech] Education policy at the University of Greenwich, 31 October 2007.

Callaghan, J. (1976) *Towards a National Debate*. [Speech] Foundation stone-laying ceremony at Ruskin College, Oxford, 18 October 1976.

Chang, H-J. (2011) *23 Things They Don't Tell You about Capitalism*. London: Allen Lane.

Chitty, C. (2004) *Education Policy in Britain*. Houndmills: Palgrave Macmillan.

DfE (2010a) *Academies Bill*. London: The Stationery Office. Available online at http://www.publications.parliament.uk/pa/cm201011/cmbills/057/2011057.pdf (accessed 10 September 2012).

Gray, J. (1998) *False Dawn: The delusions of global capitalism*. London: Granta.

Hayek, F. von. (1991) *The Road to Serfdom*. London: Routledge.

Lawton, D. (1992) *Education and Politics in the 1990s: Conflict or consensus*. Lewes: Falmer Press.

Mulready-Jones, M. (2011) There is no such thing as a 'free school' for Hackney. London: Hackney Citizen. Available online at http://hackneycitizen.co.uk/2011/03/14/there-is-no-such-thing-as-a-free-school-for-hackney/ (accessed 3 March 2012).

Rose, J. (2006) *Independent Review of the Teaching of Early Reading*. London: DfES.

Rose, J. (2009) *Independent Review of the Primary Curriculum: Final Report*. London: DfE. Available online at https://www.education.gov.uk/publications/standard/AbouttheDepartment/Page3/DCSF-00499-2009 (accessed 10 September 2012).

Stiglitz, J. (2010) *Freefall: Free markets and the sinking of the global economy*. London: Allen Lane.

Wolf, A. (2011) *Review of Vocational Education: The Wolf Report*. London: DfE.

Chapter 2

Children, families, communities and the state

Catherine A. Simon

Introduction

This chapter explores the place given to children, families and communities in two different political agendas. It begins with the radical changes brought about by the New Labour Government in the 13 years following 1997. The social policy agenda Every Child Matters (ECM) marked a significant shift in the relationship between the state and those it governed. This continued under the 2010 Conservative/Liberal-Democrat Coalition. Both administrations used the business and voluntary sectors to open up and modernize public welfare provision. For New Labour, emphasis on community involvement was intended to enhance a sense of public ownership of reform and to make services more directly accountable to those who used them. The rights and responsibilities of service-users could be set out clearly: for example, parents in their engagement with schools. 'Modernization' allowed for the influx of private finance in the funding of state services in order to alleviate pressures on the public purse. The Coalition Government took this further and promoted social action for the benefits of community empowerment, together with a renaissance in local rather than state institutions in determining policy at the district level. This was depicted as 'the Big Society' as opposed to 'big government'. However, rather than the loosening of state control over public services that these measures promised, the state not only extended its influence into the areas of family and community life previously untouched by government, it increased its powers over local decision making with its mobilization of non-elected bodies and individuals, particularly in education and schools.

Background

The legacy of New Labour

'Dear Chief Secretary, I am afraid there is no money' (BBC, 2010b) was Liam Byrne's note to his successor chief secretary to the Treasury after the 2010 general election. It gave the Coalition Government a headline on the £160bn budget deficit they inherited, but it would be unfair to suggest that this was New Labour's only legacy after 13 years in power. 'Education, education and education' had been Tony Blair's slogan in the 1997 general election and, indeed, there was no shortage of education policies from New Labour during their term in office. Tomlinson (2005: 192) charts some 44 'acts, reports and events' between 1997 and 2000 alone. Underpinning these reforms was a deep-seated concern about the persistent rise in social exclusion since the 1980s of certain individuals and communities. The Social Exclusion Unit in December 1997 was one of the first measures to address this. A plethora of social policy reforms was intended to raise individuals, families and communities out of poverty and into work. The disadvantaged poor were targeted with incentives to take responsibility and preventative action for change. The Department for Education and Skills (DfES) was adopted as the chief ministry through which many of these reforms were implemented.

Sure Start Local Programmes (SSLPs) offered parents of the very young (primarily young mothers) a means to achieve social mobility. Sure Start was an early-years intervention policy directed initially at locations where the market in pre-school provision had not penetrated, namely each of the 20 per cent most deprived neighbourhoods in the United Kingdom. Described as 'a radical cross departmental strategy' (Glass, 1999: 257), Sure Start promoted collaboration between government and local communities. Children's centres offered a range of services and advice with the convenience of being under one roof. Locally led and managed, they brought together partnerships across public, private and voluntary agencies. The intention was to build on services already available locally, offering an integrated approach to service delivery. Core services were:

- outreach services and home visiting;
- support for families and parents;
- good quality play, learning and child care;
- primary and community healthcare and advice about child health and development;
- support for those with special needs.

(Glass, 1999: 258)

Communities could respond to local need by including additional services such as general advice, training for parents in key skills and debt counselling. The model was later extended with the aim of establishing 3,500 children's centres across all communities by 2010.

A policy of 'extended schools' continued the Sure Start model into compulsory schooling, making use of the nationwide infrastructure of school facilities. By 2010 all schools were to operate as extended schools, offering services to children and families. Schools, either individually or in clusters, were to be open from 8 am to 6 pm for 48 weeks of the year. This involved head teachers brokering, marketing and running a 'core offer' of services and enrichment activities in partnership with local authorities and local providers. The offer included a varied menu of activities combined with childcare in primary schools, parenting support, and community access to school facilities (Wallace *et al.*, 2009: 4).

Both initiatives formed part of the ECM agenda (DfES, 2003), New Labour's flagship policy for children, their families and communities. Following the abuse and death of eight-year-old Victoria Climbié in 2000, the government unveiled this radical and far reaching social policy agenda as a response to what Lord Laming in his report on the case described as the 'gross failure' of the child protection and welfare system (Laming, 2003: s1.18). ECM acknowledged the complexity and interconnectedness of welfare issues, emphasizing prevention and intervention rather than cure. ECM permitted the development of two specific policy strands central to New Labour's modernizing agenda. First, it aimed to tackle the perceived inadequacies of the welfare system set out in Lord Laming's report by uniting services across professional and sector boundaries to achieve greater efficiency and effectiveness. As no one service could realistically tackle the complex problems of certain children and families or their communities, a more holistic service delivery approach was called for. Multi-agency working was promoted as a commonsense response to family and community need. The assumption was that all agencies working for improved outcomes for children and young people, such as schools, health, housing and youth justice, would work together. The intended outcomes for all children following engagement with these newly aligned public services were that they were safe, healthy, able to enjoy and achieve, to make a positive contribution to society and to achieve economic well-being in adulthood.

Second, multi-agency working enabled government to modernize the welfare state, moving away from the old 'top-down', hierarchical model of public administration to a 'partnership/network' model of New Public Management (NPM) where traditional sector boundaries are blurred by 'joined-up' working between service providers. The role of local authorities changed from their traditional advisory role to one of commissioning and facilitating services across the sectors. 'The children's workforce' was developed by rationalizing aims, qualifications and standards, overseen by the Children's Workforce Development Council (CWDC). New types of professionals emerged, and a new language of targets, early intervention, aims and outcomes adopted.

In essence, New Labour continued a process that had begun as early as the 1970s (Tomlinson, 2005: 3). NPM represented a model of localism based on a strong belief in family and community 'empowerment' and responsibility. Modernization allowed for greater diversity of schooling, the promotion of academies and changes to teacher professionalism. Reforms were underpinned by the ideology of the 'Third Way', an attempt to marry social democracy with market capitalism (see Chapter 1). However, the reality was increased bureaucracy and greater centralization of government control. In spite of its commitment to addressing issues of child poverty and social exclusion, New Labour failed to stem the tide of widening economic inequality and stagnating social mobility for bottom strata communities (see Chapter 4).

All change: The Conservative/Liberal Democrat Coalition

The general election of May 2010 resulted in a coalition agreement between the Conservatives and Liberal Democrats, an uneasy alliance given the different political traditions of the two parties. British Conservatism stands for tradition, and values the institutions of the monarchy, the family, property ownership and the Anglican Church as guiding forces in society. Historically it holds a right-of-centre political position, although modernizers in the party, including David Cameron, hold a centre-right position, advocating a more liberal, 'compassionate Conservative' stance with an interest in general well-being and social responsibility. Former leader, Iain Duncan Smith, pioneered the Centre for Social Justice, an independent think tank dedicated to concerns of social responsibility and justice. Liberal Democrats, on the other hand, spring from a centrist or left-of-centre tradition. They have argued for electoral reform, progressive taxation and civil liberties. A strong emphasis on social liberalism again emphasizes the role of the state in promoting social justice.

Cameron: Big Society versus big government

New Labour created a massive increase in central control. 'Big Society' represents the antithesis of 'big government'; a move from 'state action to social action' (Cameron, 2009).

The approach was twofold: first making opportunity more equal, primarily through education reforms, and second, actively making a stronger and more responsible society. The project invokes an active, rather than passive, role for the state in:

> [G]alvanizing, catalyzing, prompting, encouraging and agitating for community engagement and social renewal. It must help families, individuals, charities and communities come together to solve problems. We must use the state to remake society. We must use the state to stimulate social action.

Big Society amounts to empowering communities to construct services tailored to their own needs through decentralization and localism. The emphasis is on promoting social action, particularly through philanthropy, volunteering, charitable donation, and continuing New Labour's drive to open public services to greater competition and involvement from the charitable and voluntary sectors. The focus was on the personal and collective benefits accrued from such engagements across all communities, rather than the targeted and interventionist agenda. New Labour had used children and families as the rationale for, and the means of, social policy reform. Big Society looks to strengthening and renewing civic institutions such as the family, the Church, unions and activist organizations to mediate between the needs of individuals and the state that could provide for them.

The Big Society is not a new concept, resonating with religious notions of community engagement and support, particularly Christian traditions of social care, philanthropy and stewardship. The report on the Big Society published by the House of Commons Public Administration Committee (2011) noted links with the nineteenth-century cooperative movement, the work of Saul Alinsky and the social action of 1930s Chicago, as well as the theory of social capital popularized in Putnam's (2000) book *Bowling Alone*. The contention is that there is strength and value in reciprocal social networks developed through family, friendships and working relationships, representing both a public and a private good. However, the stock of social capital has been diminishing as social bonds have weakened during the latter half of the twentieth century. David Cameron, while in opposition, commissioned a report from the Centre for Social Justice. *Breakdown Britain* (Social Justice Policy Group, 2006) argued the case for a deficit nation that needs mending; the preferred model was third-sector organizations (TSOs), charitable and voluntary organizations that demonstrate 'independence, enthusiasm, innovation, commitment and diversity' (ibid.: 20).

> The welfare society has been breaking down on the margins, and the social fabric of many communities is being stripped away. Although this has been increasingly accepted by commentators and academics in recent years, a defensive complacency, akin to attitudes towards Britain's industrial decline in the 1970s, has characterized our reaction to this problem. Too many either do not care or feel powerlessness to do anything about it.
>
> (ibid.:14)

Blond (2010: 72) suggests that this anomie has occurred at both civic and social levels through the breakdown of trust, to the extent that the ideals expounded by Edmund Burke of a civic, religious, political or social middle, which acted as a balance between the demands of individuals and the power accrued by the state in delivering them, has now gone. What is called for is a resurgence of civic and community action based on a renewed understanding of the values of community and mutual reciprocity.

The model of localism promoted in the Big Society project is underpinned by a philosophical belief in aspects of communitarianism, reciprocal altruism and the preservation and/or creation of institutions that maintain and promote civic values and cooperation, rather than simply 'rolling back' the state and allowing community organizations to fill the vacuum. The emphasis on institutions (including schools) and tradition (from which our civic/moral values emerge) distinguishes this form of localism from New Labour's NPM.

The Localism Act (HMG, 2011a) offers a legal framework for the Big Society project with the aim of devolving greater powers to councils and neighbourhoods, and giving local communities more control over housing and planning decisions. There is the potential for greater community involvement in decision making via referenda called for by the local authority or local residents, including the election of local mayors in certain authorities and the ability of local community and voluntary groups to challenge service provision. Local authorities are given greater flexibility in relation to social housing, local business rate relief and the protection of services and facilities threatened by closure. Plans for the outworking of the Big Society are contained in the Open Public Services White Paper (2011) (HMG, 2011b) organized around five 'key principles': choice, decentralization, diversity, fairness and accountability. One view of this process is that it divests the public sector of its responsibility for service provision. Lord Adebowale (Adebowale, 2010), for example, warns of the US experience which found that volunteerism alone could not provide reliable, dependable public services. This raises important questions about the role of the state, the provision of welfare services, underlying assumptions driving the shift from governing to local governance, and the impact this has on power, citizenship and democracy.

One way of exploring these questions is to take the example of English local authorities. Since the 1988 Education Reform Act, local authority responsibilities for schools have changed from managing, supporting and advising on locally initiated projects to supporting the understanding and delivery of national initiatives such as the National Curriculum or the National Literacy and Numeracy strategies. Parental choice and league tables involved local authorities in policing school admissions to ensure a fair distribution of pupils across schools within their boundaries. With the merger of education and children's services under the ECM agenda, local authorities gained a commissioning rather than provider role, and they found themselves forced to engage in partnerships outside the public sector for the delivery of services. Furthermore, since 1988 the number of schools for whom local authorities are responsible has diminished considerably, as more and more schools became academies and 'opted out' of local authority control, a process that quickened under the 2010 Coalition Government.

Superficially, localism is government devolving powers to local communities and institutions such as schools. For Giddens (2002, cited in Olssen et al., 2004: 211) localism is the 'freedom to do things differently', offering flexibility and opportunities for innovation. It is more inclusive of people in the democratic process and encourages democratic citizenship. If centralism represents inefficiency and bureaucracy, localism stands for greater competence in the management of public services. Olssen et al. (2004: 212) critique this notion of localism. Local community groups and institutions are unequal in power and influence, but equality, professional standards, expertise and justice all require uniformity in both provision and enforcement. Localism celebrates difference and diversity, but challenges fairness and equality. The state's role is to facilitate and coordinate, while allowing schools to make their own decisions. In reality, the state still effects control; power is merely reorganized via networks and partnerships rather than reduced, and may even be increased in attempts to iron out the inequalities in power relationships within and between local authorities and partners (Olssen *et al.*, 2004: 212–3). Thomson (2011: 95) goes further, suggesting that the localism agenda has reduced democratic citizen activity at the level of the local authority. Elected members of councils and committees have less say in decisions about local services as provision is devolved to non-elected private or voluntary organizations.

Academies and free schools: The Big Society in education

Changes in governance and state control in the Big Society are evident in education. Academies and free schools ('independent schools' within the state sector, part financed by private capital with control vested in the governing bodies with representatives from industry) began as city technology colleges under Thatcher. New Labour's academies introduced new kinds of partnerships with the private and voluntary sectors for establishing and running state schools in inner city areas. 'City academy' status provided freedom from local authority control and from the national curriculum beyond the core subjects; and the ability to set pay awards and admissions policy. Self-determination was balanced by legal requirements to be non-selective, to comply with Ofsted regulations and to be run on a not-for-profit basis. The Coalition Government's Academies Act (HMG, 2010) extended these allowances yet further, in line with the Big Society agenda. All schools could apply for academy status, including primary schools, special schools and pupil referral units (PRUs), not just those with an Ofsted rating of 'failing', as had been the case under New Labour. The Act extended this model of governance to parents, teachers, voluntary and private organizations so that they could apply to set up a new 'free school' in response to local demand or need; only an academy can be set up by such individuals or community bodies.

Modelled on Swedish free schools and US charter schools, the first free schools opened in England in September 2011 and, according to the DfE, operate as 'all-ability state-funded schools set up in response to what local people say they want and need in order to improve education for children in their community' (DfE, 2012). Together with university technology colleges and trust schools, they add to the growing number of schools operating outside local authority control. Each of these types of school has different legal status and governance arrangements. Their relationships to local and central government and to other schools are also different. The funding agreements and contractual arrangements with the academy trust are made directly with the Secretary of State. These agreements set out the framework within which the academy must operate and require seven years' notice of termination.

It is too early to know how far free schools impact local communities and parents in addressing local need and empowerment, but early indications suggest that parent and community involvement is less significant than government might have anticipated. While some, like the Bristol Free School, were set up by parents, most have come about through partnership with other organizations or groups including academy chains and, as such, contribute to the development of network governance. Ball and Junemann (2011) explore the complex web of social, political and business relationships that weave financial capital with philanthropy across party divides. They name such organizations as ARK, E-ACT and the Garfield Weston Foundation whose key personnel are also actors in other aspects of government advisory groups, finance and think tanks. Many have links to charity banking, micro-finance and venture philanthropy, as well as 'edubusinesses' – companies interested in for-profit opportunities arising from the out-sourcing of state services (ibid.: 57). These networks extend beyond national boundaries, for example in links with US charter schools. It is these powerful groups and networks, rather than individual parents or teacher groups, that influence policy in the running of free schools, and this brings into question the real nature of parent and community empowerment and self-determination.

Whither vulnerable children?

Absent from the discourse on academies and free schools is the emphasis on vulnerability and disadvantage which underpinned New Labour's social and education policies. Under the Coalition Government, education policy returned to teacher recruitment, training and standards and to maintaining international competitiveness. This was signalled by the rebranding of the Department for Children, Schools and Families (DCSF) into the Department for Education (DfE). Although maintaining responsibility for children's services, the Secretary of State, Michael Gove, wished to 'refocus' the department 'on its core purpose of supporting teaching and learning' (BBC, 2010a). Gove diminished the central role given to schools by New Labour in the battle to tackle generational poverty and worklessness, in line with Conservative traditionalist political beliefs.

However, Liberal Democrat Sarah Teather, Minister of State for Children and Families, set out the Coalition Government's policies for children and young people in 2010 (All Party Parliamentary Group for Children, 2010). These measures revealed more radical and social liberal politics. The Childhood and Families Taskforce examined areas such as parental leave and flexible working, support for disabled children and those affected by family breakdown, and the commercialization and sexualization of children. Funding for Sure Start was ring fenced with the intention of returning it to its original purpose of early intervention among the neediest families. Funding for 16–19-year-olds was also protected through the pupil premium. Free childcare for three- and four-year-olds was extended, and a further 20,000 early-years places were found for disadvantaged two-year-olds. The Early Years Foundation Stage (EYFS) came under review. Other reviews during the first 18 months of the coalition included Frank Field's review on poverty and life chances, Graham Allen's review on early intervention, and the Eileen Munro (2011) review of child protection. Alan Milburn has also led work on the question of social mobility (see Chapter 3).

The proliferation of reports suggests a continuation of rather than a break with New Labour's social policy, although the methods of policy implementation via new partnerships and networks changed. Multi-agency or integrated working remained for those in the front line of service delivery, and in many ways the emphasis on network governance and localism appeared to strengthen this approach, even in the face of fierce reductions in funding. It was the removal of education from the cross-departmental approach to policymaking for children and families that made a significant statement and highlights the tensions in political ideology between the two parties of the coalition. For Conservatives the universal service of schools was no longer considered the means of delivering a child-focused social policy, but a test bed for the new localism – the Big Society agenda.

Conclusion

This chapter has addressed a number of issues in government policy for children, families and the community from New Labour to the Conservative/Lib Dem Coalition. New Labour policy on children, families and communities was deployed to modernize welfare state provision via NPM and multi-agency working. The delivery of welfare services was opened up to other public, private and voluntary organizations while accountability measures increased. This led ultimately to a significant ingression of government influence into family and community life. In contrast to big government, coalition policy promoted an active citizenry via the Big Society and a reaffirmation of the traditional institutions of British society. Whereas the rhetoric of community empowerment continued under the coalition, the tightening of central government control continued in the funding for academies, a diminution of the democratic voice for citizens and the widening influence of international and global players in local education and education policymaking. Policy intent towards children, families and communities shifted from one of empowerment for social mobility to a redistribution of state power among a wider, non-elected group of political and philanthropic actors. This raises significant questions about the role of the state in relation to welfare provision, education and schools, and has implications for civil democracy, equality and social mobility, community empowerment and self-determination.

Summary points

- No political policy is neutral: it emerges from party political beliefs and ideologies.
- Government policy on children, families and communities has been significant, particularly since 1997, but for different political ends.
- New Labour focused on modernizing the welfare state and intervening in the lives of individuals and communities in order to enhance social mobility.
- The Coalition Government, influenced by Conservative ideology, sought to mobilize community and voluntary organizations and reinstate the powers of traditional institutions for social change.
- The power of the state over the lives of individuals has increased, while certain powers have been redistributed to non-elected individuals or groups rather than devolved to local communities.
- Academies and free schools are examples in education of the Big Society.
- There are implications in education and social policy for the exercise of civil democracy, equality and social mobility.

Questions for discussion

- To what extent did central control increase under New Labour and Coalition governments, despite the stated aim of increasing local democracy?
- Does the Big Society represent a significant policy change, or merely a development of the ECM agenda to modernize the welfare state under a different guise?
- What has been the impact of academies and free schools on the education landscape?

- How far has the introduction of business groups and charities into education changed the role of government in providing state education?

Recommended reading

Ball, S.J. (2007) *Education plc: Understanding private sector participation in public sector education*. London: Routledge.
A comprehensive account of privatization in education.

Hatcher, R. and Jones, K. (eds) (2011) *No Country for the Young*. London: Tufnell Press.
A critique of coalition education policy and social justice; including European as well as UK perspectives.

Simon, C.A. and Ward, S. (2010) *Does Every Child Matter?* Abingdon: Routledge.
A political critique of New Labour's Every Child Matters agenda.

Tomlinson, S. (2005) *Education in a Post-welfare Society* (2nd edn). Maidenhead: Open University Press.
A detailed and accessible account of New Labour under Tony Blair.

References

Adebowale, V. (2010) 'The Big Idea'. *Ethos* 20 April 2012. Available online at http://www.ethosjournal. com/archive/item/198-the-big-idea (accessed 28 April 2012).

All Party Parliamentary Group for Children (2010) Coalition Policy on Children and Young People. London: All Party Parliamentary Group for Children. Available online at http://www.ncb.org.uk/ media/156103/100712sarahteatherminutes.pdf (accessed 22 September 2012).

Ball, S.J. and Junemann, C. (2011) 'Newtork Governance and Coalition Education Policy'. In: R. Hatcher and K. Jones (eds) *No Country for the Young*. London: Tufnell Press.

BBC News (2010a) Department for Education Returns in Coalition Rebrand. Available online at http://news.bbc.co.uk/1/hi/8679749.stm (accessed 28 April 2012).

BBC News (2010b) Treasury Chief's Note to Successor: There's no money left. BBC, 7 May. Available online at http://news.bbc.co.uk/1/hi/uk_politics/8688470.stm (accessed 28 April 2012).

Blond, P. (2010) *Red Tory: How left and right have broken Britain and how we can fix it*. London: Faber and Faber.

Cameron, D. (2009) *The Big Society:* [Lecture] Hugo Young Lecture Tuesday 10 November 2009. Available online at http://www.conservatives.com/news/speeches/2009/11/david_cameron_the_big_society. aspx (accessed 28 April 2012).

DfE (2012) *Free Schools. Available online at* http://www.education.gov.uk/schools/leadership/typesof-schools/freeschools (accessed 28 April 2012).

DfES (2003) *Every Child Matters*. Nottingham: DfES.

Glass, N. (1999) 'Sure Start: The development of an early intervention programme for young children in the United Kingdom'. *Children and Society* 13(4): 257–64.

HM Government (2011a) *Localism Act 2011*. National Archives. Available online at http://www.legislation. gov.uk (accessed 28 April 2011).

HM Government (2011b) Open Public Services White Paper, Available online HYPERLINK "http:// www.official-"www.official-documents.gov.uk (accessed 02.09. 2011).

HM Government (2010) *Academies Act 2010*. National Archives. Available online at http://www.legislation. gov.uk/ukpga/2010/32/contents (accessed 28 April 2012).

House of Commons Public Administration Select Committee (2011) *The Big Society*. London: The Stationery Office.

Laming (2003) *The Victoria Climbié Inquiry*. Norwich: The Stationery Office.

Olssen, M., Codd, J. and O'Neil, A. (2004) *Education Policy: Globalisation, citizenship and democracy*. London: Sage.

Putnam, R.D. (2000) *Bowling Alone: The collapse and revival of American community*. New York: Simon and Schuster.

Social Justice Policy Group (2006) *Breakdown Britain: Interim report on the state of the nation*. London: Social Justice Policy Group.

Thomson, P. (2011) '"The Local" and its authority: The coalition, governance and democracy'. In R. Hatcher and K. Jones (eds) *No Country for the Young*. London: Tufnell Press.

Tomlinson, S. (2005) *Education in a Post-welfare Society* (2nd edn). Maidenhead: Open University Press.

Wallace, E., Smith, K., Pye, J., Crouch, J., Ziff, A. and Burston, K. (2009) *Extended Schools Survey of Schools, Pupils and Parents: A qualitative study of the perceptions, and usage of extended schools*. London: Ipsos MORI, DCSF.

Chapter 3

Social mobility and education

Richard Riddell

> Our schools should be engines of social mobility, helping children to overcome the accidents of birth and background to achieve much more than they may ever have imagined. But, at the moment, our schools system does not close gaps, it widens them.
> (Michael Gove, Introduction, *The Importance of Teaching,* White Paper DfE, 2010: 6)

Introduction

Michael Gove is the most recent Secretary of State for Education to express frustration at the (apparent) inability of schools in England to ensure that children can achieve their highest possible ambitions, irrespective of their personal circumstances and social backgrounds. The 2010 Coalition Government, like its Labour predecessor, introduced a range of policies and interventions intended to increase *social mobility*. This chapter explores what we mean by social mobility, looks at the record of the UK, examines the performance of schools in promoting opportunity, the transmission of advantage and disadvantage, and briefly introduces aspects of the policies of the two governments that have been in power in recent years. The chapter concludes with a brief discussion of the opportunities available to young people as the UK economy assumes an 'hourglass' shape over the next ten years.

Opportunities in the UK

The balance of opportunities and the social ladder

All societies have a structure: in one such as ours, we come into contact with a range of complex institutions beyond the family which govern our lives. These include preschools and schools, hospitals, universities, companies, shops, banks, local and national government, sports and leisure organisations, sometimes the police and law courts. We occupy different positions in relation to each of these organisations depending on the *stage* of our lives – children, adults – and on *what we are doing* at the time – teachers, customers, patients, and so on. These different positions give us hugely disparate amounts of access to wealth, power and influence over how our society is run.

In other words, we occupy differing social, political and economic positions: one way of looking at a society is through the *balance of opportunities* available to us (Bottero, 2005). Alternatively, we can look at this as a *social ladder:* if we climb it, we achieve greater success; we better ourselves. The Coalition Government's *Social Justice Strategy* (DWP, 2012) is intended to ensure 'people are able to move up the social ladder, regardless of background' and 'everybody can put a foot on that ladder', irrespective of the hardship in their lives or any problems they have suffered (DWP, 2012: 4).

Social mobility

It is possible to measure changes in people's social and economic position over time – this is what social mobility is. It can be measured in terms of (real terms) income – *income mobility* – or in terms of occupation – *occupational mobility*. In addition, social mobility can be *intergenerational* – a comparison of how a current generation has done in relation to its parents, and *intragenerational* – the extent to which individuals are able to improve their position over their own lifetime. Social mobility can be *relative* – how likely it is that people from particular backgrounds can reach certain social or income groups (usually higher ones), and *absolute* – overall, how far one generation has done better than its parents.

In the contribution that education might make, we may be interested in both occupational and income mobility, but particularly in relative and intergenerational mobility: how people's occupations are better than those of their parents. This is the Coalition Government's view (Cabinet Office, 2011).

How does the UK do?

Between generations, there will be some people who achieve higher social and economic status than their parents and those whose position declines relative to their parents. Equally, many people will maintain a similar social status to their parents. The Panel on Fair Access to the Professions (2009), or the Milburn Report as it is often termed, was commissioned by the Labour Government to examine whether access to the professions was currently fair and based on merit, or could be more so in the future. Some of the data commissioned for the report examined social mobility rates by looking at the percentage of men and women over the twentieth century who, when aged over 25, were in higher occupations than their fathers. This data showed that, in successive generations born from 1900 onwards, *upward* social mobility increased steadily until it was nearly 30 per cent more for the generation of men born in 1958, and for women it increased for those born from the 1930s onwards, and who were entering the labour market after World War II. But the figure for women was less than a third of that for men. This increasing pattern, in effect until the 1970s, was echoed in many other countries, including the United States (Blanden *et al.*, 2005).

But there has been a decline in intergenerational mobility *since* the cohort born in 1958. One of the most commonly quoted comparisons made is that between this cohort, now in their fifties, and the cohort born in 1970, now in their forties. There are quite a lot of data on these two cohorts. Milburn quoted a slight decline in upward social mobility between these two cohorts. We also know some other things about them: for those born in 1958, 31 per cent of men in the lowest income quartile (25 per cent) had fathers in the same, while 35 per cent of those in the highest quartile did so. For the cohort born in 1970, these figures had become 35 per cent and 42 per cent respectively. It was 'becoming harder for young men of working class backgrounds to elevate their social positions and less likely in the professional classes that they would reduce theirs' (Riddell, 2010: 148). To put it another way, for both these cohorts it was eight times more likely for the son of a father in Social Class I or II than the son of a father in Social Class V.[1] Although many would continue to achieve better jobs, for most of them it would be to an adjacent part of social structure (Woods *et al.*, 2003) and few would go straight to the top. But that does not mean that some people cannot, and do not! But it is less likely, more difficult and there are more obstacles in their paths.

Internationally, the UK does not compare well. Despite this apparent decline, the UK still has better rates of mobility than the US, but is behind West Germany (the timescale for these figures predates reunification), Finland, Canada, Denmark, Sweden and Norway (Blanden *et al.*, 2005). Worse, some of the things that hold children back – such as coming from more deprived backgrounds – seem to have a greater effect on English children than on those in other countries. And attainment gaps widen, particularly after the age of eleven (Sutton Trust, 2011).

The role of the education system

Social class and achievement

The role of the education system is important because the key to a higher status job in twenty-first century Britain is achieving higher qualifications. But it would seem the less deprived you are, the more likely you will succeed educationally, and hence socially and occupationally. In other words, the effects of deprivation maintain current levels of social status.

The diagram at Figure 1 is taken from a comprehensive summary of the evidence on deprivation and attainment published by the Department for Children, Schools and Families (DCSF, 2009). It shows the contrast in educational outcomes between children entitled to free schools meals (FSM) – the most common, but not the only, measure of deprivation – and all others. Further, it shows the odds for children of achieving particular measures (such as 5 A*–Cs at GCSE) who are not entitled to FSM compared with those who are (see Chapter 4).

This is not just about deprivation, however. This useful summary also examines some of the differences in educational outcomes by socio-economic status. One of the most shocking statistics it quotes is that children from lower socio-economic groups – who may very well be cared for, fed and clothed properly by their parents – with high levels of cognitive functioning at the age of 22 months, are overtaken during the primary years by children from higher socio-economic groups who had lower levels of cognitive functioning at the start.

So deprivation depresses attainment outcomes, and in the UK its effects are more damaging and last longer. At the same time, *social class* is also significant. So the question for all working in schools, if they wish to increase social mobility, is what they can do to narrow the gap between these differing outcomes for children.

So, to put it another way, if you are living in poverty, or just have an ordinary, working class job, your children are less likely to do well at school compared to those children of more well-heeled parents with better jobs. And this makes it less likely that they will go to university and obtain a higher status, better paid, professional job. And then the same cycle will hold for their children.

The reason the Milburn Report (Fair Access Panel, 2009) was commissioned by the Labour Government, and why Alan Milburn himself was invited by the Coalition Government to monitor its progress on social mobility, was that fair access to the professions,

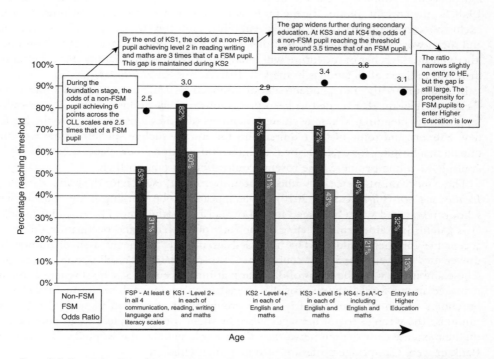

Figure 3.1 Free school meals attainment gap from early years to higher education (DCSF, 2009: 25)
Adapted from DCSF (2009) Deprivation and Education, the Department for Education, protected by Crown copyright.

based on merit and not wealth, was considered an important matter on which to move social mobility forward. This is because the major professions, such as medicine or the law, have always been seen as routes to social respect and status, partly because they have had entrance requirements and qualifications. They have been something to aspire to.

A further key finding of the report, however, was the disproportionate percentage of members of the 'top professions' that attended independent schools: more than 50 per cent of journalists on national papers and top city solicitors, 75 per cent of senior judges and nearly 70 per cent of top barristers, and 70 per cent of finance directors in top companies. On average, only 7 per cent of children attend these fee-paying, selective schools.

Given the age of senior members of these professions, many of these data, as the report says, date back to what was happening in the 1960s and 1970s; but Milburn also found from Sutton Trust data that younger professions schooled in the early 2000s were predominantly from the independent sector. Most professions had made some progress since the 1980s (though not much), except for the medical profession (no change) and journalism, where the figures had gone backwards.

In terms of family wealth, the 'typical young professional' (born in 1970) grew up in a family with an income 27 per cent above the national average – as might be expected if independent school fees needed to be paid – as opposed to 17 per cent for those born in 1958. So the current trend is for the professions to become more rather than less socially exclusive, creating a barrier to social mobility. But this trend also affects teaching and social work – traditionally professions with members from a variety of backgrounds: 'the typical … teacher of the future will today be growing up in a family that is better off than two in three of all families in the UK' (Fair Access Panel, 2009: 19).

In addition to the independent school connection, Milburn identified some other social mechanisms that tended to keep professions socially exclusive. One was so-called 'opportunity hoarding', whereby current members of professions tend to raise the bar for new entrants; and some of the requirements for entry – such as spending time working unpaid in a hospital, for example, or as an intern on a national newspaper – could only be available to young people whose parents could afford to support them.

These mechanisms were also found in the author's own research for the book, *Aspiration, Identity and Self-Belief* (Riddell, 2010). What appeared to be working in the independent schools researched was a 'managed model of social reproduction'. The (mainly) middle-class parents had a determined view of the sorts of education and occupation that were acceptable for their children. This included attendance at one of a small number of universities – fewer than 50 per cent of the 24 so-called 'top' Russell Group universities. These ambitions were the focus of discussion at home, echoed at school where a micro-managed, mono-focal path was provided to 'getting in' to one of these universities. Helped by choice of school, peer and friendship groups were controlled in such a way as to minimise the wrong sorts of messages heard by these young people. Parents commented on their extensive use of their networks – for example, people who worked at Rothschild's Bank or were Cambridge professors – to help their children.

Does this matter?

It needs to be remembered that if you are entitled to FSM you are less likely to achieve the entrance requirements for an independent school or the prestigious universities that host medical schools. And these professionals are the ones that govern our country (MPs over 30 per cent, top civil servants 45 per cent), run universities (vice chancellors 20 per cent), inform us about current affairs (journalists 54 per cent) and decide whether we will go to prison or not for serious crimes (top judges 75 per cent).

As the Sutton Trust (2009) eloquently said in their evidence for Milburn:

> Who holds the positions of power and influence in our society is important for two connected reasons. Firstly, it sheds light on how accessible routes are to those professions, and reflects inequalities in our education system which means that the type of school attended and the family background of children are such powerful predictors of future life chances. Secondly, it highlights the very particular experiences and standpoints that such influential people bring to their positions. This is particularly important for those professional elites making judgments that affect the whole of society. What experience of education do the politicians who direct our state school system have? How in touch with the concerns of the population are those judges who have been educated in environments serving a minority of the population? Which issues do newspaper editors judge to be important when deciding the stories to promote for public debate? And, importantly, can the professions spot

potential in young people with social backgrounds very different to those of their membership?

(Sutton Trust, 2009: 10)

What the elites in our country represent – socially, ethnically and in terms of gender – may be important. Are we really 'all in this together', for example? But there is more recent evidence emerging (Brown *et al.*, 2008) that recruitment to future top jobs in transnational companies – those with the capability of moving money and largely production globally generally where they please, so the elites of the elites – emanates from a very small number of 'top' universities. So the independent schools – and the parents who send their children there – are right about their current future prospects.

Tackling social mobility – what can be done educationally?

Improving social mobility has been a key priority for both the Coalition and the Labour Governments, especially after Gordon Brown became Prime Minister in 2007. The following two quotations illustrate the similarity of their aspiration:

> This is the modern definition of social justice: not just social protection but real opportunity for everyone to make the most of their potential in a Britain where what counts is not where you come from but what you aspire to become, a Britain where everyone should be able to say that their destiny is not written for them, but written by them.

(Cabinet Office, 2009: 1)

> [N]o one should be prevented from fulfilling their potential by the circumstances of their birth … [This is] a vision for a socially mobile country.

(Cabinet Office, 2011: 5)

These statements were made by politicians in their respective introductions to the *New Opportunities* white paper of the Brown Government, published in January 2009, and the *Opening Doors, Breaking Barriers* Social Mobility Strategy of the coalition, published in April, 2011. Although the aspirations may appear similar, how the two governments see implementation could not be more different.

Nevertheless, several aspects of our society must be considered for intervention if levels of social mobility are to be increased, all of them considered to a degree by both governments. One of these, of course, is the education inequality – by socio-economic background (and gender and race) – that prevents equity in access to better jobs, promoted opportunities and social status (see Chapter 5). Very often educational attainment to particular levels is necessary for the next step to be taken in career trajectories. As Milburn points out, more and more professional jobs now require a degree, so that all the educational steps up to university and then entry into professions need to be tackled by social mobility strategies.

But both governments have been aware of the need to start much earlier. The importance of very early intervention, before the age of three, has been the recommendation of three reports commissioned in the early stages of the Coalition Government: two reports by Graham Allen on Early Intervention (Allen, 2011a, 2011b) and one by Frank Field on ending child poverty (Field, 2010). Their conclusions have been reflected in the published report on social justice strategy (DWP, 2012), see page 22, and the Government's own report on child poverty (DWP, 2011). An important early action of the Coalition Government was to extend the entitlement of three- and four-year-olds to early-years education to the most disadvantaged two year olds. This must be set against cuts in the Early Intervention Grant, as it was called, made by central government to local authorities to support their early-years provision.

Nevertheless, against the background of reducing the government's budget deficit, funding was found for this new entitlement to intervene in the circumstances of disadvantaged children as part of the 'fairness premium' (Cabinet Office, 2011). There are two other components: first, the 'pupil premium', an allocation of extra funding to primary and secondary schools – for the first year on the basis of FSM – to help schools combat the disadvantage graphically illustrated in Figure 1. Schools were given advice on how to spend this (see Higgins *et al.*, 2010) and were obliged to give account of their work in this area. It was also possible for schools serving disadvantaged communities to bid for project funding from a national 'education endowment fund'.

Both governments saw – rightly – that raising attainment in schools more generally remained a crucial contribution to improving social mobility. The question of what schools might do has already been raised in this chapter, and both governments discussed school reforms in their strategies. There are many similarities in attitudes towards schools between the two governments. The effectiveness of encouraging much greater numbers of schools to become academies – state independent schools funded directly by central government – is contested, but such a change is in its early stages. The importance of a new increased floor target to disadvantaged children – the minimum that schools should achieve – 50 per cent 5 A*–Cs at secondary – has yet to be established so soon after its introduction. Both these Coalition Government developments originated with the previous government.

The third component of the 'fairness premium' was a National Scholarship Scheme whereby universities were allocated funding to be made available to disadvantaged students in order to ease their access to higher education (HE). This was part of fundamental reform of HE set out in a white paper (BIS, 2011) whereby all funding for most universities came from student fees, that students would be able to pay by taking out loans provided nationally on a subsidised basis. It may not be possible to disentangle the effectiveness of the National Scholarship Scheme from the effects of the reforms overall and this will not be known for several years; but its effects on professional recruitment, either way, are important.

A year after the publication of its social mobility strategy, in an update (Cabinet Office, 2012), the Coalition Government published a series of 'social trackers'. These are seventeen indicators to measure progress to a fairer society and include attainment by children entitled to FSM, and progression to HE by social background.

An additional continuity between the two governments has been the work done with the professions themselves. Both were keen to promote wider access, through encouraging *non*-graduate access (a key recommendation of Milburn) and encouraging companies of national standing to establish scholarship schemes and relationships with schools serving disadvantaged communities. A voluntary body, the Gateways to the Professions Collaborative Forum, set up under the Labour Government, was continued and reconstituted under the coalition. Under its auspices, in 2011, an organisation called Professions for Good (www.professionsforgood.com) was launched, which was a 'public information campaign, made up of a collaboration of the representative bodies for the UK's largest professions'. 'Together', they say, 'we seek to unite the leading professions to maximise their contribution to a fairer society, a strong economy and better informed policy making' (professionsforgood.com website). The results of their work will be of interest.

Future change

So much of this policymaking is recent that it is not possible to say whether it will work or not. Educationally, there is a consensus that all phases – from birth to the end of university education and beyond – are necessary and relevant. School reform in particular, but not exclusively, is contested and controversial and, whatever your views on what schools can do to counter the effects of poverty on the attainment of children, a much wider range of policy interventions is necessary to counter the non-school effects that are no less important.

Neither government proposed to tackle the effective mechanism for a small proportion of the population that links independent schools to certain universities and future professional positions; and, of course, access to power, wealth and influence. If all schools serving disadvantaged communities brought all their students up to the attainment levels of those from more advantaged backgrounds, then there may be some equity in admission to university.

Milburn was relying on there being up to seven million new professional and managerial jobs by 2020; however, this was an estimate made before the 2008 recession, but at least two million new jobs now seem likely (Wilson and Homidou, 2011). The next decade will also see considerable retirements from the 1958 cohort of professionals which, as Milburn says, benefited from a huge expansion of professional jobs – a changing UK occupational pattern.

The shape of the UK economy is undergoing another drastic change and is assuming an 'hourglass' shape (Hackett *et al*, 2012; Sissons, 2011) whereby there is an expansion of jobs requiring advanced skills (broadly graduate and above equivalent), reflected in these figures; a contraction of jobs requiring the equivalent of A level, GCSE Level or Level 2 or 3 vocational qualifications, and an expansion of routine, unskilled unqualified labour. This new shape will require more rather than fewer graduates (Hackett *et al*, 2012); many will have professional or managerial status.

This may achieve greater social mobility – what John Goldthorpe (2007) called a 'structural' change, rather than one resulting from greater social equity. There will be more people in the UK from a wider range of backgrounds in these jobs – indicators will change, without much government intervention.

But then there will be a new set of questions. Has the new economy now reached out to the *most* deprived in our midst? And for young people becoming engineers, barristers, solicitors and journalists from working-class backgrounds, will there be opportunities for them to develop throughout their careers, take on the most challenging and rewarding work, and generally, achieve the 'tops' of their professions as measured by the Sutton Trust?

Note

1 Social classes I to V were the classifications used before the current NS-SEC (National Statistics Socio-Economic Classification) scheme was adopted in 2001, and which is used, for example, by UCAS.

Summary points

- All societies have a range of social and economic opportunities available to individuals.
- The movement between opportunities for individuals and between generations is termed 'social mobility'.
- Social mobility is not high in the UK; it is difficult to reach the highest echelons of society from the lowest, and always has been.
- The education system in the UK widens with age the differences between children from less and more privileged backgrounds; it makes social mobility more difficult.
- In recent years in the UK, major professions have become more rather than less socially exclusive.
- All governments in the UK are committed to increasing social mobility. This involves all changes at all stages of education.

Questions for discussion

- How would you define a fair society? Are the 'social trackers' helpful here?
- Thinking about the lives of children who are living in poverty, how might this affect their ability to participate and do well in school and afterwards? What can schools do about it?
- What government interventions could promote social mobility? Will they work?

Recommended reading

This sets out the coalition's strategy, giving up-to-date figures for the UK, and discusses work across government. Look out too for the updates (the first one came out in 2012).
Cabinet Office (2011) *Opening Doors, Breaking Barriers: A Strategy for Social Mobility*. London: Her Majesty's Government. Available online at www.thecabinetoffice.gov.uk (accessed 30 April 2011).

References

Allen, G. (2011a) *Early Intervention: The next step*. London: Her Majesty's Government. Available online at http://www.dwp.gov.uk/docs/early-intervention-next-steps.pdf (accessed 24 August 2011).

Allen, G. (2011b) *Early Intervention: Smart investment, massive savings*. London: Her Majesty's Government. Available online at http://www.dwp.gov.uk/docs/early-intervention-next-steps.pdf (accessed 24 August 2011).

BIS (2011) *Higher Education: Students at the heart of the system*. London: BIS. Available online at http://www.bis.gov.uk (accessed 28 June 2011).

Blanden, J., Gregg, P. and Machin, S. (2005) *Intergenerational Mobility in Europe and North America; A report supported by the Sutton Trust*. London: LSE.

Bottero, W. (2005) *Stratification: Social division and inequality*. Abingdon: Routledge.

Brown, P., Lauder, H. and Ashton, D. (2008) *Education, Globalisation and the Knowledge Economy – A commentary by the Teaching and Learning Research Programme*. London: TLRP. Available online at http://www.tlrp.org (accessed 10 March 2011).

Cabinet Office (2009) *New Opportunities: Fair chances for the future.* Norwich: The Stationery Office. Available online at http://www.hmg.gov.uk/media/ (accessed 19 January 2011).

Cabinet Office (2011) *Opening Doors, Breaking Barriers: A strategy for social mobility.* London: Her Majesty's Government. Available online at http://www.thecabinetoffice.gov.uk (accessed 30 April 2011).

Cabinet Office (2012) *Opening Doors, Breaking Barriers: A strategy for social mobility – Update on progress since 2011.* London: Her Majesty's Government. Available online at http://www.thecabinetoffice. gov.uk (accessed 28 May 2012).

DCSF (2009) *Deprivation and Education: The evidence on pupils in England – Foundation Stage to Key Stage 4.* London: Department for Children, Schools and Families. Available online at http://www. education.gov.uk/publications (accessed 11 April 2012).

DfE (2010) *The Importance of Teaching – Schools white paper 2010.* London: DfE. Available online at http:// www.education.gov.uk (accessed 30 August 2011).

DWP (2011) *A New Approach to Child Poverty: Tackling the causes of disadvantage and transforming families' lives.* London: Her Majesty's Government. Available online at https://www.education.gov.uk/publi- cations/eOrderingDownload/CM-8061.pdf (accessed 24 August 2011).

DWP (2012) *Social Justice – Transforming lives.* London: Department for Work and Pensions. Available online at http://www.dwp.gov.uk/social-justice (accessed 10 April 2012).

Ferri, E., Bynner, J. and Wadsworth, M. (eds) (2003) *Changing Britain, Changing Lives – Three generations by the turn of the century.* London: Institute of Education, London University.

Field, F. (2010) *The Foundation Years: Preventing poor children becoming poor adults: The report of the Independent Review on Poverty and Life Chances.* London: Her Majesty's Government. Available online at http:// webarchive.nationalarchives.gov.uk/20110120090128/http://povertyreview.independent.gov.uk (accessed 24August 2011).

Goldthorpe, J. (2007) *On Sociology* (2nd edn) – Vol. Two: *Illustration and Retrospect.* Stanford, CA: Stanford University Press.

Hackett, L., Shutt, L. and Maclachlan, N. (2012) *The Way We'll Work – Labour market trends and preparing for the hourglass.* London: University Alliance. Available online at http://www.university-alliance.ac.uk (accessed 10 April 2012).

Higgins, S., Kokotsaki, D. and Coe, R. (2010) *Toolkit of Strategies to Improve Learning – Summary for schools spending the pupil premium.* London: Sutton Trust. Available online at http://www.suttontrust.com (accessed 31 August, 2011).

Panel of Fair Access to the Professions (2009) *Unleashing Aspiration: The final report of the panel on fair access to the professions.* London: The Cabinet Office. Available online at http://www.bis.gov.uk (accessed 22 January 2011).

Riddell, R. (2010) *Aspiration, Identity and Self-Belief - Snapshots of social structure at work.* Stoke-on-Trent: Trentham Books.

Sissons, P. (2011) *The Hourglass and the Escalator - Labour market change and mobility.* London: The Work Foundation. Available online at http://www.theworkfoundation.com (accessed 10 April 2012).

Sutton Trust (2009) *The Educational Backgrounds of Leading Lawyers, Journalists, Vice Chancellors, Politicians, Medics and Chief Executives.* London: Sutton Trust. Available online at http://www.suttontrust.com (accessed 3 April 2012).

Sutton Trust (2011) *What Prospects for Mobility in the UK? A cross/national study of educational inequalities and their implications for future education and earning mobility.* London: The Sutton Trust. Available online at http://www.suttontrust.com (accessed 4 April 2012).

Wilson, R. and Homenidou, K. (2011) *Working Futures 2010–2020.* London: UK Commission for Employment and Skills. Available online at http://www.ukces.org.uk (accessed 10 April 2012).

Woods, L., Makepeace, G., Joshi, H. and Dolton, P. (2003) *The World of Paid Work.* In: E. Ferri, J. Bynner and M. Wadsworth (eds) *Changing Britain, Changing Lives – Three generations by the turn of the century.* London: Institute of Education, London University.

Chapter 4

Child poverty and educational attainment

Christine Eden

Introduction

This chapter examines the debates about poverty and educational achievement. It considers:

- the background theory about poverty;
- evidence of the relationship between poverty and underachievement explanations that try to account for the relationship;
- current government policy and its likely impact;
- competing models of state intervention.

Background

Debates about the social background of pupils and inequalities in educational attainment have shifted over the last 50 years. In the 1950s, 1960s and 1970s inequalities were seen to be rooted in an education system differentiated by social class which, it was hoped, would be challenged by the comprehensive system that was meant to open up educational opportunities. Since 1997 under Labour and the 2010 Coalition Governments the debate has moved to one that, while recognising the importance of income differentials, emphasises parental responsibility and the home learning environment.

The Labour Government from 1997 became known for Tony Blair's three priorities of 'education, education and education' and his claim, through high-quality education, to eradicate child poverty by 2020. The emphasis shifted from social class to poverty and social deprivation and the Labour Government from 1997 to 2010 expended considerable effort aimed at addressing child poverty and its associated evil of underachievement. It was driven both by a commitment to social justice and equal opportunity, and the need for Britain to be internationally competitive.

Child poverty is most commonly defined as children living in households with 60 per cent less than the median income. The commitment to eradicating it was fuelled by the fact that the number of children in poverty had almost doubled during the Conservative Governments of 1979 to 1997. It tried to achieve its aspirations by legislation and by spending significant sums of money to raise the income of low-income families through a range of mechanisms: tax credits; support to parents through the New Deal Programme to help lone parents into work; early-years services in the Sure Start Programme; and the Every Child Matters (ECM) agenda (HM Treasury, 2008) (see Chapter 2).

Some progress was made: over ten years there was a reduction in child poverty numbers from 3.4 million to 2.8 million and the government claimed that 'the most deprived schools have made the most (academic) progress' (DCSF, 2009: 2). The Coalition Government elected in 2010 passed the Poverty Act 2010 with cross-party support. They claimed that Labour had failed to solve child poverty, in spite of spending significant sums of money. The Prime Minister, David Cameron, set up a review into 'Poverty and Life Chances' chaired by Frank Field, a Labour MP with a lifelong interest and experience in anti-poverty strategies. His review in December 2010 argued that previous approaches to poverty had followed that of Rowntree's initial report in 1901 and had focused on income to the exclusion of other influences on life chances. Field (2010: 5) argued that the emphasis on income had 'prevented a much more comprehensive strategy emerging', and he highlighted the impact of parenting and the learning environment. In addition, the types of resources needed to eradicate child poverty were seen as unrealistic, particularly in the light of the Coalition Government's intention to cut the budget deficit.

Field's report was reflected in the Coalition Government's 2011 Child Poverty Strategy (DfE, 2011). This chimed well with the overall ideological approach of a Conservative Party that wanted to reduce the influence of the state in favour of individuals taking responsibility for their own lives, and to reduce the national fiscal deficit (see Chapter 1). The government argued that 'work, not welfare, is the best route out of poverty' (DWP, 2011: 2) and claimed the previous Labour Government had encouraged a benefit dependency, while they would ensure that 'work pays as a sustainable route out of poverty' (DWP, 2011: 3).

Evidence

The measure for poverty commonly cited in government statistics uses children eligible for free school meals (FSMs) and compares their achievement with those not eligible – 'the FSM gap'. FSMs are available to children whose parents receive income support, income-based jobseekers allowance or child tax credit. The government also used another measure, the Income Deprivation Affecting Children Indices, which refer to the area in which children live using a number of measures to rank deprivation. But the FSM characteristic is the one most commonly used in the DfE statistics and allows analysis and comparisons over time. There are criticisms of the use of FSM as a proxy for child poverty and deprivation, but it is valuable as a consistent measure across the years and starkly illustrates differences in educational achievement.

In addition to data available from the DfE website, a number of large-scale longitudinal studies trace the experiences of children growing up in the UK. These include: the Effective Pre-School, Primary and Secondary Education Project (EPPSE), the Millennium Cohort Study (MCS), the Avon Longitudinal Study of Parents and Children (ALSPAC), the Longitudinal Study of Young People in England (LSYPE) and the British Cohort Study (BCS). All provide evidence of a strong link between low socio-economic status and lower educational attainment. A number of campaigning organisations analyse this evidence and provide data which translate and interpret the DfE official data: the End Child Poverty site, Child Poverty Action Group (CPAG) and the Joseph Rowntree Foundation. Organisations such as the Institute of Fiscal Studies also provide up-to-date research, predictions and analysis of government policy in this area.

The most recent DfE data show quite clearly why there is such concern:

> In 2010/11 at KS2, 58 per cent of pupils known to be eligible for free school meals (FSM) achieved the expected level in both English and mathematics compared with 78 per cent of all other. *The gap in attainment between these two groups was 20 percentage points* in 2011 compared with 21 percentage points in 2010.
>
> (DfE, 2012: 3)

Further analysis shows differences associated with gender, curriculum subjects and special educational needs (SEN) (see Chapter 5); but in all cases there is a substantial FSM achievement gap, except in the case of children of Chinese origin eligible for FSM. Some researchers have also highlighted that children from minority ethnic groups are over-represented among poor children. Ethnic minorities make up 12 per cent of the population and 15 per cent of children, but 25 per cent of children who are in poverty (Platt, 2009: 2; Tackey *et al.*, 2011). The data on ethnicity highlight the complexity of links between poverty and attainment: the FSM gap is markedly different across ethnic groups and reminds us that children eligible for FSM can achieve good levels of attainment (DfE, 2012).

The evidence suggests that poorer children do worse on both cognitive and behavioural outcomes at both age 3 and age 5. Shockingly, by age 5 children from better-off families who have low cognitive ability at age 2 have almost caught up with high-ability children from poorer families (Waldfogel and Washbrook, 2010; Hobcraft and Kiernan, 2010). Eleven-year-old pupils eligible for free school meals are around twice as likely not to achieve basic standards in literacy and numeracy as other pupils (Josph Rowntree Foundation, 2012a, 2012b).

That early gap continues to affect children's educational achievement; early attainment is significantly linked to later outcomes throughout the educational process and explains a high proportion of the gap in attainment between the poorest and the richest at Key Stage 2 (Waldfogel and Washbrook, 2010). Feinstein argues that around 55 per cent of children in the bottom 20 per cent at age 7 (Key Stage 1) remain there at age 16 (Key Stage 4), and fewer than 20 per cent move into the top 60 per cent (Feinstein, 2003). Field (2010: 5) summarises a wide range of evidence and argues, 'schools do not effectively close that gap; children who arrive in the bottom range of ability tend to stay there'. The data show the attainment gap between those eligible and that those ineligible for free school meals becomes wider as pupils progress through the education system. This is also reflected in the data for GCSE and A levels. One of the most powerful indicators of the long-term impact lies in the fact that 60,000 state school pupils in the top 20 per cent of academic performers do not go on to higher education (CPAG, 2012).

Explanations

Research in this area recognises the difficulty of identifying causal relationships between poverty and educational achievement that are affected by gender, SEN, ethnicity, racism, neighbourhood factors, health including mental health, housing, teacher and parent expectations, peer group influences and size of family. However, some characteristics emerge repeatedly.

Income

Poverty is defined in many government and research reports as below 60 per cent of average income. As indicated above, the focus on income in the relationship between poverty and educational achievement has been challenged in recent years (Field, 2010; Goodman and Gregg, 2010). Income is only one aspect in accounting for the experiences of children in the school system. But there is evidence that poverty has a powerful influence on children's ability to respond to educational opportunities. Poverty affects children in the following ways:

- the absence of learning habits and experiences at home;
- a lack of access to computers;
- a lack of a sense of self-esteem through appropriate interactions with parents;
- poor housing;
- an unhealthy diet;
- possible mental health issues within the family;
- domestic violence;
- the stresses associated with low pay or unemployment.

These all make it potentially difficult for children to see themselves as positive learners. Low income is likely to affect parents' sense of being able to provide their children with the same advantages as those in more affluent households. Parents who are stressed about money and employment, working unsocial hours in more than one job, are likely to have less time to provide their children with an environment conducive to good educational outcomes (Blanden and Gregg, 2004).

A study on children's perspective (Horgan, 2007) shows that the way that children experience school is determined by the level of disadvantage they face, and that poorer children get used to the fact of their social position from a very early age. They accept that this will be reflected in their experience of school – that they are not going to get the same quality of schooling or of outcomes as better-off children. This was confirmed in later research by Martin and Hart (2011), which indicated that young people observing links between poverty and a lack of motivation saw these as contributing to strains on family relationships and impacting on aspirations around employment. Housing difficulties and possible moves can shatter continuity of educational experiences (CPAG, 2012). These can all impact negatively on a child's experiences of learning and make it difficult to separate material deprivation from its impact on life chances.

Home learning environment

An emphasis on the importance of the home learning environment has grown across the years, initially through the EPPE project (Sylva *et al.*, 2004, 2008). An early publication commented 'the home learning environment is only moderately associated with social class. What parents do is more important than who they are' (Sylva, 2004). Recently three influential reports have given considerable emphasis to the importance of the early years (Allen, 2011; Tickell, 2011; Field, 2010). Field notes aspects of the home learning environment as able to 'trump class background and parental income' (2010: 16).

The home learning environment covers a range of aspects of the parent–child relationship, including language development, conversation with children, interaction with them, reading to them and the time given to listening to them (Gregg and Goodman, 2010). Issues associated with low income are likely to influence the capacity of parents to offer a positive learning environment and can lead to a poor learning environment compounded by poor income. This has led to calls for early intervention to counter the poor learning environment in which children may find themselves. Evidence may be seen in the Field report and in the Coalition Government's strategy on child poverty (Field, 2010: DWP, 2011).

Parenting

An emphasis on parenting has emerged strongly in recent years. Many of the models developed by New Labour were concerned with how to encourage effective parenting, initially in a supportive framework but then moving to an increasingly orientated deficit model (see Chapter 2). The Every Child Matters (ECM) agenda was part of this concern about effective parenting, and research has shown that parental involvement has a positive effect on achievement, even when background factors such as social class and family size have been taken into account (Sylva *et al.*, 2004, 2008). Interaction between parents and children, warm, positive relationships with parents, and being interested in their children's education, are significant in increasing the child's chances as an adult of moving out of poverty (Blanden, 2006).

Early-years education

Attendance at early-years settings has also been shown to have a major effect on cognitive outcomes in childhood (Sylva *et al.*, 2008). Recent research from the EPPSE project has shown the longer term impact of attending preschool. Pupils perform better at 14 if they have attended preschool, regardless of the quality of provision they received (Sammons *et al.*, 2011). The Coalition Government maintained funding for 15 hours a week of early education for all three- and four-year-olds and expanded provision for two-year-olds; but cuts were made to children's centre budgets in two-thirds of local authorities. The evidence suggests that quality early-years settings have a long-term impact on educational outcomes, and in many ways may be easier to provide than other aspects that affect children's home environment.

Cognitive abilities

There is substantial evidence that low-income children are behind in cognitive development and one year behind in vocabulary when they enter school, with long-term consequences: 'such early gaps may affect low-income children's attitudes towards school and their aspirations for school attainment' (Waldfogel and Washbrook, 2010: 36). The work of Goodman and Gregg (2010) has focused on the significant role that attitudes and behaviours have in explaining differential progress between rich and poor children and how aspirations and attitudes are passed from parents to children. Their model of intergenerational transmission suggests that 'an important part of the story is about the transfer of cognitive abilities from one generation to the next' (2010: 11). They suggest their work helps to explain a large part of the cognitive skills gap between rich and poor children by identifying a strong relationship between the cognitive skills of parents and their children that remains after controlling for many environmental factors.

Of all the factors identified above, particularly those associated with the intergenerational transmission of cognitive skills, it is difficult to disentangle the extent to which these factors are heavily influenced by the structural inequalities which have characterised British society for many years. The cognitive skills and limitations rooted in parents' own childhood influences will themselves have been part of the way in which class inequalities shape attitudes and aspirations. Disentangling cause and effect in such complex areas is not easy.

Coalition government policies and impact

The rhetoric of the 2010 Coalition Government's approach to poverty has not translated into practice. It gave overriding priority to reducing the financial deficit by restructuring the welfare system. This was seen by many commenters as ensuring that targets to address poverty, and particularly child poverty, had no chance of being met. The decision to withdraw working tax credits from couples with children unable to increase their working hours to a new high threshold of 24 per week had a major negative impact on the finances of low-income families:

> Relative child poverty is set to increase between 2010–11 and 2015–16 by around 400,000, and absolute child poverty (as defined in the Child Poverty Act (2010) will increase between 2010–11 and 2015–16 by around 500,000.
>
> (Browne, 2012: 4)

Browne's work also points to the fact that cuts in public spending will fall heavily on some groups: he identifies particular ethnic groups, families with the lowest incomes, and non-working lone parents who are losing the most from the reforms (Browne, 2012: 3). Analyses have also shown that the impact will fall heavily on women, and this has implications for single-parent families and those families dependent upon the woman's income (Fawcett Society, 2012). *The Guardian* newspaper (2012) undertook an analysis of vacancies in the job market which showed that only 52 per cent of the positions available provided enough hours to meet the new government definition of work for a typical family. Thousands of low-income families would see their income plummet, increasing their stress levels and the consequent negative impact on children and their educational outcomes.

The 2010 Coalition Government did have policies which they claimed challenged the relationship between poverty and educational achievement, particularly through the pupil premium, but this came under attack for both its level and spread of the funding. The government also set up the Education Endowment Foundation in 2010 which was dedicated to raising the attainment of disadvantaged pupils and to breaking the link between family background and educational achievement; but its success is yet to be realised.

In addition to issues that directly relate to income, other policy developments by the Coalition Government may entrench existing inequalities. The educational divide

between the wealthy and the poorest are likely to be exacerbated by government education policies. The Sutton Trust's survey of teachers indicated that that they did not
see educational change associated with academies or free schools as contributing to
improved educational outcomes for less privileged children (Sutton Trust, 2010).

Political discussion

The evidence suggests that there is no single and simple explanation for why learners
from poor backgrounds do badly in educational terms; rather there are multiple factors
implicated at the individual as well as the social and wider society levels. But policy to
address this relationship depends on what is seen as effective and politically desirable.
The New Labour model saw children's achievement located in the way in which aspirations and attitudes are socially produced and the role of material resources in influencing
them. This saw the role of the family within the wider social and economic structure
where the state can influence material resources and provide support for good parenting
and the home learning environment.

The coalition model is different: it looks at child poverty and its associated educational
outcomes through a political prism which rejects the 'heavy hand of the state' in favour
of a focus on individual responsibility to provide 'good' parenting and a home learning
environment. It takes attention away from wider structural questions about the circumstances in which families find themselves, and how values and aspirations may be rooted
in material poverty. The Coalition Government brought together a neoliberal agenda
to contract the role of the state and empower individuals to act, while working within
a neoconservative exemplar to espouse a particular model of parenting and the home
learning environment. Claims about reducing state intervention hide the increasing invasion of the family and are in danger of leading to a deficit view of inadequate parents
whose children somehow need to be rescued.

Raffo et al. (2007) have identified three levels of policy intervention to tackle poverty:
the individual; the immediate social context (families, communities, schools and peer
groups); and underlying social structures and inequality. These levels are informed by
two perspectives, the first of which is a functionalist one that assumes that education plays
a key role in enabling societies to function properly, and another identifying that interventions would be needed across all three levels. Interventions undertaken by the Labour
Government, and then by the Coalition Government, were aimed largely at the individual and immediate social context within that broadly functionalist perspective, trying
to make the current system work more effectively.

Raffo's second 'socially critical' perspective focuses on wider structural issues: the
impact of globalisation, forms of social exclusion, the way these are reflected in health
inequalities, high levels of unemployment, poor housing and infrastructure, lack of
employment, lack of resources, public services and the way all these are likely to 'cause'
poverty. The socially critical perspective assumes that education in its current form
reflects an unequal distribution of power and resources, and that this needs to be challenged. Policies from this perspective require very different interventions than do those
issues that appear to be about individual characteristics and immediate social context
within a benign view of the current system.

The Coalition Government's is a functionalist perspective and sees challenging the
link between poverty and low educational achievement, not as transferring income within

the welfare system, but as transferring responsibility to parents and families. This risks an implicit message: poor parents lead to poor parenting. It diverts attention away from the impact of rising prices, frozen benefits and soaring unemployment. Katherine Rake of the Family and Parenting Institute argues:

> This focus on parenting skills is not matched by conclusive evidence about a decline in our standards of parenting. It also acts as a distraction – it risks diverting our attention away from the mounting pressures which modern society creates for parents.
>
> (Rake, 2012, para. 2)

Conclusion

In 2010 Brewer, commenting on the difficulties of addressing child poverty, suggested that there was a need for fiscal resources to increase state support for families with children, to improve labour market outcomes for low-income parents and to reduce inequalities in earnings (Brewer *et al.*, 2010: 55). This chapter supports that view, but argues that the current political and economic approach to child poverty does not address any of these factors.

Summary points

- There is a considerable body of evidence which shows that children living in poverty achieve poorer educational outcomes and that this educational gap grows across their school career.
- The explanations for this relationship indicate a complex interaction between a number of factors and, while important, income may not be the overriding characteristic.
- Certain groups such as women and ethnic minorities are particularly vulnerable to low income and deprivation.
- The use of concepts such as 'home learning environment' and 'parenting' can suggest a deficit model of low income families who practise inadequate parenting. Such models fail to locate poverty and social deprivation within the wider model of class and structural inequalities which are rooted in historic models of power and economic and political domination.
- Attempts by the 2010 Coalition Government to address child poverty were undermined by other aspects of their policy relating to welfare benefits, the reduction of the fiscal deficit and their model which argues for transferring responsibility for tackling poverty away from the state to individuals as participants in the labour market.
- Estimates suggest that government policies will lead to an increase in child poverty over the next five years which, given the ideological models enshrined within the government's child poverty strategy, will emphasise further parental deficit models and may encourage attacks on the 'undeserving poor'.

Questions for discussion

- How do you understand the relationship between poverty and attitudes and aspirations?
- What policies do you think could tackle the 'poverty gap' without stigmatising poor children?

- What would a socially critical perspective identify as the underlying roots of child poverty?

Recommended reading

DCSF (2008) *Impact of Parental Involvement in Children's Education.* London: DCSF. Available online at https://www.education.gov.uk/publications/eOrderingDownload/DCSF-parental_Involvement.pdf (accessed 30 March 2012).
An accessible discussion of impact of parental involvement and the importance of the home learning environment.

DCSF (2009) *Breaking the Link between Disadvantage and Attainment.* London: DCSF. Available online at http://publications.teachernet.gov.uk/eOrderingDownload/00357-2009.pdf (accessed 3 April 2012).
Gives data on rising levels of attainment for different groups and identifies strategies to further tackle the achievement gap.

Field, F. (2010) *The Foundation Years: Preventing poor children becoming poor adults: The report of the independent review on poverty and life chances.* London: DWP. Available online at http://www.nfm.org.uk/component/jdownloads/finish/74/333 (accessed 23 April 2012).
Useful for emphasis on 'the foundation years' and for references to research on impact of poverty on educational outcomes.

Goodman, A. and Gregg, P. (eds) (2010) *Children's Educational Outcomes: The role of attitudes and behaviours, from early childhood to late adolescence.* York: Joseph Rowntree Foundation. Available online at http://www.jrf.org.uk/sites/files/jrf/poorer-children-education-full.pdf (accessed 10 April 2012).
Brings together data from a range of longitudinal studies and has a clear summary of factors influencing role of attitudes and behaviour on educational outcomes.

Rake, K. (2012) *Parenting under the Microscope.* London: Family and Parenting Institute. Available online at http://www.familyandparenting.org/our_work/Parenting/Katherine+Rake (accessed 28 April 2012).
Examines the rise of scrutiny on parents and the emergence of a stigmatising narrative around deficit parenting, and suggests ideas for framing future parenting policy.

References

Allen, G. (2011) *Early Intervention: The next steps: An independent report to Her Majesty's Government.* London: Cabinet Office. Available online at http://www.dwp.gov.uk/docs/early-intervention-next-steps.pdf (accessed 12 April 2012).

Blanden, J. (2006) *Bucking the Trend: What enables those who are disadvantaged in childhood to succeed later in life?* DWP Working Paper No.31. London: DWP.

Blanden, J. and Gregg, P. (2004) *Family Income and Educational Attainment: A review of approaches and evidence for Britain.* CMPO Working Paper Series No 04/101.

Brewer, M., Browne, J., Joyce, R. and Sibieta, L. (2010) *Child Poverty in the UK since 1998–99: Lessons from the past decade.* IFS Working Paper 10/23. London: IFS. Available online at http://www.ifs.org.uk/wps/wp1023.pdf (accessed 12 April 2012).

Browne, J. (2012) *The Impact of Austerity Measures on Households with Children.* London: Institute for Fiscal Studies, Family and Parenting Institute. Available online at http://www.familyandparenting.org/Resources/FPI/Documents/FPI_IFS_Austerity_Jan_2012.pdf (accessed 23 April 2012).

Child Poverty Action Group (CPAG) (2012) 2 skint 4 school: *What does child poverty have to do with educational achievement?* London: CPAG. Available online at http://www.cpag.org.uk/2skint4school/details.htm#incomes (accessed 27 February 2012).

DCSF (2009) *Breaking the Link between Disadvantage and Attainment.* London: DCSF. Available online at http://publications.teachernet.gov.uk/eOrderingDownload/00357-2009.pdf (accessed 3 April 2012).

DfE (2010) *Child Poverty Act*. London: DfE. Available online at http://www.legislation.gov.uk/ ukpga/2010/9/pdfs/ukpga_20100009_en.pdf (accessed 12 April 2012).

DfE (2011) *A New Approach to Child Poverty: Tackling the causes of disadvantage and transforming families' lives*. London: DfE. Available online at https://www.education.gov.uk/publications/eOrdering-Download/CM-8061.pdf (accessed 12 April 2012).

DfE (2012) *National Curriculum Assessments at Key Stage 2 in England 2010/2011* (rev. edn). London: DfE. Available online at http://www.education.gov.uk/rsgateway/DB/SFR/s001047/index.shtml (accessed 23 April 2012).

Fawcett Society (2012) *Response to Latest Labour Market Statistics – 14 March 2012*. London: Fawcett Society. Available online at http://www.fawcettsociety.org.uk/index.asp?PageID=1266 (accessed 12 April 2012).

Feinstein, L. (2003) Inequality in the Early Cognitive Development of British Children in the 1970 Cohort. *Economica*: 73–97.

HM Treasury (2008) *Ending Child Poverty: Everybody's business*. London: HM Treasury. Available online at http://www.hm-treasury.gov.uk/d/bud08_childpoverty_1310.pdf (accessed 15 March 2012).

Hobcraft, J. and Kiernan, K. (2010) *Predictive Factors from Age 3 and Infancy for Poor Childhood Outcomes at Age 5: Evidence from the Millennium Cohort Study*. York: University of York.

Horgan, G. (2007) *The Impact of Poverty on Young Children's Experience of School*. York: Joseph Rowntree Foundation. Available online at http://www.jrf.org.uk/knowledge/findings/socialpolicy/2146.asp (accessed 8 April 2012).

Joseph Rowntree Foundation (2012a) *The Poverty Site: The UK site for statistics on poverty and social exclusion*. York: Joseph Rowntree Foundation. Available online at http://www.poverty.org.uk/summary/ key%20facts.shtml (accessed 8 April 2012).

Joseph Rowntree Foundation (2012b) *Educational Attainment at Age 11*. York: Joseph Rowntree Foundation. Available online at http://poverty.org.uk/25/index.shtml (accessed 14 April 2012).

Martin, K. and Hart, R. (2011) *Trying to Get By: Consulting with children and young people on child poverty*. Nottingham: NFER and Office of the Children's Commissioner.

Platt, L. (2009) *Ethnicity and Child Poverty*. London: DWP. Available online at http://research.dwp.gov. uk/asd/asd5/rports2009-2010/rrep576.pdf (accessed 12 April 2012).

Raffo, C., Dyson, D., Gunter, H., Hall, D., Jones, L. and Kalambouka, A. (2007) *Education and poverty: A critical review of theory, policy and practice*. York: Joseph Rowntree Foundation. Available online at http:// www.jrf.org.uk/bookshop/eBooks/2028-education-poverty-theory.pdf (accessed 12 September 2012)

Rake, K. (2012) *Parenting under the Microscope*. Family and Parenting Institute. Available online at http:// www.familyandparenting.org/our_work/Parenting/Katherine+Rake (accessed 28 April 2012).

Sammons, P., Sylva, K., Melhuish, E., Siraj-Blatchford, I., Taggart, B., Draghici, D. and Smees, R. (2011) *Effective Pre-school, Primary and Secondary Education Project (EPPSE 3–14): Influences on students' development in Key Stage 3: Social–behavioural outcomes in Year 9*. London: DFE-RB184b. Available online at https://www.education.gov.uk/publications/eOrderingDownload/DFE-RB184b.pdf (accessed 3 April 2012).

Sutton Trust (2010) *NFER Teacher Voice Omnibus: The government's education reforms*. London: The Sutton Trust. Available online at http://www.suttontrust.com/public/documents/the-government-s-education-reforms.pdf (accessed 2 May 2012).

Sylva, K., Melhuish, E., Sammons, P., Siraj-Blatchford, I. and Taggart, B. (2004) *The Effective Provision of Pre-school Education (EPPE) Project: Findings from pre-school to end of Key Stage 1, Final Report*. London: DfES/Institute of Education/University of London.

Sylva, K., Melhuish, E., Sammons, P., Siraj-Blatchford, I. and Taggart, B.L. (2008) EPPE 3–11: *Final Report from the Primary Phase: Pre-school, school and family influences on children's development during Key Stage 2 (Age 7–11)* DCSF-RR061. London: DCSF.

Tackey, N.D., Barnes, H. and Khambhaita, P. (2011) *Poverty, Ethnicity and Education*. York: Joseph Rowntree Foundation. Available online at http://www.jrf.org.uk/sites/files/jrf/poverty-ethnicity-education-full.pdf (accessed 7 April 2012).

Tickell, C. (2011) *The Tickell Review: The early years: Foundations for life, health and learning.* London: DWP. Available online at http://www.dwp.gov.uk/docs/early-intervention-next-steps.pdf (accessed 12 April 2012).

Waldfogel, J. and Washbrook, E. (2010) *Low Income and Early Cognitive Development in the UK.* London: Sutton Trust. Available online at http://www.suttontrust.com/public/documents/1Sutton_Trust_Cognitive_Report.pdf (accessed 1 May 2012).

Washbrook, E. and Waldfogel, J. (2011) *On Your Marks: Measuring the school readiness of children in low-to-middle income families.* London: Resolution Foundation. Available online at http://www.resolution-foundation.org/media/media/downloads/On_your_marks.pdf (accessed 18 April 2012).

Chapter 5

Gender, educational achievement and the labour market

Christine Eden

Introduction

Reports on educational results always include comments on gender differences which are given considerable publicity. An emphasis on results fits within the policy of Labour Governments and the policy has been developed by the 2010 Coalition Government to give parents as much information as possible to support their choices as consumers. Gender is an easy way of appearing to provide such information. Understanding the data on gender and achievement requires not only identifying patterns and facts, but also seeking the explanations that account for these patterns. Such explanations often focus on the processes that occur within the school and classroom. But just as important are the experiences that construct young people's expectations and identities.

This chapter aims to:

- introduce the changing nature of debates about gender and educational achievement, including the relationship between gender, social class and ethnicity;
- illustrate these relationships by drawing on recent data;
- consider explanations for these relationships;
- briefly explore the 'labour market gender gap' in terms of pay and occupational positions.

Background

Gender has always been one of the dimensions in discussions on pupil attainment, but these vary across time and place, depending on social expectations of the position of men and women in society as a whole. In the nineteenth century the Schools Enquiry Commission of 1868 compared girls' and boys' school performance and suggested that differences could be attributed to characteristic mental differences between the sexes. The Commission did not argue for a different curriculum for boys and girls, but reports during the twentieth century did argue for differentiation. In the mid-twentieth century both the Crowther (CACE, 1959) and Newsom (CACE, 1963) reports argued that the prime destination of girls was as wives and mothers and that their curriculum should reflect their future domestic role.

In the mid-twentieth century political debate centered on working-class male pupils, and various explanations were given for their disadvantage in the school system, ranging from characteristics of the home background through to the school mechanisms which stratified pupils on the basis of social class. In the 1960s and 1970s there were significant changes in articulated social values and education systems with the introduction of comprehensive schooling and the Sex Discrimination Act of 1975. Within this framework it was possible to challenge female underachievement.

The feminist movement of the time promoted subject choices for girls and a number of projects aimed to break down traditional assumptions and to promote greater access across the curriculum. Projects such as Girls into Science and Technology and Women into Science and Engineering aimed to challenge stereotypical choices within the curriculum and drew attention to the importance of enhancing girls' achievement. Feminist writers made issues of gender equality very visible and argued strongly for change to address girls' and women's disadvantage in education and in the labour market. They were not prepared to accept that there were 'essentialist' fundamental differences in the biological capacities of males and females. Feminists wanted to focus on the social explanations for gender inequality in education achievement and to consider strategies for change.

The Education Reform Act of 1988 had considerable implications for gender equality in that it established a common curriculum to GCSE level for boys and girls. While subject stereotyped choices continue to be made at A-level, the climate within which the National Curriculum was introduced and the curriculum itself has led to at least the theoretical assumption that the sciences, technology and mathematics are as much part of the curriculum for girls as they are for boys.

The publication of GCSE results in the early 1990s revealed a gender gap. This gap has continued to widen in favour of females, and even the traditional advantage of males over females in science is reducing. After a relatively short focus on girls' achievements, current discussion of gender inequality focuses on boys and the strategies that will address their underachievement, usually without looking at the wider society, its economic and power structures and where men and women are located in these.

Whether the focus has been on boys or girls, explanations of inequalities have explored aspects of the education process, but have not always stressed the social construction of gender and the way in which gender interacts with social class and ethnicity. Understanding the construction of diverse masculine and feminine identities is necessary to understand educational achievement.

Gender differences in educational achievement and the labour market

Before the introduction of GCSE examinations, gender differences were hidden: girls were often significantly outperforming boys in arts and humanities subjects and boys slightly outperforming girls in mathematics and science subjects. Once GCSEs were introduced both boys' and girls' results improved, but girls increased their performance and challenged boys' performance in mathematics and science subjects. Since the 1990s this has led to a focus on the underachievement of boys, with reports commissioned to address the problem (Ofsted, 2003; DCSF, 2009). Boys' underachievement has been presented as something that schools should be able to address rather than as symptomatic of wider problems in gender relations in society. This is in spite of the fact that gender is not the strongest predictor of attainment; social class and ethnicity reveal greater attainment gaps (DfE, 2012a, 2012b, 2012c; Cassen and Kingdom, 2007; Ward and Eden, 2009).

The gap in achievement of girls in relation to boys actually widens as pupils get older and, in the last few years, the gap in performance which had existed in favour of boys at A-level has been almost eliminated. While the gender gap exists across all key stages, this statement needs to be moderated by subject and level.

Key Stage 2 2010/11

These figures illustrate differences between subjects and levels, with boys outperforming girls at level 5 in mathematics. The largest gender gap of 12 percentage points is in English, and it is a concern about literacy in particular that has driven so much of the moral panic and concern about boys' underachievement, which is replicated in international data.

The free school meals gap

The free school meals (FSM) gap is much more shocking than that for gender. Only 58 per cent of pupils known to be eligible for FSM achieved the expected level in both English and mathematics, compared with 78 per cent of all other pupils (DfE, 2012c). This is a 20 per cent FSM gap.

Ethnicity

When the data on ethnicity are added the picture becomes yet more complex. While there is a 5 to 6 percentage point difference between the genders in the majority of ethnic groups, for the black Caribbean groups eligible and ineligible for FSM there is a gender gap of 11 per cent and 9 per cent respectively. The biggest ethnicity gap relates to the Chinese ethnic group, where 91 per cent of Chinese pupils eligible for FSM achieved the expected level in English and mathematics, compared to 65 per cent for the same category of white British, a gap of 26 per cent.

Table 5.1 Percentage of pupils achieving level 4 or above at KS2 in English and mathematics

Gender	English	Mathematics
Boys	77	81
Girls	86	80
Gender gap	11 in favour of girls	1 in favour of boys

(Source: DfE, 2012a)

Table 5.2 Percentage of pupils achieving level 5 or above

Gender	English	Mathematics
Girls	35	33
Boys	23	37
Gender gap	12 in favour of girls	4 in favour of boys

(Source: DfE, 2012a)

These statistics illustrate the complexity of making blanket statements about gender performance: subject, level, FSM and ethnicity reveal different patterns and show that some girls also underperform, which is frequently ignored.

GCSE Key Stage 4

The measure normally used here is the percentage of pupils who achieve five or more A★–C grades at GCSE or equivalent, including English and mathematics. Between 2006/7 and 2010/11 girls consistently outperformed boys, and in 2010/11 continued to do so. A total of 61.9 per cent of girls compared with 54.6 per cent of boys achieved these grades – a gender gap of 7.3 per cent. But as at Key Stage 2 (KS2) the FSM gap is much greater, with 34.6 per cent of those pupils eligible for FSM compared to 62.0 per cent of all other pupils achieving these grades – an FSM gap of 27.4 (DfE, 2012a). Table 5.3 again highlights the complexity of the relationship between gender, FSM status and ethnicity. The gaps associated with FSM and ethnicity remain much greater than those associated with gender. For white British males the FSM gap is 32 per cent and there is a startling FSM gap of 54 per cent between white British girls and girls of Chinese origin.

A-level

The gender gap continues at A-level. In 2010/11 a record 26.5 per cent of girls' entries in all subjects were at A★ or A grade, compared with 19.8 per cent of boys' entries, a gap between the sexes of 6.7 percentage points. But boys are narrowing the girls' lead at A★ and a slightly greater percentage of males (13.1 per cent) achieved three or more A grades or above at A-level compared to 12.5 per cent for females (DfE, 2012c). The number of A★ grades issued to boys has gone up from 7.9 per cent in 2009/10 to 8.3 per cent in 2010/11. Girls' performance dipped slightly from 8.3 per cent to 8.2 per cent in the same period.

A-level gendered choices

It was suggested in the introduction that the National Curriculum had removed some of the choices around gendered subjects. There are still gendered choices at GCSE, but at A-level these become more pronounced and differences exist around both subject choice and the achievement of grades, as Table 5.4 illustrates.

Certain subjects are still clearly gendered. Physics, further mathematics and mathematics are chosen by far more boys than girls, while home economics, sociology and

Table 5.3 Percentage gaining five or more A★–C grades at GCSE or equivalent including English and mathematics

	Boys eligible for FSM	Girls eligible for FSM	Boys not eligible for FSM	Girls not eligible for FSM
White British	26	31.7	58.5	65.6
Back Caribbean	33.2	42.1	45.1	58.8
Chinese	61.4	86.1	74.6	83.5

(Source: DfE 2012b)

Table 5.4 2010–11 subject choices and A★ achievement by gender

Subject	Male entrants	Female entrants	% males gaining A★	% females gaining A★
Home economics	64	304	0	3.3
Computer studies	3,277	241	3.8	5.4
Physics	23,199	6,017	10.5	11.3
Further mathematics	7,815	3,585	27.8	26.6
Art and drama	11,438	30,179	11.9	14.7
Sociology	6,925	20,575	3.9	5.2
Psychology	14,257	36,690	6.8	7.9
Economics	14,409	6,417	8.4	10.4
Mathematics	45,288	30,204	18.7	17.2
Chemistry	22,820	20,436	10.1	8.7
All subjects	36,1992	420,592	8.3	8.2

(Source: DfE 2012c)

psychology are preferred by girls. The overall percentages of males or females gaining A★ grades does not indicate significant differences between males and females, but gives a slight overall margin to males for 'all subjects'. The sort of extreme gendered choice associated with home economics and computer studies is also found in looking at applied A-level examinations, where applied engineering is taken by 214 males and 12 females, and health and social care taken by 176 males and 4,685 females. Such choices have a direct relationship to degree and career options.

In recent years there has been a growth in the numbers of females taking what have been seen as traditionally masculine subjects. This is particularly the case in mathematics where the numbers have risen from 21,171 in 2007 to 30,204 in 2011. During the same period there was an increase of approximately two thousand in the number of males taking psychology. Over the last two years girls have moved into the areas of science and mathematics to a greater degree than males have moved to more traditional 'female' subjects.

Higher education

Historically, women have been under-represented in universities. From 1992 their participation has been increasing and there are now more women than men undergraduates in the UK: 54 per cent compared to 46 per cent. There are, though, significant differences in the types of courses and universities that males and females choose, and this has implications for their options in the labour market. HESA data from 2007/08 show that over twice as many women as men choose to study education and twice as many males as women study physics. Men make up less than a quarter of those on social work, education and psychology degree courses, fewer than a third on English studies and fewer than half on languages; male qualifiers in initial teacher training make up fewer than a quarter of students. In physics fewer than 20 per cent were female, and in engineering and technology only 15 per cent were female (HESA, 2008).

There are also marked differences in women's and men's access to universities. Women are significantly over-represented in the new universities and particularly in the new universities which were originally teacher training colleges. In these institutions female students outnumber males, in some cases in the ratio of three to one. These universities are not yet seen as high status or with strong research profiles. So both subject choice and type of university have considerable impact on male and female students in access to high-status and well-paid work in the labour market (HESA, 2008).

Evans (2009) has illustrated how social class interacts with gender in influencing university choice for working-class girls for whom class and gender norms of behaviour and aspirations remain rooted within domestic and personal agendas. She shows that, for young working-class women attempting to enter prestigious social institutions, there is a tension between their commitment to the maintenance of family ties and obligations and what would be a difficult process of cultural separation. This highly gendered experience reflects the differences for working- and middle-class women and constitutes an important part of educational aspirations.

The labour market

The gender gap associated with education suggests that girls should be leaving the education system in a privileged position. But this is not the case (Rake, 2009). Equal pay legislation came into force in the UK more than 40 years ago; yet women still earn less than men with a gender pay gap of 14.9 per cent (Fawcett Society, 2011). However, it is significant that *junior* female managers are actually earning more than men at the same level, and in 2010 the Equality and Human Rights Commission reported that the pay gap was lowest for those under the age of 30 (EHRC, 2010). This may reflect a different approach to young women's willingness to accept lower pay and their more assertive approach within the labour market.

Gender and power

Women are under-represented in all positions of power and influence. More women than men go to university in the UK and the US and tend to outlive them; yet men still dominate economic and political leadership. Only five of 23 Cabinet ministers are women; 31 per cent of elected councillors are women; 13 per cent of local authority council leaders are women (Fawcett Society, 2011). The same problems exist in the world of business where only 14.2 per cent of directors in FTSE100 boards are women. Only 15 per cent of High Court judges are women and there is only one female Supreme Court Justice. In the public and voluntary sectors, where women are in the majority, women do make up 48 per cent of chief executives; just over a third of secondary school head teachers are women, although they do account for the majority of full-time teachers across Great Britain (EHRC, 2010).

Explanations

In the 1960s and 1970s, when issues about girls' achievement and access to the curriculum were seen as a problem by feminist writers, much of the debate was about challenging the way that the curriculum and learning experiences were structured in ways which reinforced primary socialisation and stereotypical sex roles. These are significant influences on the development and reproduction of gendered expectations, but this focus on social learning presented gender as a clear male/female binary construction which initially did not focus on the way social class, sexuality and ethnicity were interwoven with gender. The search for the school's role in reproducing gender stereotypes led to studies which explored the internal processes of the classroom, classroom organisation, teacher's expectations, and the nature of the curriculum, resources and assessment strategies, teaching and learning styles and the hidden curriculum. The focus on boys' underachievement led to debates about different teaching styles for boys, the feminisation of the classroom and a lack of male teacher role models, the need for boy-friendly learning materials, and suggestions that assessed coursework favoured girls. Such debates reinforced the notion of a binary view of boys and girls as learners (Connell, 2002; DCSF, 2009).

The notion that boys and girls need different sorts of learning experiences has been challenged by a perspective which emphasises the way identities are socially constructed, and this makes sense of the data provided on pages 46–8. Pupils bring with them into the classroom not just knowledge of what is expected of them as boys and girls, but also experiences rooted in other identities and subjectivities. Therefore, what we need to recognise is that there are multiple masculinities and femininities which are interwoven with social class and ethnicity (Connell, 2002; Francis and Skelton, 2005). This model highlights the diversity of behaviours and expectations and the ways in which boys and girls and young men and women construct their subjectivities and resist and challenge gender stereotypes. It also points to the complexity of how boys and girls and young men and women develop their own sense of sexual identity, including rejecting heterosexual models; how these identities are constructed within the school; and what choices they make about subjects and appropriate gendered behaviour. This emphasis on multiple identities also highlights the fact that such diverse identities are socially constructed and negotiated within schools and classrooms. Gender relations are located within a context of power rooted in hegemonic masculinity and heterosexuality which is imposed on both boys and girls, including those who resist and challenge these identities.

Various studies illustrate the way in which gender interacts with race and class in the classroom, influencing achievement, expectations and aspirations. An early study by Lees (1986) illustrated the use of sexual language and bullying to impose gender norms on girls. It showed the way that such abuse interacted with racism to create another layer of power relations between girls themselves, even while both groups were constrained by the sexual stereotyping to which they were all subjected. Mac an Ghaill (1994) argued that the loss of working-class manual occupations undermined traditional models of masculinity, leading to an erosion of confidence and a sense that education lacked relevance and value. This negative approach to education is indicated by greater rates of truancy and exclusion (Ofsted, 2003). In other research teachers report that male students exhibit greater behavioural problems in the classroom, with a group culture that sees education as undesirable (Martino and Berrill, 2003). Warrington and Younger (2007) argue that the issues associated with male underachievement relate to the tensions between the culture of the school and images of masculinity held in the local community and wider society. The dominant image of masculinity, and the street culture from which it emerges, creates an alternative culture within schools that constructs masculinity as competitive, macho and laddish, resulting in boys' gradual alienation from school. They found this to be particularly strong among white working-class boys in schools in inner cities.

A significant aspect of this imposition of gender norms lies in relationships with peer groups, constructing, policing and reinforcing hegemonic masculinity and gender stereotypes: 'being accepted by the peer group, this "halfway house between the family and the adult world" is one of the most powerful and potent forces effecting change in the adolescent' (Warrington and Younger, 2011: 2). This involves both boys and girls imitating and evaluating themselves against each other, using sanctions to promote dominant hegemonic masculinity and compulsory heterosexuality and motherhood models. For both genders such behaviours can lead to resistance to education (Smith, 2007).

Such evidence leads to a position where the issue that needs to be tackled is gender itself – how gender is constructed and reproduced within the school. This cannot be achieved by changing the proportion of male teachers or focusing on learning and teaching styles. 'It's in schools where gender constructions are less accentuated that boys tend to do better – and strategies that work to reduce relational constructions of gender that are most effective in facilitating boys' achievement' (Francis and Skelton, 2008, quoted in DCSF, 2009: 3).

Countering gender effects requires a whole-school approach to challenging gender cultures and the construction of stereotyped gender behaviour. Teachers need to challenge stereotypes, encourage pupils to challenge them, change the way in which the classroom is organised to engage boys and girls working together, address language and discourse and explore the expectations that pupils have of themselves and their own educational success.

Francis and Skelton (2005) refer to 'oppositional relationships' between boys and girls: boys gain status in their own and their peer group's eyes in a way that has a negative impact on their learning; girls are bullied about their sexuality, intimidated about their role in heterosexual relationships and subject to expectations that their futures lie in compulsory motherhood (Haywood and Mac an Ghaill, 1996; Archer et al., 2007; Francis and Skelton, 2005; Warrington and Younger, 2007). Strategies to tackle the dominant images of masculinity could have a positive impact on girls' experience of hegemonic masculinity. McCarry's (2010) research into violence among young people illustrates the way in which they endorse a model of gender in which 'men and women enter intimate heterosexual relationships which accommodate this inequality; part of normative masculinity is utilising violence as a legitimate (if undesirable) resource' (2010: 27). Her work emphasised the importance of the peer group in regulating boys' behaviour across social class, but she also suggests there are possibilities for intervening to 'facilitate the development of gender identities which have positive rather than negative implications' (2010: 28).

Conclusion

The gender gap has to be seen in the context of the even more alarming gaps associated with class and ethnicity. To address the gender gap requires challenging the power relationships that frame the social construction of gender both within the education system and wider society where men and women make choices about work and childcare. Understanding and challenging male underachievement in educational attainment needs to be accompanied by an analysis of what is happening to women in the home and labour market.

Summary points

- Educational attainment needs to be understood in association with social class and ethnicity.
- Data analysis highlights that:
  o Subject and level show different stories about the gender gap.
  o The focus on boys' underachievement masks the fact that some girls are under-performing.
  o The underachievement of white working-class boys and black Caribbean boys is marked.
  o The gaps associated with educational attainment are much greater in relation to social class and ethnicity than those associated with gender.
  o Attention is not given to areas of the curriculum where girls are less successful, such as mathematics, nor to their under-representation in physics and economics.
- Understanding the gender gap requires an analysis that sees gender as not being about fixed, binary categories but as actively constructed and susceptible to change.
- Challenging male underachievement requires tackling gender itself as an oppositional social construction rather than tinkering with the curriculum.
- An emphasis on boys' underachievement obscures the need to address women's position in the labour market.

Questions for discussion

- Why do you think data on educational attainment always emphasise the gender gap when the gaps associated with FSM and ethnicity are considerably greater?
- How do you account for the attention given to boys' underachievement in education compared to women's position and experience in the labour market?
- What can schools do to help create a positive approach to learning that challenges dominant power models of masculinity?

Recommended reading

Connell, R.W. (2002) *Gender*. Cambridge: Polity Press.
A valuable discussion of the complexity of gender relationships.

DCSF (2009) *Gender Issues in School – What works to improve achievement for boys and girls*. London: DCSF. Available online at http://media.education.gov.uk/assets/files/pdf/8/8311dcsfgender per cent20what per cent20works per cent20bmkpdf.pdf (accessed 29 April 2012)
A useful evaluation of different approaches to boys' underachievement.

Francis, B. and Skelton, C. (2005) *Reassessing Gender and Achievement*. London: Routledge.
A survey which is still valuable of a wide range of arguments on this topic.

Rake, K. and Lewis, R. (2009) *Just below the Surface: Gender stereotyping, the silent barrier to equality in the modern workplace?* London: Fawcett Society. Available online at http://www.fawcettsociety. org.uk/documents/Just per cent20Below per cent20the per cent20Surface.pdf (accessed 4 March 2012).
Good on stereotyping and impact on women's choices.

References

Archer, L., Halsall, A. and Hollingworth, S. (2007) Class, Gender, (Hetero)sexuality and Schooling: Paradoxes within working-class girls' engagement with education and post-16 aspirations. *British Journal of Sociology of Education* 28: 165–80.

CACE (1959) *15–18 The Crowther Report*. London: HMSO.

CACE (1963) *Half Our Future: The Newsom Report*. London: HMSO.

Cassen, R., and Kingdon, G. (2007) *Tackling Low Educational Achievement*. London: Joseph Rowntree Foundation. Available online at http://www.jrf.org.uk/sites/files/jrf/2063-education-schools-achievement.pdf (accessed 1 May 2012).

Connell, R.W. (2002) *Gender*. Cambridge: Polity Press.

DCSF (2009) *Gender Issues in School – . What works to improve achievement for boys and girls*. London: DCSF. Available online at http://media.education.gov.uk/assets/files/pdf/8/8311dcsfgender per cent20what per cent20works per cent20bmkpdf.pdf (accessed 29 April 2012)

DfE (2012c) *National Curriculum Assessments at Key Stage 2 in England 2010/2012* (rev. edn). London: DfE. Available online at http://www.education.gov.uk/cgi-bin/rsgateway/search.pl?keyw=081&q2=Search (accessed 30 April 2012).

DfE (2012a) *GCSE and Equivalent Attainment by Pupil Characteristics in England, 2010/11*. London: DfE. Available online at http://www.education.gov.uk/cgi-bin/rsgateway/search.pl?keyw=083&q2=Search (accessed 12 April 2012).

DfE (2012b) *GCE/Applied GCE A/AS and Equivalent Examination Results in England, 2010/11* (Rev. edn). London: DfE. Available online at http://www.education.gov.uk/rsgateway/DB/SFR/s001055/index.shtml (accessed 12 April 2012).

DfE (2012c) *National Curriculum Assessments at Key Stage 2 in England 2010/2012* (Rev. edn). London: DfE. Available online at http://www.education.gov.uk/cgi-bin/rsgateway/search.pl?keyw=081&q2=Search (accessed 30 April 2012).

EHRC (2010) *How Fair is Britain?* London: EHCR.

Evans, S. (2009) In a different place: Working class girls in higher education. *Sociology*, 43(2): 340–355.

Fawcett Society (2011) *Pay Gap Stagnant as Women's Unemployment Continues to Rise*. London: Fawcett Society. Available online at http://www.fawcettsociety.org.uk/index.asp?PageID=1257 (accessed 24 April 2012).

Fawcett Society (2012) *If We're Not at the Table, We're on the Menu. Fawcett's Facts and Stats on women and power – November 2011*. London: Fawcett Society. Available online at http://www.fawcettsociety.org.uk/documents/Women per cent20in per cent20Power- per cent20Facts per cent20and per cent-20Stats per cent20November per cent202011.pdf (accessed 12 April 2012).

Francis, B. and Skelton, C. (2005) *Reassessing Gender and Achievement*. London: Routledge.

Haywood, C. and Mac an Ghaill, M. (1996) Schooling Masculinities. In: M. Mac an Ghaill (ed.) *Understanding Masculinities* Buckingham: Open University Press.

HESA (2008) *All HE Students by Level of Study, Mode of Study, Subject of Study (#1), Domicile and Gender 2006/07*. Cheltenham: HESA. Available online at http://www.hesa.ac.uk/dox/dataTables/studentsAndQualifiers/download/subject0607.xls?v=1.0 (accessed 10 April 2012).

Lees, S. (1986) *Losing Out: Sexuality and adolescent girls*. London: Hutchinson.

Mac an Ghaill, M. (1994) *The Making of Men: Masculinities, sexualities and schooling*. Buckingham: Open University Press.

McCarry, M. (2010) Becoming a 'Proper Man': Young people's attitudes about interpersonal violence and perceptions of gender. *Gender and Education* 22(1, January): 17–30.

Martino, W., and Berrill, D. (2003) Boys, Schooling and Masculinity: Interrogating the 'right' way to educate boys. *Educational Review* 55(2): 99–117.

Ofsted (2003) *Boys' Achievement in Secondary Schools*. London: Ofsted. Available online at http://www.ofsted.gov.uk/resources/boys-achievement-secondary-schools (accessed 15 March 2012).

Rake, K. and Lewis, R. (2009) *Just below the Surface: Gender stereotyping, the silent barrier to equality in the modern workplace?* London: Fawcett Society. Available online at http://www.fawcettsociety.org.uk/documents/Just per cent20Below per cent20the per cent20Surface.pdf (accessed 4 March 2012).

Smith, J. (2007). 'Ye've got to 'ave balls to play this game sir!' Boys, Peers and Fears: The negative influence of school-based 'cultural accomplices' in constructing hegemonic masculinities. *Gender and Education* 19: 179–98.

Ward, S. and Eden, C. (2009) *Key Issues in Education Policy*. London: Sage.

Warrington, M. and Younger, M. (2007) Closing the Gender Gap? Issues of equity in English secondary schools. *Discourse: Studies in the Cultural Politics of Education* 28(2): 219–42.

Warrington, M. and Younger, M. (2011) 'Life is a Tightrope': Reflections on peer group inclusion and exclusion amongst adolescent girls and boys. *Gender and Education* 23(2): 153–68.

Chapter 6

Education and race

Stephen Ward

Introduction

Britain is a multicultural, multiracial and multi-faith society, and always has been. Like many countries in Europe its population comprises centuries of migrants: Angles, Saxons, Jutes, Vikings, Normans and Jews, as well as people from the former colonies in the Caribbean, India, Africa and Hong Kong. This chapter examines the ways in which the education system has responded to the combined effects of a diverse population and inherent racism in British society.

Understanding the issues

Race and racism

The nineteenth century scientific classification of species and types divided human beings into three 'racial' types: Caucasoid (White European), Negroid (Black African) and Mongoloid (Mongolian or Chinese). This is now discredited and 'it is widely accepted that there is no such thing as separate human races in the biological sense' (Gillborn, 2008: 2). The term 'race' is a sociological and not a biological concept: there are physiological differences between people and some characteristics, particularly skin colour, have high social significance. Skin colour is biologically a minor characteristic, but people notice it and it is the focus of racial prejudice. Prejudice is to 'pre-judge', to hold ideas about people without evidence or knowledge. Racial prejudice is to make assumptions about individual people based on traditional stereotypes: 'Asian girls are studious and hard-working; young black men take drugs and are involved in knife crime'. Any visible characteristic, including speech accent, can allow a person to be categorised and stereotyped. Irish people can suffer from a stereotype held by the English that they are of low intelligence. Stereotypes usually have some historical origin, and this one derives from the Irish migrants imported during the nineteenth century as navigational workers ('navvies') to dig the canal system in England: physical labourers who attracted the low intelligence stereotype.

However, prejudice is only a part of the problem. 'Racism' occurs where people can act on their prejudices to disadvantage others with the power to affect people's lives. A white person may decide not to give a job to a black person because they are prejudiced against black people. In British society the power to offer jobs or to sell houses mainly lies in the hands of white, often male, people. Racism, then, is a matter of the differential power between the white majority and the black minority. Racism is sometimes described simply as 'prejudice plus power'. Because power is almost exclusively in the hands of white people, it is white people who can be racist. It is possible to imagine a society in which black people have the power to act in a racist manner to disadvantage white people, but that society does not exist in Britain today.

Racism is not restricted to the attitudes and activities of individuals. Whole organisations such as schools or business companies can operate to disadvantage minority groups. This is known as 'institutional racism'. Institutional racism is usually unintended and often unnoticed. It is the tendency of the traditional majority (white) cultural choices to prevail, and is racist in *effect*. Beyond individual institutions, the whole power structure of society in Britain is dominated by white male power: the government, the House of Commons, the judiciary, the police force, boards of directors, the civil service and the education system.

The terms 'black' and 'white' are used in discussion of race. Of course, no one is literally either black or white and the terms are not intended to describe colour in the biological sense. They are *sociological* ones to designate different groups: those likely to suffer the effects of racism, and those who are not. Some individuals and groups prefer not to be called 'black' and so the term 'black and minority ethnic' (BME) groups is now commonly used.

The colonies and post-war migration to Britain

Like other European countries, much of Britain's diverse population derives from its colonial past in the eighteenth and nineteenth centuries. As we saw in Chapter 1, the industrial revolution made Britain the most powerful economy in the world, but it developed its manufacturing industries at the expense of exploited workers in the colonies. While European countries are often depicted as helping developing countries to advance, colonialism fuelled the European industrial economies and prevented the economies of Africa and India from developing. Driven by combined economic domination and religious mission, Britain controlled countries and populations in India, the Caribbean, China, the Middle East and Africa. The most notorious case was the slave trade in which goods were traded in the west of Africa for slaves who were then stacked in their hundreds in the holds of the ships to be taken to the colonial plantations of the Caribbean to work to their deaths. In India there were no slave populations, but the British used its military strength to become the supreme overlords in India's caste system, with Queen Victoria 'Empress of India'. The rank cruelty and exploitation suffered by the peoples of the colonies at the hands of their British rulers are graphically described by Newsinger (2006).

The colonial history of European nations led to the 'supremacist world view' among its white populations: the perception that there are different biological races, that some races are superior to and more intelligent than others, and that the lower races can be treated as less than human. While few would subscribe explicitly to this view now, such assumptions are built into the cultural norms of Europe, its literature and media, with the portrayal of black people as evil, as golliwogs, as minstrels and of low intelligence; it pervades the thinking and unconscious actions of white people.

After World War II, Europe needed to re-build its economies. Britain had lost 25 per cent of its material resources, and its human resources were depleted with the loss of much of its male working population. It looked to the former colonies to supply the labour. The 1948 British Nationality Act gave members of the colonies the status of 'commonwealth citizens', allowing them to work in Britain. With an economic 'pull' from the industrialised countries of Europe, there was a 'push' from the peoples who were displaced from their homes by post-colonial movements when countries were given independence. It was natural, then, for people to come to Britain – 'the mother country' – where there were well-paid jobs, housing, education, a health service and political freedom in one of the world's greatest democracies.

The post-war migrant populations arrived in Britain with hopes and ambitions of creating a new life for themselves and their families. However, they found not the wealthy and democratic utopia they had imagined, but a society which still perceived black people as its colonial subjects. The jobs turned out to be arduous and under-paid shift work: the 'shit-jobs' which white people did not want. Housing was in over-crowded slums in the poorest areas of British cities. But worse was social ostracism of overt racism. This was a time when job advertisements would include 'no blacks' and estate agents would have lists of houses which were not to be made available to 'coloureds' (Fryer, 1984).

The Race Relations Act of 1967 made it illegal for companies or individuals to 'discriminate on the grounds of race, colour or creed'. Although legislation makes explicit and overt racial discrimination illegal, it does not change deep-seated attitudes and it does not remove the implicit and covert institutional racism. That black and minority ethnic people might feel angry about their experiences in Britain should not be surprising. The post-colonial diaspora in Britain can be explained simply by the phrase 'we are here because you were there'. The Commonwealth Immigrants Act of 1968 reversed the 1948 Act by introducing restrictions on black immigration. Britain then had enough labour and it was time to start closing the door to black immigration. In the 1970s, Britain was to join what is now the European Union (EU) which allowed free migration of workers into Britain from Europe, but, of course, those were mostly white.

Schooling and race

Assimilation and integration

Gillborn (2008) categorises the different responses of the education system to post-war immigration. In the 1950s and 1960s, schools in the inner cities found themselves with a diverse range of pupils from the West Indies, India, Pakistan and Hong Kong. The first response was to see such pupils as 'a problem': some didn't speak English, had different religions, ate different food and knew little of 'British culture'. The response became known as 'immigrant education': to try to 'assimilate outsiders' into the existing culture of the school system, mainly by teaching English. *They* needed to be changed to fit into existing school practices. Racism was overt and acceptable in British society, and the perception of BME children in this way was normal. 'Assimilation' was more than an attitude; it defined policies on schooling and race. For example, language teaching neglected the pupil's first language. English was to 'replace' the first language, without having regard to the fact that children used their first language to communicate within their family (Houlton, 1985).

While education policy sought integration through assimilation, voices in the wider social and political context resisted integration and, in the 1960s, opposition to immigration was rife. In 1968, Enoch Powell, Conservative MP for Wolverhampton South-West and Shadow Minister for Defence, gave an infamous speech in Birmingham warning that immigration would lead to racial conflict and that Britain's streets would 'run with rivers of blood'. The speech was highly inflammatory and he was removed from the shadow cabinet. These views are now expressed by racist nationalist groups such as the British National Party (BNP). The latent xenophobic fear of 'foreigners' can be fuelled by right-wing politicians. Margaret Thatcher (1978) was careful not to speak openly against immigration. However, in a television interview before the 1979 general election which brought her to power, she spoke of people's fear of being 'swamped' by different cultures.

Multiculturalism and cultural pluralism

The mid-1970s brought a change of view about BME pupils among sections of the education community as the concept of a multiracial and multicultural society grew. Rather than Britain being a single (white) society and culture into which immigrants should be made to fit, it was recognised that it comprises different 'races' and cultures, and always has done. The Labour Government's Race Relations Act in 1976 set up the Commission for Racial Equality to support minority groups. In education BME pupils were not to be regarded as a problem. Rather, schools should take account of different cultural origins and adjust to accommodate them. It should make provision for children to continue to learn and become literate in their first language as well as in English. The curriculum should include BME children's 'cultures': the music of the Caribbean, the history of India, world religions including Islam and Sikhism (Arora and Duncan, 1986). Multicultural education was not just to accommodate ethnic minority pupils; it should enhance the education of all pupils by enriching their learning with knowledge of other cultures and understanding the nature of the society in which they are growing up. The school should be a microcosm of a harmonious society in which different peoples live in social cohesion, sharing each other's cultural assets. The school should build links with its community: send messages in the community languages, get members of the community to take part in school activities and gain the trust of BME parents.

During the 1970s and early 1980s multicultural education gained a foothold in the consciousness of teachers and local authority officers. While there was no central government policy on multicultural education, there was recognition that minority ethnic pupils were underachieving in the education system, and in 1976 the Labour Government launched a public enquiry into the causes of underachievement led by Sir Anthony Rampton. The report in 1978 startled both the political and educational world by finding that the underachievement of black and minority pupils was caused by racism among individual teachers and institutional racism in the school system (Rampton, 1981).

Anti-racist education

Rampton found what education academics and sociologists had long argued: that the problem in schools was not black pupils, but racism in the system. Teachers held negative stereotypes of black pupils: black boys are good at sport, but cannot be expected to be good at mathematics. The deficit view of African-Caribbean pupils is a part of the European world view and the covert racism in society. Black writers added their voices. Coard (1979) argued that teachers' low expectations of black pupils lower their achievement and the system then classifies them as 'sub-normal'; Stone (1981) argued that learning about steel bands and the history of the Caribbean was useless for African-Caribbean pupils. What was required was a curriculum which taught pupils to read and to do mathematics so that they could compete in the employment market. Black people, she insisted, don't want to be depicted as exotically-clothed, interesting musicians who eat spicy food; they want proper jobs and power in society. Multicultural education 'exoticised' the lives of black pupils by learning about 'samosas, saris and steel bands' and did not recognise the wider racist social context in which black children lived (Troyna, 1984). While black children at school might be in a friendly microcosm of a liberal and tolerant multicultural society, outside the school, or even in the school playground, they would be subjected to racial abuse and violence, as shown in research by Troyna and Hatcher (1992).

Anti-racist education rejects the problematisation of the black child and questions the notion that ethnic groups can live together harmoniously without recognition of the power differences between black and white groups. Pupils need an understanding of the workings and effects of white racism (Epstein, 1992). Anti-racist educators argue that it is the racism pupils learn from their parents and culture, together with the power structure of institutional racism, which disadvantage black people. Schools need to counter the effects of racism in the classroom and the playground and eliminate the institutional racism of the school. The school should have an 'anti-racist' policy to counter racism:

- racial abuse should be explicitly forbidden;
- all incidents of racial abuse should be identified, recorded and acted upon;
- staff should be made aware of racism and its effects;
- the curriculum should include teaching about race and racism;
- the progress of BME pupils should be monitored;
- the school should endeavour to include black members among its staff.

While multicultural education was largely about the curriculum, anti-racist education looked to the school in society. Schools cannot operate in isolation to address the societal problem of white racism; instead it is the whole political and power structure of society which needs to be changed. Black people need to be included in the power structure, as MPs, judges, company directors, head teachers and chief executives. This is a left-wing radical idea, and the strongest form of anti-racism is Marxist in its origin (Cole, 2008). In fact, much of the impetus for both multicultural and anti-racist approaches to education came from the left-wing Labour-controlled local urban authorities in England: Liverpool, Leeds, Manchester, Bristol (Avon Local Education Authority [LEA]) and, above all, the Inner London Education Authority (ILEA).

Conservative opposition

The Thatcher Government of the 1980s had no time for the radicalising tendencies of anti-racism. Thatcher wanted economic revolution: getting the trade unions under control and allowing neoliberal free market capitalism to operate (see Chapter 1). A reaction to her policies were the so-called 'race riots' across England's inner cities. They began with a police drugs raid on the Black and White Café in St Paul's, Bristol, in April 1980; spontaneous resistance among the black community erupted into street violence, stone-throwing and over-turning police cars. The scenes were replicated in Toxteth in Liverpool and, more dramatically with petrol bombs, in Brixton, South London. The riots were depicted by sociologists as black resistance to white oppression, originating in slavery and colonialism and continued by racial disadvantage in 1980s England (Sivanandan, 1982). The government-commissioned enquiry into the riots concluded that they were, indeed, the effects of urban poverty and disadvantage: 'complex political, social and economic factors' created a 'disposition towards violent protest' (Scarman, 1982: 34). Scarman also pointed to the effects of 'racial disadvantage' and 'racial discrimination', but rejected the notion of 'institutional racism'. He warned, though, that positive discrimination was necessary to prevent racial disadvantage becoming an 'endemic, ineradicable disease threatening the very survival of our society' (ibid.: 36).

Anti-racist education grew within this highly charged political context of race riots, and the Conservative Government under Thatcher saw the actions of local authorities and teachers as 'left-wing activism'. There were criticisms that officers and advisers were sent into schools as 'race spies', checking on those teachers who did not adopt anti-racist policies (Ward, 1998). The Conservative Government wished to end the control of local authorities and 'activists', and it did this through the 1988 Education Act. Chapter 1 shows how the Act took control from local authorities through local management of schools (LMS). Its effect was also to limit the equal opportunities policies of the left-wing authorities. But the most effective means of eliminating multicultural and anti-racist education came with the National Curriculum and national testing. It created an overwhelming list of priorities for schools which struggled to implement the new curriculum and to prepare pupils for the new tests. There was nothing in the new curriculum to require schools to address racism, and the statutory orders emphasised an Anglo-centric focus with, for example, little on colonialism and slavery in the History curriculum. Government policy did not forbid multicultural or anti-racist education, but simply marginalised it. The 1980s and early 1990s saw a struggle by those committed to a just and equal society against a powerful white establishment in which the government overtly and covertly resisted efforts to eliminate racism in the education system.

New Labour and equal opportunities

The New Labour Government of 1997, which was to have the first ever black member of its cabinet, brought a revival for anti-racism with the Macpherson Report (1999) into the death of Stephen Lawrence. Stephen was an African-Caribbean 16-year-old murdered by a gang of white youths while waiting at a bus stop with friends in London: a prime example of a racist killing. When the (white) police officers were called they failed to pursue the white culprits. Macpherson regarded the policing as an example of 'institutional racism' where the police's perception of the incident had been framed by their expectations of black people. The failure by senior officers to investigate the matter further was evidence that such perceptions were a structural feature of the organisation: institutional racism was inherent in the London Metropolitan Police Force. Previous governments had refused to understand or to acknowledge racism in society, but the then Home Secretary, Jack Straw, agreed that institutional racism was inherent in society and should be eliminated. (In 2012 further evidence was found to convict two suspects of the killing. However, later the same year brought more accusations of racist behaviour among members of the Metropolitan Police Force.)

The result of the Macpherson Inquiry was the Race Relations (Amendment) Act in 2000 (OPSI, 2000) which required all organisations, including schools, to ensure equality of opportunity on grounds of race. This 'duty' is different from previous requirements which had been constructed by local authorities or individual schools in that it is enshrined in legislation. It requires schools to have a policy on race equality, to monitor their activities to ensure that there is no racial bias and to have an action plan to eradicate inequality. For the first time, there was policy at government level for countering racism. When the Labour Government was again elected in May 2001 with a strong majority and the race relations legislation was in place, it seemed that society would progress to equality and pluralism. It was only a few months later, on 11 September 2001, that the world picture was to change.

2001 – Confusion and retreat

The reaction in western societies to the attack on the World Trade Centre in New York in September 2001 brought a wave of anger and fear about Islam (Islamophobia) and an international 'war on terror'. The struggles of the 1980s and 1990s had been to gain recognition of the social and educational effects of racism by a right-wing government. After 9/11 the debate became global as the cultural and religious divide between east and west opened up and began to legitimate articulated opposition to multiculturalism. The government's recognition of institutional racism, which had been such a step forward in 2000, began to weaken. Gillborn (2008: 131) points out that the Labour Government backed away from its commitment to eradicating racism. In 2004 the new Home Secretary, David Blunkett, described 'institutional racism' as 'a slogan that missed the point'. The riots of the 1980s were reflected in similar riots in the North-West of England in 2001 (Cantle, 2001; Ouseley, 2001) and race-inspired riots in London and other cities in August 2011.

Opposition to multiculturalism ranges from the crude insistence of nationalist groups such as the BNP that Britain should be kept for the whites and not be over-run by other cultures. But a surprising critique of the multicultural society came from Trevor Phillips, the black chair of the Commission for Racial Equality. He spoke against the maintenance of separate ethnic groups, arguing that multiculturalism was dividing society and that Britain should become more of a singular nation in which there is a greater sharing of the same values:

> The fact is that we are a society which, almost without noticing it, is becoming more divided by race and religion. We are becoming more unequal by ethnicity … there are some simple truths which should bind us together
>
> (Phillips, 2005)

Another form of opposition to multiculturalism during the 2000s was the reaction against 'asylum seekers'. This became a major issue in the mass media in which the government was accused of allowing supposedly 'bogus' asylum seekers into the country. The government responded by making severe limitations on immigration. The 7/7 bombings in London in July 2005 reinforced the opposition to cultural pluralism and made the government even more anxious to be managing the 'terrorist threat'. The over-reaction by the Metropolitan Police in the shooting of the Jean Charles de Menezes, the Brazilian-born electrician who was mistaken for a terrorist, typified the level of anxiety. Immigration became a major issue in the 2010 general election, with Conservatives claiming that migrant workers from the EU were limiting the employment prospects for the British. The subsequent limitations on immigration imposed by the 2010 Coalition Government were another symptom of the reaction against a multicultural society.

Conclusion

The issue of race in education has lived through continuing racial tensions in society. Government policy since 2001 has been to emphasise 'cultural cohesion'. In 2004, those being given British Citizenship were required to demonstrate their ability to speak English. Ceremonies for those gaining British Citizenship required people to swear an oath of allegiance to 'Her Majesty Queen Elizabeth the Second, her Heirs and Successors, according to law' (UK Border Agency, 2004). There has been a move from a strong, but brief, commitment to countering institutional racism in schools and society to a policy of social cohesion which marginalises the attention to racism. Governments have reacted to right-wing pressures in the media and society for 'social cohesion' with an emphasis on 'Britishness' and similarity, rather than on the preservation of cultural differences.

One of the major cultural variations in British society has been along religious lines. Religious differences have always been a part of the multicultural debate with demands for the rights of religious groups to maintain their faith and to have it enshrined in the school system with Muslim or Sikh schools, or at least to allow for dedicated religious practices within mainstream schools. These are discussed further in Chapter 7.

Summary points

- Britain always has been a multicultural and multiracial society defined by its colonial past.
- The education system has moved through different phases: assimilationist, multi-culturalism and anti-racism.
- There is a strong political dimension to these issues, and right-wing governments have resisted anti-racism.
- Recent political approaches aimed at 'cultural cohesion' have evaded the core issue of racial disadvantage.

Questions for discussion

- Because racism is about the exercise of power, is it mainly the responsibility of white people in Britain?
- Should schools teach children about race and racism?
- What can schools do to address the issue of institutional racism?

Recommended reading

Gillborn, D. (2008) *Racism and Education: Coincidence or conspiracy*. London: Routledge.
An up-to-date survey of the issues of racism in education and explains 'critical race theory'.

Institute of Race Relations (1998) Available online at http://www.irr.org.uk (accessed 12 April 2012).
See the IRR website for a weekly update on global events on race.

Strand, S. (2007) *Minority Ethnic Pupils in the Longitudinal Study of Young People in England (LSYPE)*. London: DCSF. Available online at http://education.gov.uk/publications/eOrderingDownload/DCSF-RR002.pdf (accessed 12 April 2012).
Strand gives a detailed analysis of the achievement of BME pupils.

Troyna, B. and Hatcher, R. (1992) *Racism in Children's Lives: A study of mainly white primary schools*. London: Routledge.
Troyna and Hatcher's research provides telling examples of black children's experiences in Britain.

See also the campaigning organisation *Show Racism the Red Card*. Available online at http://www.srtrc.org/ (accessed 24 May 2012).

References

Arora, R.K. and Duncan, C.G. (1986) *Multicultural Education: Towards good practice*. London: Routledge.
Cantle (2001) *Community Coherence: A report of the independent review team chaired by Ted Cantle*. London: Home Office.
Coard, B. (1979) *How the West Indian Child is Made Educationally Subnormal in the British School System*. London: New Beacon Books.
Cole, M. (2008) *Marxism and Educational Theory: Origins and issues*. London: Routledge.
Epstein, D. (1992) *Changing Classroom Cultures: Aantiracism, politics and schools*. Stoke-on-Trent: Trentham.
Fryer, P. (1984) *Staying Power: The history of black people in Britain*. London: Pluto Press.
Gillborn, D. (2008) *Racism and Education: Coincidence or conspiracy?* London: Routledge.
Houlton, D. (1985) *All Our Languages*. Leeds: E.J. Arnold.
Macpherson, W. (1999) *The Stephen Lawrence Inquiry, CM 4264-1*. London: The Stationery Office. Available online at http://www.archive.official-documents.co.uk/document/cm42/4262/4262.htm (accessed 8 April 2012).
Newsinger, J. (2006) *The Blood Never Dries: A people's history of the British Empire*. London: Bookmarks Publications.
Office of Public Sector Information (OPSI) (2000) *Race Relations (Amendment) Act*. London: OPSI. Available online at http://www.opsi.gov.uk/acts/acts2000/ukpga_20000034_en_1 (accessed 8 April 2012).
Ouseley (2001) *Community Pride, Not Prejudice: Making diversity work in Bradford*. Bradford: Bradford County Council.
Phillips, T. (2005) *After 7/7: Sleepwalking to segregation*. [Speech] Manchester Council for Community Relations, 22 September.
Rampton (1981) *West Indian Children in our Schools: Interim report of the Committee of Inquiry into the education of children from ethnic minority groups*. London: HMSO.
Scarman (1982) *The Scarman Report: The Brixton disorders 10–12 April 1981*. Harmondsworth: Penguin.
Sivanandan, A. (1982) *A Different Hunger: Writings on black resistance*. London: Institute of Race Relations.
Stone, M. (1981) *Educating the Black Child in Britain*. London: Fontana.
Thatcher, M. (1978) *World in Action Television Programme*. [Interview] Granada Television, Manchester, 27 January 1988.
Troyna, B. (1984) Multicultural Education: Emancipation or containment. In: L. Barton and S. Walker (eds) *Social Crisis and Educational Research*. Buckingham: Croom-Helm.
Troyna, B. and Hatcher, R. (1992) *Racism in Children's Lives: A study of mainly white primary schools*. London: Routledge.
UK Border Agency (2004) *Citizenship Ceremonies*. London: UK Border Agency. Available online at http://www.ukba.homeoffice.gov.uk/britishcitizenship/applying/ceremony/ (accessed 12 May 2012).
Ward, S. (1998) Intercultural Education and Teacher Education in the United Kingdom: A case of reversible decline. *European Journal of Intercultural Education Studies 9(1)*: 41–54.

Chapter 7

Religious and cultural plurality in education

Denise Cush

Introduction – religious and cultural plurality?

In today's 'globalised' world it is more important than ever to prepare children and young people to live and work alongside others who may not share the same beliefs, values or customs, and to provide the resources for pupils to develop their own beliefs, values and identity in the light of those of their family, society and the wider world. These are the main aims of the subject called 'religious education' in the UK. Religion is often in the news and public affairs, so much so that some have started referring to living in a 'post-secular' society. A more accurate description of British society would recognise that it is Christian and secular and plural and spiritual in complex and changing ways (Woodhead and Catto, 2012). The number of students in England taking GCSEs and A-levels in religious studies has increased impressively year on year. Recent research reveals that young people in Britain are remarkably tolerant of diversity and that young people throughout Europe want to learn about religious and cultural plurality (Jackson, 2011). The Equality Act 2010 for England, Scotland and Wales includes 'religion or belief' as one of the 'characteristics' for which public bodies have a duty to avoid discrimination and promote understanding. The Council of Europe (2008) recommends that all young people should learn about religious diversity.

It is simply a fact that human beings have different views on fundamental issues concerned with the meaning and purpose of our lives, human nature and destiny, the nature of reality, reliable authorities and sources of knowledge, ethical issues from war to abortion, and the purpose of education. Skeie (1995: 84) has distinguished between 'plurality' as a descriptive term for this situation (another term frequently used is 'diversity') and 'pluralism' which is used to refer to an evaluative position (usually positive) on the fact of plurality.

'Religion' and 'culture'

The chapter links 'religious' and 'cultural' plurality because the two are sometimes indistinguishable. The terms 'culture' and 'religion' are in common use, but there is no agreement over what these words mean: whether they refer to the same dimension of human experience or two distinct areas, or whether they are useful terms at all. They tend to become confused with concepts such as 'ethnicity', 'nationality', 'community' and 'identity'. Some have suggested that the word 'religion' could be replaced by 'culture' as both can refer to the beliefs, values and customs of particular groups. However, as 'cultures' are usually viewed as human constructs, this would be difficult for some adherents to accept. From a believer's point of view, a distinction can be made between 'religion' (the eternal truths) and 'culture' (the changeable social context). We talk of 'religions' adapting to different 'cultures' or making changes in what is merely 'cultural'. Yet in practice there is often no agreement as to what counts as 'religion', and what as 'culture'. For example, ordaining women as priests, monogamy, not cutting one's hair, or honouring ancestor spirits and local gods may be viewed as religious or as cultural, or the distinction may not be made.

'Culture' tends to be defined as the learned aspects of being human. It includes language, customs and beliefs, and is passed on from one generation to the next by means of socialisation and education. The way in which we use the word 'culture' can suggest that there are distinct 'sets' of language/customs/beliefs to which an individual 'belongs', or is even sometimes 'torn between' two of them. On the one hand, 'cultures' can be seen as essentially different and having different educational needs. This can (and did, in South Africa under apartheid) lead to separate provision for different categories of pupils. On the other hand, 'cultures' can be viewed as fluid, internally diverse and contested, influenced by and influencing other cultural streams (Jackson, 1997). An individual therefore does not so much 'belong' to 'a culture', but is influenced by and engaged with a number of cultural streams. A culture is in this view more like a language you learn than something you 'are'. Cultures are not only challenged and changed by interactions with other cultures, but may be criticised from within. Jackson's (1997) research with young Hindus in Britain reveals them, not as negatively 'caught between two cultures', but as having the 'multiple cultural competence' to navigate successfully multiple cultural streams (see Chapter 20).

'Religion' is notoriously difficult to define. Definitions focussing on belief in God or the supernatural leave out many traditions. Westerners, influenced by Christianity, Protestantism and the Enlightenment, tend to think of religion as being about 'beliefs', but in other contexts people focus more on practice, values or identity. Similarly, the division into clearly distinguished 'isms' – Buddhism, Hinduism, Christianity, Islam – is seen by many as an artificial construct of nineteenth century western thinking. In reality 'religions' are internally diverse, and the dividing lines between them are not clear, particularly in non-western (e.g. Indian) traditions or post-modern manifestations such as 'new age'. In many non-European languages there is no word that translates into the English 'religion', or way of distinguishing between 'religious' and 'non-religious'; there is just how people live their lives. Thus the current trend in academic circles is to view the term 'religion' as a tool for analysis, rather than having any real relationship to reality 'out there'.

A further problem with the term 'religion' is that for many people it has negative overtones, associated with controlling authorities, 'meaningless ritual' and fanatical terrorists. Or, they may be afraid of venturing into an area where it is easy to cause offence. Misunderstandings occur between those who view religion as a matter of belief and opinion that can be a topic for debate, and those for whom religion is a crucial part of identity: what for one person is a critical (or even idle) questioning of an idea is for the other a vicious personal attack. 'Spirituality' tends to be seen as less threatening and it has been suggested (Heelas and Woodhead, 2005) that there has been a 'spiritual revolution' in society, meaning a turn from 'organised religion' to individual, subjective 'spirituality'.

Recent research with students and staff in universities (Weller *et al.*, 2011) supports this thesis, with 'spirituality' scoring more highly than worldviews other than Christianity or the non-religious. Research with young people reveals that, for those who identify with a tradition, it is an expression of identity, and that for both religious and non-religious students the most common attitude is a tolerant acceptance of other people's beliefs and customs based on a strong commitment to human rights.

Responses to cultural and religious plurality: Multicultural/intercultural education

The term 'multicultural education', can refer to any attempt on the part of education to respond to cultural plurality, or particular approaches which can then be contrasted with other approaches such as 'anti-racist' (see Chapter 6). The idea behind 'multicultural education' – much discussed in the 1970s and 1980s – was that cultural diversity should be appreciated and reflected in the school curriculum. Music, art and literature should include examples of African, Indian and Chinese origin, as well as European; history, geography and religious studies should be worldwide not just national; mathematics and science should emphasise the contributions of non-western peoples such as 'Arabic' numerals. 'Multicultural education' has been criticised for being superficial and for failing to address the real roots of racism and discrimination, and sometimes for making relationships between different groups worse by stressing differences and reinforcing stereotypes (see Chapter 6). The term 'multicultural society' might suggest that several discrete cultures exist in competition, a reason why some dislike the phrase. Instead the term 'intercultural' has become popular, to reflect that 'cultures' are fluid, changing and interacting, with exciting new 'hybrids' emerging all the time.

International diversity of religion in education

Worldwide, the response by state-funded education systems to the plurality of 'religious' and 'non-religious' beliefs, values and customs is varied, but can be summarised into three basic options: the *secular*, the *confessional* and the *non-confessional*. Simply put, this means either having no religious education, having religious education with the primary aim to nurture children in the religion of their heritage, and religious education that aims to be open, multi-faith and unbiased.

The term *secular* is used here to mean an education system that does not officially include consideration of religions as a subject on the timetable. This does not imply that pupils, teachers and parents are not themselves religious. The United States of America (USA) takes this secular option in state-funded schools, in spite of being one of the most 'religious' countries in the world. Other countries that currently take the 'secular' option in state-funded schools include France (except Alsace and part of Lorraine), Russia, Albania, China and Japan.

Some of the most common arguments for excluding religion from the curriculum are:

- it is too personal and private and should be left to the family and community;
- it is impossible for teachers to be impartial in such a contested area;
- students may be open to proselytising by teachers, persuaded to adopt a particular religious, anti-religious or agnostic stance;

- any study risks highlighting areas of difference and conflict between people;
- academic evaluation might seem to criticise pupils' religious and cultural heritage;
- any presentation in school is bound to be so simplified that it misrepresents and stereotypes the tradition in question;
- religions may include views unacceptable to the values underpinning liberal education.

In the USA, the major consideration is that the First Amendment to the 1787 Constitution sought to protect religious freedom by instituting a complete separation between 'church' and 'state' so that there was 'no establishment' of religion. This has been interpreted as meaning that no public funds can be used for teaching about religions in schools, and thus no religious education. However, this clause was interpreted differently in different eras, and in different states. An important ruling in 1963 made it clear that it is only promoting a particular religion that is ruled out, rather than teaching about religion. The increasing awareness of plurality has led several states, such as California, to include teaching about religions in the history or social studies syllabus. However, there are no teachers specially qualified to teach religious studies, and many teachers leave religion out. Nevertheless, some such as Moore (2007) argue that the religious freedom of the USA is only really guaranteed by education which includes learning about religions. So 'religion' increasingly finds some place in a general humanities curriculum, though not as a discrete subject. Even in China, religion is now dealt with as an aspect of geography (Nanbu, 2008), and it could be argued that the teaching of Marxist beliefs is a form of *confessional* belief education.

Many of the countries of Europe take the *confessional* approach to religious education. This means that schools contribute to the nurturing of children within the particular faith tradition of their family, or what is deemed to be the heritage of the country. There are many variations. Religious education can be compulsory or optional, the syllabus can be decided by the state or the churches/groups concerned or a partnership of both. There may or may not be an alternative subject, such as 'ethics', for the 'non-religious'. It can be taught by the ordinary class teacher or by paid or unpaid church workers coming into school. Where one particular tradition forms part of the dominant construction of national identity – Catholicism in Poland, Orthodoxy in Romania or Greece – that tradition forms the basis of the syllabus. Where there is more awareness of diversity, separate religious education classes may be offered for the main groups represented. For example, in the majority of German Länder there is choice between Protestant and Catholic (and sometimes Muslim) religious education, and in Finland until 2003 there was a choice between Lutheran or Orthodox religious education and 'ethics' for the non-religious. In spite of the confessional label, many European educators in practice take a more open approach as they seek to connect with the actual worldviews and experience of their pupils (Larsson and Gustavsson, 2004).

A growing minority of countries take the *non-confessional* approach and attempt to provide a religious education that is open, balanced and impartial, and is seeking to educate children about religion rather than promote a particular religion or religion in general. The countries with the longest experience of this are Sweden, England, Wales and Scotland, which have pioneered non-confessional multi-faith religious education since the late 1960s. More recently, they have been joined by Norway, South Africa and

Namibia, and for students over 16 ('upper secondary') in Denmark, and the Swiss canton of Zurich. South Africa, which made the decision to take the non-confessional route in 2000, has decided to call the subject 'religion education' to emphasise that it does not have the aim of 'making people religious'.

Some of the most common arguments for including religion in the curriculum are:

- the majority of people in the world are 'religious', it is crucial to understand this important component of their identity, and religions are very powerful forces in world affairs;
- religion is intertwined with culture, so it is impossible to appreciate history, art, music, architecture, laws, customs and morality without understanding religion;
- ignorance is often the root of prejudice and conflict; knowledge assists understanding and appreciation of diversity;
- students need the opportunity to reflect on their own beliefs and values, and a vocabulary with which to do so;
- students need the opportunity to critically evaluate their inherited beliefs and values and conditioning by society;
- if religion is omitted there may be an implicit anti-religious bias to the curriculum, causing children from religious backgrounds to feel excluded;
- one (or more) religions may be the truth.

It is possible to construct arguments in favour of the secular, the confessional, and the non-confessional approaches to education as being the best way to ensure freedom of religious belief and to promote harmony rather than conflict. However, ignorance is a dangerous option. An increasingly plural world calls for a positive approach to plurality of beliefs and values.

Positive pluralism

'Positive pluralism' is a term coined by the author in 1991 to describe an approach which sees the plurality of religious and non-religious beliefs, values and customs as a positive resource for the human race. Outlined in Cush and Francis (2001), it was developed from practical experience in an English context. The positive pluralist approach is based upon 'epistemological humility': your own sincerely held views, beliefs, values and customs, need not mean that you have nothing to learn from others, even when their views differ greatly. Schools should respect the religious and cultural backgrounds of all pupils, whether religious or not, but also accept that these perspectives are open to debate and critical evaluation in the *public* forum that is education. This is *not* to maintain that all views/beliefs/traditions are 'equally valid', a position that no one really holds when pressed, or to teach *universalism*: the belief that all religions are the same really, just different paths to the same goal, as these are themselves confessional positions.

It is argued here that religious education should take a non-confessional, multi-faith (and non-faith) approach, which attempts to be, as far as is humanly possible, impartial and empathetic, where all children are taught together, and where no single tradition is privileged in terms of its truth claims. Plurality within the so-called 'religions' and interactions and hybridity between them need to be recognised. The non-confessional approach means learning *about* religions and non-religious views rather than learning *to be* 'religious'. It does not rule out, and indeed encourages and facilitates, students exploring and developing their own perspectives on religious issues and questions, whether or not these perspectives turn out to be the same as their family/community heritage or any previously recognised worldview.

Religious education in England

In England, non-confessional religious education is well established, and was an early advocate and location for multicultural education. Religious education has been a compulsory subject in the school curriculum since 1944. It was established as non-confessional in 1971 (Schools Council, 1971), and reinforced as part of the 'basic curriculum' in 1988. The 1988 Education Reform Act, repeated in the 1996 Education Act, requires religious education to 'reflect the fact that the religious traditions in Great Britain are in the main Christian, while taking account of the other principal religions represented in Great Britain' (1996 Education Act section 375.3). This is open to a variety of interpretations as to which religions are included and what proportion of the syllabus is spent on each. Religious education is not technically part of the National Curriculum, as each local authority must produce an 'Agreed Syllabus' for use in its schools. The parties agreeing the syllabus are the Church of England, other faiths and other Christian denominations, teachers' representatives and elected members of the local authority. The *local* nature of the syllabus allows for considerable 'grass roots' involvement, and the local Standing Advisory Council on Religious Education (SACRE) has been a forum for different faith communities to meet and get to know each other. Religious education is a subject from which parents can withdraw their children on grounds of conscience, a right which is seen by some as anachronistic, and by others as an important human right.

Recently, there have been moves towards more national uniformity. In 1994 two 'Model Syllabuses' were produced as guidance for local syllabuses (SCAA, 1994) and in 2004 the Non-Statutory Framework for Religious Education (QCA, 2004) appeared, and was welcomed by the majority of the 'Religious Education (RE) community' including faith communities with their own schools, and some Humanist organisations. This document recognises the importance of including non-religious perspectives and traditions other than the 'major world religions'. It has ambitious learning objectives which stress critical thinking and links with other subjects and global issues. From 2008, the *New Secondary Curriculum* produced many examples of how RE could work alongside other subjects to produce 'compelling learning experiences' for pupils. A further document, *Religious Education in English schools: Non-statutory guidance* DCSF (2010) was produced just before the change of government in 2010.

Reports from Ofsted (2007, 2010) the Religious Education Council (2007) and major research projects such as Glasgow University's (2010) *Does RE Work?* have identified strengths and weaknesses in the current position of RE. Strengths include the popularity of the subject with pupils, the contribution to intercultural understanding, the contribution to critical thinking and enquiry skills and success at exam level. Weaknesses include limited initial and continuing teacher training, the lack of timetable time and budget compared with other subjects, standards and assessment and confused expectations. The 2010 Coalition Government reviewed the National Curriculum and stated that RE would continue to be statutory, and locally rather than nationally organised. There has been an expansion of new categories of schools – academies and free schools, funded by central rather than local government – which do not have to follow either the National Curriculum or the Locally Agreed RE syllabus, but may view these as 'benchmarks'. This may cause problems for local SACREs. RE has been omitted from the list of subjects included in the so-called 'English Baccalaureate' (see Chapter 1). These and other measures have caused concern to the Religious Education Council; however agreement (but no funding) was given for the Council to produce a review of RE in parallel with the National Curriculum Review.

The situation in England is complicated by the presence of state-funded 'schools with a religious character', some categories of which are allowed to provide their own *confessional* religious education. This provides a case study of the complexities which arise in the area of religion, culture and education.

The 'faith schools' debate

Internationally, Christian churches and religious organisations such as Buddhist monasteries pioneered education for the poor as well as the rich. Many countries, including Great Britain, have private schools independently funded by religious groups. However, the history of education in England has given rise to the existence of state-funded 'faith-based' schools. In 1870, when state education was introduced, it supplemented rather than replaced the voluntary provision by religious groups, and some state assistance was given to allow the voluntary schools to survive and meet basic standards (see Chapter 1). This is known as the 'dual system'. The 1944 Education Act established two categories of state-funded voluntary schools, a distinction which still persists today, with the addition of 'foundation schools', 'academies' and 'free schools'. The two important categories until recently have been 'voluntary controlled' (VC) and 'voluntary aided' (VA) schools. The former is controlled by the local authority from which it receives all its funding. These schools must follow the non-confessional Locally Agreed Syllabus for religious education, but as a reflection of their original foundation may conduct denominational worship. The VA category receives the majority of its funding from the local authority, but in return for providing some of the funding itself, the religious body is allowed to provide religious education of a confessional, denominational nature, as well as worship in the tradition to which it belongs. Academies and free schools may have a faith-based foundation and make their own decisions about RE and worship, depending on their funding agreements.

'Faith-based' schools have become controversial in recent years. Both the Church of England and the 1997–2010 Labour Governments were in favour of increasing the number of such schools. They are popular with parents and perceived as obtaining good academic results. Since 1998, 11 Muslim, one Hindu and four Sikh schools have gained VA status. Racism, and in particular Islamophobia, colours the discussions in the media. Far more people opposed separate Muslim schools than separate 'Church' schools (43 per cent to 27 per cent in a 2001 MORI poll), expressing fears that separate Muslim schools might be 'training grounds for terrorists' (see Chapter 6).

State-funded faith schools account for roughly one third of primary schools (6,203 of 16,884) and one sixth of secondary schools (631 of 3,310). Of the total, 4,605 are Church of England and 2,001 Roman Catholic, the rest being counted in single figures or tens, the next largest group being Jewish schools at 39 (all figures from 2011).

If the system was started from scratch, perhaps the fully comprehensive pluralist community school would work best for equality in diversity. However, many faith-based schools are trying to make up for the disadvantages of segregation by making links with other schools, and by following multi-faith and multicultural curricula. In 2005, all the 'major faith communities' made a written agreement with the then Department for Education and Skills that it was important for schools with a religious character to teach about faiths other than their own.

Related areas: Moral education, citizenship, worship

Other areas of school provision which need to take account of cultural and religious plurality are spiritual development, moral education, personal and social education, health education, and citizenship education. Often these are attempted without thinking through the full implications of cultural and religious diversity and real disagreement on fundamental issues. There is also the issue of the practice of prayer and worship in school. In England, the attempt to provide non-confessional religious education is compromised by the legal requirement for community schools to provide daily 'collective worship' which is 'wholly or mainly of a broadly Christian character'. There is the possibility of parental withdrawal from this and complex ways in which schools can be exempted from this requirement, but it remains a difficult area.

Conclusion

There are many ways in which religious and cultural plurality impact upon education and there needs to be a subject in the school curriculum to deal directly with this area of human experience (Cush, 2007). It should allow students to learn about and respect the beliefs, values and customs of others and to develop their own, either within a heritage tradition or in critical opposition to it. It is currently called 'religious education', but it possibly needs a new name. It is unlikely to be achieved as a small part of another subject such as history, social studies or citizenship and needs to be taught by specialist teachers knowledgeable about the traditions and skilled in appropriate pedagogies. In the words of Schreiner (2001), talking about Europe, but applicable to the world:

> RE can elaborate a critical potential in a civil society through its international, ecumenical and inter-religious dimension. This would contribute to a sustainable Europe in which the diversity of religions and cultures is not a burden but an enrichment to co-habitation

(Ibid.: 266)

Summary points

- It has become increasingly recognised that it is important to address religious and cultural plurality in education.
- There is a complex and contested relationship between 'religion' and 'culture'.
- Educational provision worldwide takes different approaches to addressing religious and cultural diversity.

- An approach through 'positive pluralism' is suggested as a way forward.
- Religious education policy in England is outlined up to 2012.
- The question of whether the state should fund faith-based schools is addressed as an example of a current issue at the interface between religion and education.

Questions for discussion

- What is the relationship between religion and culture? Can religious education contribute to intercultural education?
- What is the place of faith-based schools in a plural democracy? Should the state fund such schools?
- How can schools ensure that pupils from all religious/non-religious/cultural backgrounds feel included?
- Should religious education be included in the school curriculum? If so, what should be its aims, content and methods?

Recommended reading

Copley, T. (1997) *Teaching Religion: Fifty years of religious education in England and Wales*. Exeter: University of Exeter Press.
A comprehensive history of religious education in England and Wales.

Grimmitt, M. (ed.) (2000) *Pedagogies of Religious Education*. London: McCrimmons.
A very useful collection, with a critique of the major pedagogies of religious education in Britain today.

Jackson, R. (1997) *Religious Education, an Interpretive Approach*. London: Hodder.
One of the best theoretical discussions of religious education, from one of the leading UK professors, with much on religion and culture.

Jackson, R. (2004) *Rethinking Religious Education and Plurality Issues in Diversity and Pedagogy*. London: RoutledgeFalmer.
Addresses many of the issues in this chapter as well as examining current pedagogies.

QCA (2004) *Religious Education: The non-statutory national framework*. London: QCA.
Although 'non-statutory' for reasons of local accountability explained above, this gives a widely shared picture of religious education in England.

References

Council of Europe (2008) *Recommendation CM/Rec (2008): 12 of the Committee of Ministers on the dimension of religious and non-religious convictions within intercultural education*. Strasbourg: Council of Europe Publishing. Available online at https://wcd.coe.int/ViewDoc.jsp?id=1386911&Site=CM (accessed 13 September 2012).

Cush, D. (2007) Should Religious Studies Be Part of the State School Curriculum? *British Journal of Religious Education* 29(3): 217–27.

Cush, D. and Francis, D. (2001) Positive Pluralism to Awareness, Mystery and Value: A case study in RE curriculum development. *British Journal of Religious Education* 24(1): 52–67.

DCSF (2010) *Religious Education in English Schools: Non-statutory Guidance 2010*. Available online at http://publications.teachernet.gov.uk/default.aspx?PageFunction=productdetails&PageMode=publications&ProductId=DCSF-00114-2010 (accessed 13 September 2012).

DfEE (1996) *Education Act 1996*. London: HMSO. Available online at http://www.legislation.gov.uk/ukpga/1996/56/section/375 (accessed 13 September 2012).

Glasgow, University of (2010) *Does Religious Education Work?* Glasgow: University of Glasgow. Available online at http://www.gla.ac.uk/schools/education/research/currentresearchprojects/doesreligiouseducationwork/ (accessed 14 September 2012).

Heelas, P. and Woodhead, L. (2005) *The Spiritual Revolution: Why religion is giving way to spirituality.* Oxford: Blackwell.

Jackson, R. (1997) *Religious Education, an Interpretive Approach.* London: Hodder.

Jackson, R. (2011) Religion, Education, Dialogue and Conflict. *British Journal of Religious Education* 33(2): 105–9.

Larsson R. and Gustavsson, C. (eds) (2004) *Towards a European Perspective on Religious Education.* Uppsala: Artos.

Moore, D. (2007) *Overcoming Religious Illiteracy: A cultural studies approach to the study of religion in secondary education.* New York: Palgrave Macmillan.

Nanbu, H. (2008) Religion in Chinese Education: From denial to cooperation. *British Journal of Religious Education* 30(3): 223–45.

Ofsted (2007) *Making Sense of Religion.* London: Ofsted. Available online at http://www.ofsted.gov.uk/Ofsted-home/Publications-and-research/Browse-all-by/Education/Curriculum/Religious-education/Secondary/Making-sense-of-religion (accessed 13 September 2012).

Ofsted (2010) *Transforming Religious Education: Religious education in schools 2006-2009.* Manchester: Ofsted.

QCA (2004) *Religious Education: The non-statutory national framework.* London: QCA.

Religious Education Council of England and Wales (2007) *Religious Education Teaching and Training in England: Current Provision and Future Improvement. The Report of the REC's RE Teaching and Training Commission.* London: Religious Education Council.

SCAA (1994) *Religious Education: Model syllabuses.* London: SCAA.

Schools Council (1971) *Religious Education in Secondary Schools, Schools Council Working Paper 36.* London: Evans Methuen

Schreiner, P. (2001) Towards a European Oriented Religious Education. In: H. Heimbrock, C. Scheilke, and P. Schreiner (eds) *Towards Religious Competence: Diversity as a challenge for education in Europe.* Munster: Comenius Institute.

Skeie, G. (1995) Plurality and Pluralism: A Challenge for Religious Education. *British Journal of Religious Education* 17(2): 84–91.

Weller, P., Hooley T. and Moore, N. (2011) *Religion and Belief in Higher Education: The experiences of staff and students.* London: Equality Challenge Unit.

Woodhead, L. and Catto, R. (2012) *Religion and Change in Modern Britain.* London and New York: Routledge.

Chapter 8

Social and educational inclusion

Tilly Mortimore

Introduction

Are your school days a time you like to remember, or something you'd rather forget? Think back to those days and what was good about them: games in the playground? Having a laugh with your friends? Your most positive memories are probably connected with being a member of a group, feeling good about being included. Or were you ever chosen last, the one that others wouldn't work with, never shared secrets with, and walked home alone? This is exclusion at its simplest, most fundamental level, with the stress and anxiety that affect children's ability to learn and to thrive.

This chapter explores the lifelong impact of exclusion/inclusion. It examines ways in which mechanisms in society exclude certain groups and individuals, how this exclusion manifests at broader levels throughout society, the factors that can increase the likelihood of people being denied the benefits that contemporary society can offer.

Definitions

We need to move beyond personal memories towards an understanding of 'inclusion' as applied within the fields of education or sociology. The term 'inclusion' is frequently linked with education:

> Inclusive education is part of a human rights approach to social relations and conditions. The intentions and values involved relate to a vision of the whole society of which education is a part. Issues of social justice, equity and choice are central to the demands for inclusive education.
>
> (Morris, 2001: 59)

This 'rights' approach is equally applicable to social inclusion. Nind *et al.* (2003) state:

> If we wish to develop inclusion we need to accept all individuals having control of their own lives, having a say in the running of organisations that represent them and affecting the processes of the institutions that dominate much that happens to them and around them.
>
> (2003: 6)

In education this means,

> [V]aluing all children irrespective of the type or degree of impairment ... restructuring the institution to remove barriers so teaching and learning take place so all children can be valued for who they are, participate, interact and develop their potential.
>
> (Rieser, 2001: 175)

This calls for a radical reappraisal of the structure of schools and colleges. Inclusive thinking is radical thinking and inclusion was established at the heart of government social policy by the New Labour Government's Social Exclusion Task Force (SETF) in 2006 to extend opportunities to those who suffer exclusion and deprivation. The SETF, abolished by the Coalition Government in 2010, adopted this definition of social exclusion:

> Social exclusion is about more than income poverty .... (It) is an extreme consequence of what happens when people don't get a fair deal throughout their lives, often because of disadvantage they face at birth, and this disadvantage can be transmitted from one generation to the next.
>
> (Cabinet Office, 2007)

In August 2011, 15,000 young people participated in riots across England. The independent panel appointed to explore the background suggested, 'the key to avoiding future riots is to ensure that everyone feels they have a stake in society (Lewis, 2012: 2). Might the riots be an extreme consequence of exclusion?

Who is at risk?

The range of categories of people at risk of exclusion includes:

- people living in poverty, at risk of violence, family abuse or illness, affected by environmental degradation or war;
- children at risk of violence or abuse, oppressed minorities whose mother tongue is not the dominant language, 'looked after' children, child labourers or travellers;
- people who are pregnant, caring for relatives or young children;
- girls;
- people with disabilities;
- learners whose schools, curricula or teaching is inadequate or unsuitable.

(Booth, 1999)

Some categories apply only to specific individuals; others, such as old age, affect almost anyone. Exclusion is dynamic: changes in circumstance push many people into one of the categories at some stage in their lives; children can become homeless through family breakdown or can get into trouble with the law. Such circumstances can lead to school exclusion, which contributes to illiteracy among the population in young offenders' institutions and prisons. Sixty per cent of the young people from the 2011 riots had literacy difficulties; 30 per cent had experienced school exclusions (Lewis, 2012). The slope towards exclusion is a slippery one. Percy–Smith (2000) cites seven factors:

1. economics;
2. social difficulties;
3. politics, having no voice;
4. environment, deprived or decaying neighbourhoods;
6. individual aspects, disability, ill health or learning differences;
7. spatial dimensions, excluded groups compete for space in degraded surroundings;
8. group membership of one of the 'at risk' groups.

The Equalities Review (2007) highlighted particular combinations of group membership and specific trigger points, such as transition to school or a caring role for a baby or relative. It aimed to help individuals to become resilient in such circumstances. Considering how exclusion might work for disabled people helps us to appreciate what exclusion can mean for individuals. Mechanisms within society operate to oppress and disempower particular people and to exclude them from the social and economic benefits of contemporary life. The human rights agenda demands equal entitlement to human and material resources for everyone. It politicized and liberated many disabled individuals, and their stories reflect the experience of other excluded groups, such as women or black people. These changes have affected ways of thinking and working in education.

Disabilty and inclusion

Two things influenced current philosophical, ethical, social and political approaches to disability: first, the late twentieth-century struggle for emancipation by three oppressed groups: black people through the Civil Rights movement, women via feminism and gay and lesbian groups through Gay Pride (see Chapter 4). Second, the academic discipline of disability studies emerged, driven by the experiences of disabled activists, academics and people working to further the interests of vulnerable learners. Foucault (1980), Barton (1996) and Shakespeare (1998) explored the ways disability is perceived, constructed and represented, how the current model reflects thinking about disability and how it affects the expectations and treatment of people with impairments.

A 'model' is a representation of reality through which we interpret the world. It includes ideas, pictures, practices and systems constructed to encourage shared understanding. For example, Elizabethans represented their world as a 'Great Chain of Being' created out of chaos by the Christian God. God sat at the top of the chain and each link had power over the one below. If the order was threatened, the world would return to chaos. This worldview informed much of Shakespeare's imagery and ideas: in Macbeth, the killing of the king results in unnatural happenings throughout the world of people, animals and the elements. The world was 'theocentric', the social order was preordained and aspirations beyond one's 'place' meant danger for all. The model shaped and restricted the ways in which Elizabethans saw things and people.

Models of disability have influenced attitudes in the western world. A crucial element was the distinction between what is 'normal' and what is 'other': what is like me, and therefore 'family', what is not and therefore 'alien'. This 'normal'/'other' distinction shapes our responses to excluded groups such as refugees, travellers, immigrants or other ethnic minorities whom we subsequently dehumanize and render less worthy to share our prosperity.

Archaeology provides evidence of the existence of disability from the Neanderthal period and one utilitarian argument suggests that, in societies where survival is precarious, any individual unable to contribute would be disposed of as a liability. However, Barnes's (1996) exploration of historically cultural attitudes to disability reveals societies where people with impairments are both supported and valued. Prejudice against people with impairments is not universal; responses were culturally produced by a complex relationship between the beliefs of the society and its social and economic structure.

The war-like, slave society of Ancient Greece glorified the physical toughness and perfection expressed in Greek statuary and the Olympic Games. Its obsession with bodily perfection generated bias in western society against people with impairments. Those with disabilities received little help in classical society. The Christian church in Europe took the view that any individual not created in the perfect image of God was the product of the devil and a punishment for sins of mankind (Barnes, 1998). The notion was popularized through folk tales about changelings, dwarves, giants and ugly sisters, and epitomized in the works of Shakespeare and other writers. The depiction of the impaired body created an impression of abnormality, damage and powerlessness, or focused upon the hidden impairment of the 'diseased' mind. Think of the fate of Victor Hugo's *Hunchback of Notre Dame*, Shakespeare's black-hearted, hunchbacked *Richard III*, the hook-handed Captain Hook in *Peter Pan* or the blinded and dependent Mr Rochester in *Jane Eyre*.

Disability frequently signified moral ambivalence, evil, or childlike dependency. Dwarves and the 'feeble minded' were the butt of jokes. Visits to Bedlam or the 'lunatic asylum' became entertainment and, by the Victorian era, the freak show was flourishing. Terms such as 'spastic' and 'moron' became insults. Darwin's theories of evolution, natural selection and the survival of the fittest produced Social Darwinism: the philosophy of sending the weak to the wall to benefit the majority. The Eugenics movement linked idiocy, poverty and criminality to heredity; it argued that these 'degenerates' threatened society, should be kept separate to avoid contamination and sterilized to prevent their reproduction. These ideas were taken to the logical extreme by the Nazi party in Germany.

In the UK in 1870 the introduction of universal compulsory schooling increased pressure on schools facing an influx of children from poorer families. The Egerton Royal Commissions of 1886 and 1889 (Copeland, 2003) suggested 5 per cent of urban children were incapable of elementary education and divided the school population into two unequal groups. 'The dull and deficient' (Copeland, 2003: 45), defined as 'imbeciles', were identified by medical examination and placed in special schools with limited curricula. Some had impairments, but many more learning 'disabilities' sprang from social, economic and environmental exclusion – poverty, orphan status, and heart and lung diseases, alongside brutal teaching and classroom discipline.

The treatment of such children epitomizes a 'medical model' of disability rooted in the individual's biology. It regards personal impairment and the individual's failure to adapt to society as the cause of disability. People are diagnosed by experts, medical or quasi-medical, who see all difficulties from the perspective of treating patients. Disabled people are allocated the permanent sick role (Oliver, 1990), denied a voice, relieved of responsibility and expectations. They are rendered dependent on 'experts' and forced to be the 'victim'. Experts make decisions about where they are educated, where they live, their employment, support or benefits available, and whether they can have children. The individual is pressured to cooperate, to abandon an impaired state that is regarded as 'less than human', to be rehabilitated into 'normal' functions or to be dismissed as 'incurable'. Dehumanized, they are regarded as 'other' and punished by being excluded from ordinary life. This model is oppressive, frequently involving dominance and absence of choice. Up to ten years ago, people with disabilities were excluded from decision making for their community care plans. The model imposes both practical restrictions and a 'discourse of disadvantage' onto people with disabilities. It is sometimes termed the 'disadvantage' model.

This medical model produces a society that segregates and establishes 'special' facilities away from community life, encouraging patronizing attitudes, pity and fear. It has fuelled the market for the 'disability industry' (Barnes, 1996), particularly within education. It has encouraged media representation of people with disabilities as 'other', dependent and of low social account. Some charities use vulnerable images to incite in potential donors a mixture of pity and guilt. They create a dependent relationship between the (usually) non-disabled charity helpers and the disabled 'helped', reducing the need for the state to be the prime mover in enabling people with disabilities to reach their potential.

The medical model predominated throughout much of the twentieth century. Although still apparent within some medical, educational and social service professions, it has been robustly challenged. The 1970s saw struggles for civil liberties in which people with disabilities increasingly participated. The contribution of social and economic structures to the oppression of people with impairments was highlighted. The UK Union of Physically Impaired People Against Segregation (UPIAS, 1975) insisted that disabled people should speak for themselves, rejecting the practice of 'experts' pronouncing on their behalf. UPIAS highlighted discrimination against disabled people through denial both of the material benefits of education and the economy, and by the prejudice arising from cultural representations of disabled people as 'other'.

Postmodern theories from philosophers such as Foucault (1980) emphasized the destructive nature of current 'representations' of disability. Barton (1996) states that 'disabled people's history needs to be viewed as part of an increasing struggle to establish and maintain positive self-identities' (1996: 58). He distinguishes the individual's impairment from the nature of disability and quotes the statement of Fundamental Principles of Disability taken from UPIAS and the Disability Alliance (1975):

> In our view, it is society which disables physically impaired people. Disability is something *imposed* on top of our impairment by the way we are unnecessarily isolated and excluded from full participation in society. Disabled people are therefore an oppressed group in society.
>
> Thus we define *impairment* as lacking part or all of a limb, organ or mechanism of the body; and *disability* as the disadvantage or restriction of activity caused by a contemporary social organisation which takes no or little account of people who have physical impairments and thus excludes them from participation in the mainstream of social activities. Physical impairment is therefore a particular form of social oppression.
>
> (UPIAS, 1975: 14, quoted in Barton, 1996: 56)

This is the 'social model', shifting the 'problem' from the impaired individual to the way society is organized. It blames the social and individual attitudes and behaviours that create physical and conceptual barriers to oppress disabled people. The social model has been emancipatory: it argues for the dismantling of barriers and grants individuals the power and responsibility to make decisions about their future. It also emphasizes that representations of disabled people as 'other', tragic or helpless victims are learned prejudices. Morris (2001) explains the role played by 'rights' in the social model: 'Our vision is of a society which recognizes our rights and our value as equal citizens rather than merely treating us as the recipient of other people's good will' (ibid.: 10).

However, the social model has been criticized for reducing everything to economics, neglecting the stories and voices of disabled people and taking little account of the physical experience of living with impairments that cannot be solved by social manipulation. Social and medical models have been diametrically opposed in their representation of disability, and some suggest that placing the lived experiences of people with disabilities back in the picture risks reinforcing a 'medical tragedy' perspective. However, the voice of disabled people is increasingly being heard.

A new 'affirmative' model (Swain and French, 2000) has emerged, inspired in particular by the Disability Arts Movement. It challenges 'normality and otherness' and promotes the building of positive collective identity through membership of campaigning groups such as the Disabled People's Movement. In common with other affirmative models, such as Black Power, it can be expressed by the slogan 'proud, angry and strong' (ibid.: 573).

Disability legislation

The challenge to the medical model underlies recent legislation. The 1995 Disability Discrimination Act, the Disability Discrimination Act (DDA, Part IV, 2001) and the SEN Code of Practice (2001) outlawed discrimination in the workplace, public life and educational and training contexts. It required that people with impairments receive the same opportunities as the rest of the population, making institutions legally responsible for raising staff awareness, identifying an individual's disability and taking reasonable steps to prevent less favourable treatment for any reason relating to impairment. In 2010, most of the duties in the DDA were replaced by the Equality Act. It defined disability as physical or mental impairment having a substantial and long-term adverse effect on the person's ability to carry out normal day-to-day activities. The Public Sector Equality Duty (2011) obliges schools to eliminate discrimination and improve equality of opportunity by countering prejudice, removing barriers, meeting the needs of disabled pupils and encouraging their participation in the life of the school. Schools are required to publish information to demonstrate their compliance.

Impact of the social model on education in the UK

In 1978 the Warnock Report (Warnock Committee, 1978) shifted the emphasis from 'within-child' medicalized difficulties towards a learner's educational needs. It acknowledged that barriers prevented children from full participation in educational experience and inspired the legislation underpinning the emergence of the inclusive school. The SEN (special educational needs) Code of Practice (DfES, 2001) demanded that the requirements of children with SEN should be met, normally in mainstream schools or settings with full access to a broad, balanced and relevant education covering the National

Curriculum. The child's views should be taken into account and parents should play a vital role. Labour Government (1997–2010) policies were committed to inclusive education, placing all students together in mainstream schools.

Inclusive education

'Inclusion', however, is no easy option. Bailey (1998) suggests that inclusive education is

> being in an ordinary school with other students following the same curriculum at the same time, in the same classroom, with the full acceptance of all, and in a way that makes the student feel no different to other students.
>
> (ibid.: 179)

Rieser (2001) distinguishes between 'integration' and 'inclusion'. Integration is simply a matter of locating children in a mainstream school and expecting them to change and adapt to school life. 'Inclusion' requires the institution to be reframed to 'remove barriers so teaching and learning take place so all children can be valued for who they are, participate, interact and develop their potential' (ibid.: 175). Inclusion is a radical concept demanding reorganization of school life to create suitable learning support for the whole student population. There are implications for governors, managers, teachers, support staff, parents and children.

The Labour Governments promoted change. The Qualifications and Curriculum Authority (2000) structured inclusive practice into the curriculum. The *Index for Inclusion* (Booth and Ainscow, 2002) enabled schools to audit their progress towards inclusion. Ofsted (2004) imposed mandatory training in inclusion on inspectors. However, the reality of contemporary school life (Nind *et al.*, 2003; Cigman, 2007) means that, despite the drive for inclusion and the rise in the number of children with disabilities in mainstream schools, change remains partial and inconsistent.

There are three reasons for this. First, the drive towards inclusion coincided with increasing emphasis on competition, consumerism and individual choice, generated by successive Conservative, Labour and Coalition administrations (see Chapter 1). Concern to raise standards and test scores fuelled a move away from child-centred approaches towards a test-driven 'standards' agenda. The presence within a school of high numbers of children with SEN reduces the proportion of children gaining higher scores in SATS or GCSE in the 'raw-score league tables' (Rouse and Florian, 2006). Teachers are asked to celebrate diversity in the classroom while being castigated when their test results compare unfavourably with other schools. Despite evidence to the contrary (Farrell *et al.*, 2007) fears that the presence of pupils identified as having additional support needs (ASN) may lower the results of other pupils becomes a justification for excluding these pupils from mainstream schools.

Second, do students with disabilities benefit academically from full inclusion? A literature review by Hornby *et al.* (1997) is unclear and, despite the introduction of a National Pupil Database (NPD) tracking the attainments of individuals, problems of research methodology undermine the reliability of comparisons (Florian *et al.*, 2004). The only clear conclusion is the need for appropriate training for teachers to build confidence in their abilities and to remove underlying prejudices against disabled people.

Third, in 2005 Baroness Warnock herself expressed doubts about fully inclusive provision. Research (Cigman, 2007) suggests that some children can be equally disadvantaged by compulsory placement in the mainstream. Some parents of children with/without disabilities are ambiguous about inclusion and some senior management in local authorities (LA), academies and schools consider 'standards' agendas incompatible with full inclusion. Removal of the need for individual assessment of a child's profile may risk reducing levels of specialist support knowledge available for individuals with varying impairments. Pressure groups frequently promote the use of a particular 'label' (e.g. Specific Learning Difficulty/dyslexic) in the interests of individual children. Although there is agreement over the radical nature of true 'inclusive education', much remains contested. Is inclusion compatible with the maintenance of specialized schools? Can the medical and social models be reconciled? Does inclusion really lead to raised standards and rights for all?

One major question is the 'dilemma of difference' (Warnock, 2005). Cigman (2007) explains;

> We either treat all children as essentially the same, which means treating them as fairly as possible but with the risk of neglecting individual differences, or we treat them differently, with the consequence that some are better off than they would otherwise have been, but there is a risk of being unfair by devoting more resources or expertise to some than others.
>
> (Cigman, 2007: xxii)

Conclusion

Education, although prime, is not the sole factor in preventing exclusion New Labour's Every Child Matters ECM) agenda (2004) acknowledged the spectrum of circumstances underpinning exclusion/inclusion, recognizing the need to improve access, engagement and participation by creating stronger links across education, social and health care to prevent vulnerable individuals falling through the cracks. It drew upon ideas implicit in the models discussed here to train professionals to cooperate to remove barriers to participation for all vulnerable individuals.

The Green Paper on SEN and Disability (DfES, 2011) suggests a 0–25 education, health and care plan to enhance the quality of life for children and their families and to offer equal life chance outcomes for young people as they move into adulthood. Although the emphasis remains upon strong cross-agency partnerships between services, families, children and young people, the Green Paper privileges the voice and choices of the parent, including a personal budget for parents to choose and manage their own services from the range of voluntary and local sector organizations. This is not always welcomed, particularly since it coincides with the reduction of LA influence, both as a mediator between central government policy, parents and schools, and as a monitor of the quality of interventions with cuts to specialist LA support teams and the use of independent providers. Will children face an 'army of chancers, cherry pickers and snake-oil merchants' (Garner, 2012: 2)? Or will this be the 'radically different system to support better life outcomes for young people' suggested by the government (Teather, 2011)? The jury remains out over the impact of Coalition Government policy on the experiences of the people it aims to reach (see Chapter 2).

Summary points

- Inclusion means valuing all people alike, regardless of their situation or group membership, and restructuring social and economic institutions to remove barriers, allowing all to participate, to interact and to develop their potential. It demands critical awareness of how certain groups can be stigmatized as 'other' and lose their right to access the fruits of our society.
- Particular 'triggers' might put an individual temporarily or permanently into a group vulnerable to exclusion.
- The impact of socially constructed models to represent particular groups, such as those with disabilities, contributes to their exclusion.
- Coalition Government policies, legislation, resources and practices aim to develop a more inclusive society where professional groups cooperate closely; yet there remain many tensions, complicated by untested policies, which raise further questions as to the outcomes for vulnerable people.

Questions for discussion

- What triggers affect those at risk of exclusion?
- Can medical and social models of disability truly be reconciled?
- Can educational inclusion work?
- How can we deal with the 'dilemma of difference'?
- What are the barriers to the implementation of The Equality Act?

Recommended reading

Barton, L. (ed.) (1996) *Disability and Society: Emerging issues and insights,* Harlow: Addison Wesley Longman.
A fascinating and accessible selection of chapters by leading thinkers across the disability studies arena.

Booth, T. and Ainscow, M. (2011) *Index for Inclusion: Developing learning and participation in schools* (2nd edn). Bristol: Centre for Studies in Inclusive Education (CSIE). Available online at http://www. csie.org.uk (accessed 12 May 2012).
Practical guidance on implementation of inclusive practices.

Cigman, R. (ed.) (2007) *Included or Excluded. The challenge of the mainstream for some SEN children.* London: Routledge.
A collection of essays exploring contested areas.

Nind, M., Rix, J., Sheehy, K. and Simmons, K (eds) (2003) *Inclusive Education: Diverse perspectives.* London: David Fulton.
Contains the voices of many stakeholders within this debate; accessible and challenging.

References

Bailey, J. (1998) Australia: Inclusion through categorisation. In: T. Booth and M. Ainscow (eds) *From Them to Us: An international study of inclusion in education.* London: Routledge.

Barnes, C. (1996) Theories of Disability and the Origins of the Oppression of Disabled People in Western Societies. In: L. Barton (ed.) *Disability and Society: Emerging issues and insights.* Harlow: Addison Wesley Longman.

Barnes, C. (1998) The Social Model of Disability: A sociological phenomenon ignored by sociologists? In: T. Shakespeare (ed.) *The Disability Reader: Social sience perspectives*. London: Cassell.

Barton, L. (ed.) (1996) *Disability and Society: Emerging issues and insights*. Harlow: Addison Wesley Longman.

Booth, T. (1999) Viewing Inclusion from a Distance: Gaining perspective from comparative study. *Support for Learning* 14(4): 164–8.

Booth, T. and Ainscow, M. (2002) *Index for Inclusion: Developing learning and participation in schools*. Bristol: Centre for Studies in Inclusive Education (CSIE). Available online at http://www.eenet.org.uk/resources/docs/Index%20English.pdf (accessed 12 May 2012).

Cabinet Office (2007) *Context for Social Exclusion Work*. Available online at http://www.cabinetoffice.gov.uk/social_exclusion_task_force/context/ (accessed 15 October 2007).

Cigman, R. (2007) *Included or Excluded. The challenge of the mainstream for some SEN children*. London: Routledge.

Copeland, I.C. (2003) Integration versus Segregation: The early struggle. In: M. Nind, J. Rix, K. Sheehy and K. Simmons (eds) *Inclusive Education: Diverse perspectives*. London: David Fulton.

DfES (2001) *Special Educational Needs: Code of practice of schools, early education practitioners and other interested parties*. London: DfES.

DfES (2004) Every Child Matters: Change for children. Nottingham: DfES.

DfES (2011) Support and Aspiration: A new approach to special educational needs and disability. Nottingham: DfES.

Equalities Review (2007) *Fairness and Freedom: The final report of the Equalities Review*. Available online at http://www.theequalitiesreview.org.uk/equality_review.pdf (accessed 11 November 2007).

Farrell, P., Dyson A., Polat, F., Hutcheson, G. and Gallannaugh, F. (2007) The Relationship between Inclusion and Academic Achievement in English Mainstream Schools. *School Effectiveness and School Improvement* 18(3): 335–52.

Florian, L., Rouse, M., Black-Hawkins, K. and Jull, S. (2004) What Can National Data Sets Tell Us about Inclusion and Pupil Achievement? *British Journal of Special Education* 31(3): 115–21.

Foucault, M. (1980) The Politics of Health in the Eighteenth Century. In: C. Gordon (ed.) *Michel Foucault: Power/knowledge*. Brighton: Harvester.

Garner, P. (2012) Editoria. *Support for learning* 27(1): 2–3.

Hornby, G., Atkinson, M. and Howard, J. (1997) *Controversial Issues in Special Education*. London: David Fulton.

Lewis, P. (ed.) (2012) *Reading the Riots. Investigating England's summer of disorder*. Guardian; LSE. Available online at http://www.guardian.co.uk/uk/2011/sep/05/reading-riots-study-guardian-lse (accessed 25 April 2012).

Morris, J. (2001) *Having a Say, That Kind of Life: Social exclusion and young disabled people with high levels of support needs*. London: Scope.

Nind, M., Rix, J., Sheehy, K. and Simmons, K. (eds) (2003) *Inclusive Education: Diverse perspectives*. London: David Fulton.

Oliver, M. (1990) *The Politics of Disablement*. Basingstoke: Macmillan.

Percy-Smith, J. (ed.) (2000) *Policy Responses to Social Exclusion: Towards inclusion*. Buckingham: Open University Press.

Rieser, F. (2001) The Struggle for Inclusion: The growth of a movement. In: L. Barton (ed.) *Disability, Politics and the Struggle for Change*. London: David Fulton.

Rouse, M. and Florian, L. (2006) Inclusion and Achievement: Student achievement in secondary schools with higher and lower proportions of pupils designated as having special educational needs. *International Journal of Inclusive Education* 10(6): 481–93.

Shakespeare, T. (ed.) (1998) *The Disability Reader: Social science perspectives*. London: Cassell.

Swain, J. and French, S. (2000) Towards an Affirmation Model of Disability. *Disability and Society* 15(4): 569–82.

Teather, S. (2011) Letter to Head Teachers and Chairs of Governors. DFE. Available online at http://media.education.gov.uk/assets/files/pdf/ (accessed 25April 2012).

UPIAS (1975) (UNESCO, 1994) *Fundamental Principles of Disability*. London: Disability Alliance.

Warnock Committee (1978) *Special Educational Needs: The Warnock Report*. London: DES.

Warnock, M. (2005) *Special Educational Needs: A new look*. London: Philosophy of Education Society of Great Britain.

Chapter 9

Education for democracy

Political contexts for learning citizenship

Howard Gibson

Introduction

This chapter provides an overview of citizenship and education for democracy in England. It explains the backdrop to New Labour's initiative in 2000, and locates the particular form that citizenship education took within a historical context. This it attributes to economic and social policies that sought to increase the 'responsibility' of individuals and ensure that schools became sites for social regeneration and renewal, countering the worrying trend towards what some saw as civic and political apathy. The chapter suggests, however, that the role given to schools to develop young citizens may mean that they are now charged with an insurmountable task. Many of the problems facing what Crick (QCA, 1998) called 'modern democracies' may actually originate in combined issues: the decline in power of the nation state with the growth of global capitalism; the problem of developing a cohesive society where, as Putman (2000) put it, people 'bowl alone' or see themselves as belonging to disparate ethnic groups with multiple transnational identities; and the problem of a lack of trust in politicians and the political process.

The birth of citizenship education in England

The concern for citizenship education is not recent in English schools. During the early part of the twentieth century the Moral Instruction League endeavoured to influence government provision for state education (Wright, 2007). Between the two world wars the Association of Education in Citizenship lobbied with a similar purpose, as did the Council for Education in World Citizenship (Whitmarsh, 1974; Heater 2003). In response to such pressure the Ministry of Education (1949) published a pamphlet in 1949 entitled *Citizens Growing up: At home, in school and after* (HMSO, 1949). However not until the 1980s when Bernard Weatherill, then speaker of the House of Commons, called for a Commission on Citizenship was there a 'theme' for citizenship added to the curriculum in England, though in practice it was largely neglected by schools because of its non-statutory nature.

In 1998, however, there was a step change and the Crick Report drew upon T. H. Marshall's model of civil, political and social rights for citizenship (Marshall, 1950). *Education for Citizenship and the Teaching of Democracy in Schools* (QCA, 1998) comprised three aspects: social and moral responsibility; community involvement and political literacy; or, more simply, the learning of values, social action and politics. It became the model providing the underlying rationale for the 2002 statutory Programme of Study for Citizenship in secondary schools and for the optional Guidelines for PSHE and Citizenship at primary level (see Manley, 1992; QCA, 1998, 2002). These were later revised by the QCA to augment the economic and global dimensions of learning (QCA, 2007).

However, despite the enthusiasm to strengthen the social and political commitment of young people in schools, citizenship education and education for democracy in the 1990s has been subject to criticism. Much of this is attributable to the pragmatism underpinning its creation and to issues that make questionable some of its assumptions. In Scotland and Wales, for example, as in other parts of the world, distinct forms of citizenship education have emerged that place greater emphasis upon the community and upon curriculum provision for all stages of primary and secondary education. The next section explains the specific cultural and political backdrop to the particular form that citizenship education took in English schools.

Neoliberalism, social regulation and citizenship education

Clues to its character are to be found in the policies of Margaret Thatcher during her period in office as prime minister between 1979 and 1990. In a seemingly inconsequential interview for *Woman's Own* magazine in 1987 she declared: 'There is no such thing as society: there are individual men and women, and there are families' (Thatcher, 1987). For some her statement seemed to encapsulate the age, the individualism of self-seeking consumers and the Hobbesian belief that life was 'nasty, brutish and short' for the unsuccessful (Hobbes, 1996). Such philosophical underpinnings were combined with policies that would 'roll back the state', that is, diminish the role it had played since the end of World War II in providing services such as public transport, unemployment benefit or free dental care (see Chapter 1). Now individuals were told to rely more upon their own willingness and ability to 'survive', and for markets to provide solutions to individual needs. For those who were unfortunate or without sufficient wit to understand the nature of this Darwinian game, there would always be a minimum of state provision and, as in Dickensian times, philanthropy. In essence then, some commentators epitomised the age as dominated by self-seeking, wealth-creating adventurists whose concern as citizens for society seemed limited to voluntary and occasional acts of compassion:

> The active citizen of Thatcherism was a law-abiding, materially successful individual who was willing and able to exploit the opportunities created by the promotion of market rights, while demonstrating occasional compassion for those less fortunate than themselves – charity rather than democratic citizenship was to be the main instrument of 'active citizenship'.
>
> (Faulks, 2006)

The election of Tony Blair as the Labour Party prime minister from 1997 to 2007 changed little regarding the assumptions about the benefits of a 'modern dynamic economy' (Blair, 1998). In 1998 Blair coined the phrase 'the Third Way' in an attempt to position his government at the centre of politics. It should not be too far to the left, where it had been traditional for the state to intervene in people's lives for reasons of social equity by taxing the rich more heavily to pay for the needs of the poor. And neither should it be too far to the right, where it might be accused of identifying too closely with his ideological enemies in the Conservative Party who seemed to deny that 'society' existed independently of competing individuals. The Third Way was an attempt to gain credence from the broadest political footing with a new concept of citizenship central to the programme: 'Rebuilding Britain as a strong community, with a modern notion of citizenship at its heart, is the political objective for the new age' (Blair, 1993) (see Chapter 2).

Behind the rhetoric of 'strong community' were two fundamental policies: an economic one associated with neoliberalism, and a social one that emerged in a series of political discourses on individual responsibility, opportunity and citizenship. The economic one was essentially a development of Thatcherism and asserted that free competition was the most effective basis for market forces to ensure quality and efficiency. It meant the deregulation of the labour market and a reduction in the role of law and the state to optimise productivity and generate new economic growth. It also meant privatisation, in which the public sector would be sold off or joined in public–private partnerships through the construction of market proxies in the residual public sector with the aim of encouraging competition. Schools, for example, would compete for pupils and funding. It also meant free trade beyond the nation's borders to encourage the mobility of capital and labour as well as the abolition of tariffs, subsidies and control on foreign investments in order to stimulate global market forces. And, to enable individuals to make choice, the move towards indirect taxation and a reduction in basic income tax (see Jessop, 2002; Whitty, 2002; Olssen et al., 2004).

The social regulatory part of the Third Way was closely linked with the economic one and was designed to prepare citizens for the move away from a historical over-dependency on the welfare state. Because of its cost, inefficiency and failure to eliminate poverty, the policy was needed, it was said, to move people from the old 'welfare state' to a 'workfare' regime; one in which people were trained in the necessary skills and given incentives to find employment, or attract disincentives if they didn't (see Chapter 3). The press described the policy as 'a hand up rather than a hand out' (*The Guardian*, 2005). At the same time there was a move towards 'personal empowerment', 'opportunity' and 'individual responsibility' for, it was stressed, there are 'no rights without responsibilities' (Giddens, 1998). In essence, then, the Keynesian welfare state was gradually to be replaced by a Hayekian workfare regime where the state's role was to create the necessary economic and social structures for the successful operation of the market; one where individuals would increasingly need to compete and plan for themselves as individuals, take opportunities where they found them and, at the same time, become more active and responsible with regard to their civic obligations.

The school curricula emerging from central government mirrored these broad policy objectives. On the one hand, Personal Financial Capability (DfEE, 2000a, 2000b; DfES, 2007) and Enterprise and Entrepreneurial Education (Gibson, 2008; Davies, 2002; DfES, 2005) were aimed at addressing the requirement that pupils be taught the skills necessary for survival in a neoliberal economy. On the other hand, citizenship education was devised to help with the social regulatory part of the policy. For some these curricular initiatives were thought appropriate and upbeat responses to pressures upon the nation state, and for the need to renew civic virtues and address growing concerns with crime, social order and political apathy. For others, however, citizenship education was yet another example of the state using the school curriculum as a tool for social engineering. In 1921, for example, shortly after World War I and its economic legacy, a time of high unemployment and burgeoning class warfare, the government commissioned the Board of Education to consider ways in which the English curriculum could be used to unite 'a divided nation'. The report was called *English for the English*.

> An education fundamentally English would, we believe, at any rate bridge, if not close, this chasm of separation. The English people might learn as a whole to read their own language, first with respect, and then with a genuine feeling of pride and affection... Such a feeling for our own native language would be a bond of union between classes, and would beget the right kind of national pride. Even more certainly should pride and joy in the national literature serve as such a bond.
>
> (Board of Education, 1921: 22)

The desire to 'bond' the nation through an English curriculum in the 1920s reflects the call today for citizenship education to tackle contemporary social ills and a growing disillusionment with the political process. Because citizens are said to have become increasingly apathetic as voters, disenchanted with political parties and cynical about the sleaze and sound bites emerging from those in public office, some have seen citizenship education as a quest for 'social glue'. They argue that sticking society together is necessary because we live in fragmenting times where social capital, the network that underpins connectivity between people cooperating and working together, has dwindled (see Putnam, 2000). Prime Minister Cameron's answer to the problem was for the nation to coalesce around what he called 'the Big Society' (see Chapter 2). *The reason for this is that* 'the state has promoted not social solidarity, but selfishness and individualism' (Cameron, 2009): 'We need to create communities with oomph – neighbourhoods who are in charge of their own destiny, who feel if they club together and get involved they can shape the world around them' (Cameron, 2010).

Opposition parties and trade unions largely dismissed the idea with Labour's Ed Balls saying that far from uniting the nation it was no more than a cynical attempt 'to dignify its cuts agenda, by dressing up the withdrawal of support with the language of reinvigorating civic society' (Byrnes, 2010). Even the Archbishop of Canterbury claimed that 'we need reassuring that the Big Society isn't just an alibi for cuts, and a way back to Government just washing its hands' (Williams, 2010). Schools, then, are left with citizenship education and the highly ambitious task of generating mutual bonds and stimulating civic commitment in the younger generation. In the next section we ask whether schools' role as agents of social regeneration and civic renewal is realistic.

Explainiing citizens' disengagement with politics

Is citizenship education an appropriate response to national apathy and civic renewal with political life? Despite evidence to suggest that voter turnout is historically low and that the political parties have been haemorrhaging members for the last 50 years, some would dispute the assumption that the populace is apathetic. This was just the approach an influential pressure group took in 2006. Helena Kennedy QC, Chair of the Power Inquiry funded by the Rowntree Charitable Trust, agreed with the government that low participation in formal politics was 'a serious problem threatening to undermine our democracy' but strongly disagreed about the interpretation of the evidence. She argued:

> When a government presides over two of the lowest general election turnouts and the two biggest street demonstrations since 1945, it's time to start asking and answering hard questions about why politics is failing to engage with the people of Britain through the traditional channels.
>
> (Kennedy, 2006)

The Inquiry reported that

> [C]ontrary to much of the public debate around political disengagement, the British public are not apathetic. There is now a great deal of research evidence to show that very large numbers of citizens are engaged in community and charity work outside of politics.
>
> (Power Inquiry, 2006: 16)

It concluded by suggesting that disengagement with politics 'is NOT caused by an apathetic and uninterested public with a weak sense of civic duty' (ibid.: 17) but, rather, by the convergence of political parties upon the centre ground and by citizens feeling that the processes of formal democracy fail to offer them sufficient influence over political decisions because of the incremental growth in the power of the government executive.

Second, and linked to this, political disengagement may be inversely related to the public perception of an increase in 'sleaze', 'spin', 'dumbing down' and the 'sound bite' that has come to be associated with British political life in recent years: 'There is evidence that the increasing number of people abstaining from the electoral process do so less out of a disengagement with politics than with a contempt for politicians' (Lewis *et al.*, 2005: 3). In recent years examples of sleaze might include former Prime Minister Blair's interviews with the police regarding the 'cash for honours' investigation; his difficulties accounting for the interpretation of the Attorney General's advice regarding the legality of the war in Iraq; the suspicion that multinationals' interests may have guided major political decisions in the UK, as with the testing of GM crops; MP Jeffrey Archer's imprisonment for perjury; MP Peter Mandelson's mandatory resignation as government minister followed by his rebirth as a European one; Home Secretary David Blunkett's paternity affair, his resignation, questionable dealings with DNA Bioscience and subsequent second resignation from the cabinet; the furore over MPs expenses, and so on.

The Power Inquiry concluded that the level of animosity felt towards politicians, the main political parties and the key institutions of the political system was 'extremely high and widespread' (Power Inquiry, 2006: 16). Furedi (2004) has suggested that spoon-feeding the British public with synthetic 'sound bites' is counterproductive and that the attempt to augment postal voting during general elections is merely a substitute for genuine debate and participation.

Third, the effect of global capitalism upon democracy has not been dealt with properly in government documents on citizenship education. Bottery (2003) has argued that the more the state withdraws under the banner of neoliberalism, the less citizens will feel a sense of commitment to it. By implication, David Cameron's Big Society initiative was misguided. Anderson has suggested that globalisation has seriously challenged the traditional territorial bases of liberal democracies and that this makes them vulnerable.

> Globalisation is putting democracy in question and is itself being questioned as undemocratic. Its border crossings are undermining the traditional territorial basis of democracy and creating new political spaces which need democratising. 'Global forces' are disrupting the supposedly independent, sovereign states and national communities which have provided democracy's main framework. And these 'global forces' are apparently beyond control or, more specifically, beyond democratic control. The political implications are wide reaching and far from clear.
>
> (Anderson, 2002: 6)

In other words, one of the consequences of globalisation has been a decline in the economic, political and social effectiveness of nation states (Giddens, 1998). As private multinational corporations have become more powerful they have affected the success or otherwise of national economies. Nation states have lost at least some of their autonomy as multinational corporations, and supra-state political institutions such as the EU or the IMF have usurped their power, while economic power outruns political power and political control is lost to global markets. With the rise of transnational corporations Hertz has gone so far as to argue that because modern democracies are now resigned to the fact that multinational companies are taking the place of elected governments, and because businesses are so dependent upon the loyalty of their customers, shopping may now be more effective than voting in effecting political change. 'None of it is good for democracy', she adds (Hertz, 2001: 7).

A fourth factor that may explain political disengagement is the complex nature of British identity today. Because of globalisation, post-colonial migration and increasing population mobility, many citizens now have multiple identities (see Kymlicka, 2003; Kerr et al., 2002). Today, for example, one can be English, British, a Muslim, a member of the EU, and have a simultaneous commitment to another country by birth or by marriage. In consequence, says Parekh (2002), the state today is too plural and diverse to consist of a single people:

> Since it is constantly exposed to external influences and its members do not share a moral and cultural consensus, it cannot aspire to be a single cultural unit and base its unity on the cultural homogeneity of its citizens. It cannot claim to embody and legitimate itself in terms of their sense of collective identity either, both because many of them no longer place much emphasis on their national identity or privilege it over their other identities, and because some of them increasingly have and cherish transnational ties and identities.
>
> (ibid.: 53)

The consequence is sometimes 'fundamental' for democracy. For example, one of the effects of the publication of Salman Rushdie's *The Satanic Verses* (1988) was a Muslim fatwa placed upon the author together with book burnings and demonstrations around the UK concerning its allegedly blasphemous content. It also confirmed the juxtaposition of different ideologies or 'fundamentalisms' and the fragility of formerly self-evident 'British principles': freedom of speech versus blasphemy.

Conclusion

An NFER survey in 2008 emphasised that, while 'the important fact to underline about the introduction of citizenship education is that one of its key aims is the development of young people's trust' (NFER, 2008: 30), it witnessed just the opposite, namely, 'declining levels of trust in authority figures and institutions, including family and teachers' (DCSF, 2008: vii). To understand this, one would need to set aside simplistic invective regarding the duty of young citizens to participate in their local community and become more active, responsible and charitable (QCA, 1998: 2.11). Instead, there would need to be devised a curriculum for citizenship that attempted to give pupils a far broader understanding of the complex causes of political disengagement, such as the seeming *antipathy* to the formal political process but *not* apathy to politics *per se*. For example, the deficit of trust and the seeming lack of genuine encounter in the discussion of policy formation, from taking the nation to war to increasing university fees, despite promises not to; an understanding of the complex relationship of the media with a modern democracy and the power of important figures like Rupert Murdoch; the effects of globalisation upon the power of democracies to be authoritative on the international stage in the presence of dominant multinational companies; the changing, complex nature of British identity and what it might mean to be a citizen of this country today; and so on.

Summary points

- Bernard Crick was commissioned by David Blunkett, Secretary of State for Education at the time, to report on *Citizenship and the Teaching of Democracy in Schools* (1998). This led in September 2002 to the addition of Citizenship Education as a statutory part of the secondary school curriculum.
- Reports from Ofsted suggest that the quality of teaching of citizenship education is at best patchy. Studies from the NFER show that pupils' trust in politicians is still low and that their 'active involvement' in political or civic activities is at best uneven or inconsistent.
- Accounting for the historical rise of citizenship education in England is interesting because it helps set the policy within the broader remit of a move to neoliberal economics and an accompanying social agenda that emphasises 'individual responsibility' and 'civic duty'. It may be that schools facing the challenge of social regeneration and civic renewal may find it not only ideologically unsound but an insurmountable goal.

Questions for discussion

- If you were a teacher, how would you go about stimulating your pupils' awareness of, say, global warming and manage to escape the brickbats of 'modern Puritanism', 'scaremongering' or 'political bias' from your ideological enemies?

- The Crick Report refers to a distinction between 'justice' and the 'law'. Unfortunately his committee didn't expand on the ramifications of this distinction. You try. Say your pupils wished to march to Parliament to demonstrate about the government's 'unjust' involvement in a war, would you let them?

Recommended reading

Breslin, T. and Dufour, B. (eds) (2007) *Developing Citizenship: A comprehensive introduction to effective citizenship education in the secondary school.* London: Hodder Murray.
A good overview of how citizenship education is taught in English secondary schools.

Citizenship Foundation. Available online at http://www.citizenshipfoundation.org.uk (accessed, 2 April 2012).
An important website supported by the Law Society that raises questions like 'What is citizenship and why teach it?', although you may dispute its suggestions.

One of Crick's many papers since his 1998 report. In this one he expands on the nature of democracy.

Crick, B. (2007) Citizenship: The political and the democratic. *British Journal of Educational Studies* 55(3): 235–48.

Faulks, K. (2006) Education for Citizenship in England's Secondary Schools: A critique of current principle and practice. *Journal of Education Policy* 21(1): 59–74.
A well-developed critique of policy and the curriculum for citizenship education.

References

Anderson, J. (2002) Questions of Democracy, Territoriality and Globalisation. In: J. Anderson (ed.) *Transnational Democracy: Political spaces and border crossings.* London: Routledge, pp. 6–380.

Blair, T. (1993) Why Modernisation Matters. *Renewal* 1(4).

Blair, T. (1998) The Third Way: New Politics for the New Century. *Fabian Pamphlet 588*, London: The Fabian Society.

Board of Education (1921) *The Teaching of English in England (The Newbolt Report).* London: HMSO.

Bottery, M. (2003) The End of Citizenship? The Nation state, threats to its legitimacy, and citizenship education in the twenty-first century. *Cambridge Journal of Education* 33(1): 101–22.

Byrnes, S. (2010) How do you create a 'big society'? *The New Statesman* (20 July). Available online at http://www.newstatesman.com/blogs/the-staggers/2010/07/society-chorus-singing-others (accessed 12 March 2012).

Cameron, D. (2009) *The Big Society [Speech, Tuesday, 10 November].* Available online at http://www.conservatives.com/Default.aspx (accessed 12 March 2012).

Cameron, D. (2010) *Big Society Speech [Speech] The Prime Minister on the Big Society, 19 July.* Available online at http://www.number10.gov.uk/news/big-society-speech/ (accessed 12 March 2012).

Davies, H. (2002) *A Review of Enterprise and the Economy in Education.* London: HMSO.

DCSF (2008) *Citizenship Education Longitudinal Study (CELS): Sixth Annual Report young people's civic participation in and beyond school: Attitudes, intentions and influences* (Research Report DCSF-RR052). Nottingham: DCSF Publications.

DfEE (2000a) *Financial Capability through Personal Financial Education: Guidance for schools at Key Stages 1 and 2.* London: DfEE/QCA.

DfEE (2000b) *Financial Capability through Personal Financial Education: Guidance for schools at Key Stages 3 and 4.* London: DfEE/QCA.

DfES (2005) *Education and Skills: Presented to Parliament by the Secretary of State for Education and Skills: Cm 6476.* Norwich: HMSO.

DfES (2007) *Key Stage 3 Curriculum Review: Mastering the basics, creating greater flexibility, protecting the classics.* Available online at http://www.dfes.gov.uk (accessed 5 February 2007).

Faulks, K. (2006) Rethinking Citizenship Education in England: Some lessons from contemporary social and political theory. *Education, Citizenship and Social Justice* 1(2): 123–40.

Furedi, F. (2004) *Where Have all the Intellectuals Gone? Confronting 21st century philistinism.* London: Continuum.

Gibson, H. (2008) Ideology, Instrumentality and Economics Education: On the secretion of values within philanthropy, financial capability and enterprise education in English schools. *International Review of Economics Education* 7(2): 57–78.

Giddens, A. (1998) *The Third Way: The renewal of social democracy.* Cambridge: Polity Press.

Guardian, The (2005) A hand up, not a handout, 21 November.

Heater, D. (2003) The Origins of English Thinking about Citizenship Education. *Teaching Citizenship* 6: 40–3.

Hertz, N. (2001) *The Silent Takeover: Global capitalism and the death of democracy.* London: Heinemann.

Hobbes, T. (1996) *Leviathan.* Oxford: Oxford University Press.

Jessop, B. (2002) *The Future of the Capitalist State.* Cambridge: Polity.

Kennedy, H. (2006) *Announcement at Launch of Power Inquiry Report.* Available online at http://www.tiscali.co.uk/voter/index10.htm (accessed 29 May 2012).

Kerr, D., McCarthy, S. and Smith. A. (2002) Citizenship Education in England, Ireland and Northern Ireland. *European Journal of Education* 37(2): 179–91.

Kymlicka, W. (2003) Two Dilemmas of Citizenship Education in Pluralist Societies. In: A.Lockyer, B.Crick and J.Annette (eds) *Education for Democratic Citizenship: Issues in theory and practice.* Aldershot: Ashgate.

Lewis, J., Inthrorn, S. and Wahl-Jorgensen, K. (2005) *Citizens or Consumers? What the media tell us about political participation.* Maidenhead: Open University Press.

Manley, R. (1992) Citizenship, Voluntary Organisations and the State. In: E.Baglin-Jones and N.Jones (eds) *Education for Citizenship: Ideas and perspectives for cross-curricular study.* London: Kogan Page.

Marshall, T.H. (1950) *Citizenship and Social Class and other Essays.* Cambridge: Cambridge University Press.

Ministry of Education (1949) *Citizens Growing up: At home, in school and after.* London: HMSO

NFER (2008) *CCitizenship Education Longitudinal Study (CELS): Sixth Annual Report Young people's civic participation in and beyond school: Attitudes, intentions and influences.* Nottingham: DCSF. Available online at http://www.teachingcitizenship.org.uk/dnloads/dcsf-rr052.pdf (accessed 18 September 2012).

Olssen, M., Codd, J. and O'Neil, A-M. (2004) *Education Policy: Globalization, citizenship and democracy.* London: Sage.

Parekh, B. (2002) Reconstituting the Modern State. In: J. Anderson (ed.) *Transnational Democracy: Political spaces and border crossings.* London: Routledge.

Power Inquiry (2006) *Power to the People – The Report of Power: An independent report into Britain's democracy.* York: The Power Inquiry/Rowntree Trust.

Putnam, R. (2000) *Bowling Alone: The collapse and revival of American community.* New York: Simon and Schuster.

QCA (1998) *Citizenship and the Teaching of Democracy in Schools: Final Report of the Advisory Group on Citizenship (Crick Report).* London: QCA.

QCA (2002) *Programme of Study for Citizenship.* London: QCA.

QCA (2007) *Programme of Study for Citizenship.* Available online at http://www.lawyersinschools.org.uk/uploads/Citizenship_Curriculum_Key_Stage_4.pdf (accessed 2 April 2012).

Rushdie, S. (1988) *The Satanic Verses* London: Penguin.

Thatcher, M. (1987) There is no such thing as society: there are individual men and women, and there are families. *Woman's Own* (31 October).

Whitmarsh, G. (1974) The Politics of Political Education: An episode. *Journal of Curriculum Studies* 6(2): 133–42.

Whitty, G. (2002) *Making Sense of Education Policy: Studies in the sociology and politics of education*. London: Sage.

Williams, R. (2010) Two and a half cheers for the Big Society. *The Telegraph* (24 July). Available online at http://www.telegraph.co.uk/news/religion/7907830/Dr-Rowan-Williams-Two-and-a-half-cheers-for-the-Big-Society.html (accessed 12 March 2012).

Wright, S. (2007) Into Unfamiliar Territory? The Moral Instruction Curriculum in English Elementary Schools 1880–1914. *History of Education Researcher* 79: 31–40.

Global and environmental education

Chapter 10

Globalisation and the knowledge economy

Robin Shields

Introduction

This chapter discusses globalisation and analyses its implications for education. Specifically, it examines a convergence of educational policy and practice that has taken place over the last century; in virtually every country on earth education is now provided by national governments through a system of formal schooling. There is remarkable similarity in this model of schooling, despite vast differences in countries' cultures, histories and economies. The chapter examines and compares several theoretical accounts of the globalisation of education and looks at the concept of the 'knowledge economy' and increasing emphasis on international achievement tests (e.g. PISA and TIMSS) as a case study.

The global expansion of schooling

Studying globalisation and education can be difficult due to the ambiguous and contested concept of 'globalisation' itself. While the term originates in the field of economics, describing an increase in international trade, economic interdependence and the power of transnational corporations, it has been applied to a wide range of social science disciplines, including anthropology, sociology, and the study of education. Even more controversial than the term are its effects and consequences. Some (e.g. Friedman, 2006) claim that globalisation is ultimately beneficial, creating an egalitarian 'flat world' in which individuals' circumstances and opportunities are determined by merit and ability rather than the country of their birth. However, others describe globalisation as a form of 'global pillage' (Giddens, 1999: 16) in which the spread of global capitalism increases economic inequality and destroys environmental resources. Reflecting this, Stiglitz (2002: 214) claims that 'globalisation today is not working for many of the world's poor. It is not working for much of the environment. It is not working for the stability of the global economy'.

Ritzer (2011) likens globalisation to a 'McDonaldisation' of society: the company's golden arches are associated with a standardised fast-food menu that varies little from New York to Shanghai. This epitomises a larger trend in which transnational corporations (e.g. McDonalds, Apple, Ikea, HSBC) and their cultural symbols and ideology attain global reach, leading to economic integration, social convergence and cultural homogenisation. However, on the topic of global expansion the fast-food super-chain could learn a great deal from the relatively modest primary school. As an institution, formal schooling has undergone a remarkable global expansion, reaching the most far-flung corners of the earth. Schools have spread to remote areas of the Himalayas and African Sahara even more quickly than other changes that are usually associated with 'development' or 'modernity', such as electricity, healthcare and physical infrastructure.

Despite vast differences in countries' histories, cultural contexts and economic circumstances, the way in which education is delivered shows little variation. Throughout the world, the great majority of students attend schools that are funded by their government; internally schools are organised into classrooms, staffed by professionally certified teachers who deliver a standard set of curriculum subjects. Furthermore, education systems around the world change in similar ways. For example, initiatives to decentralise educational management away from the government can be found in countries as diverse as the United States, Nepal and El Salvador, becoming a 'mantra that is recited regardless of the circumstances of specific settings' (Mullikottu-Veettil and Bray, 2004: 224).

Recognising these trends and commonalities, Steiner-Khamsi (2004: 3) argues that countries are 'gradually converging toward an international model of education'. This 'international model' is so ingrained that it constrains which set of policies and practices is considered legitimate. For example, a government that did not provide schooling to its citizens would probably be denounced as a cruel dictatorship; a curriculum that did not include science or mathematics could be rejected as worthless. This 'international model' supersedes its historical forerunners; for example, indigenous models of education in India (e.g. Vedic schools and Buddhist monastic education) date back thousands of years, yet to speak of 'education in India' today implicitly excludes these traditions. Although the curriculum is standardised into a common set of subjects, in many cases it lacks functional relevance. For example, students in landlocked countries learn about marine biology; those in the tropics learn about snow; children who will work in agriculture learn to calculate compound interest (Meyer *et al.*, 1997). Thus, the globalisation of education is accompanied by its own set of paradoxes and dysfunctions.

Global expansion is a surprisingly recent phenomenon. Benavot and Riddle (1988) estimate that in 1870 only one third of children in the world attended primary school; by 1950 this number had increased to approximately one half. According to the most recent UNESCO (2011) data, 88 per cent of children in the relevant age group are enrolled in primary schools. The Education for All (EFA) movement (see Chapter 11) represents a culmination of this trend, aiming to universalise enrolment in primary schools throughout the world. Facilitated by international organisations and supported by over 150 national governments, the EFA movement creates a normative and ethical argument for the expansion of education that is global in scope.

Although globalisation itself is an ambiguous and contested term, its application to education yields a set of clearly defined issues and questions. The globalisation of education is associated with an expansion of formal schooling to virtually every country on earth, combined with strong similarities in curricula, convergent policy trends, and an increasing role for international organisations (for example the United Nations and the World Bank). However, the meaning and significance of these empirical phenomena are fiercely contested in competing theoretical conceptualisations of globalisation.

Explaining the globalisation of education

Although the empirical manifestations of the globalisation of education are relatively uncontested, there is a great deal of debate over why this expansion has occurred and what it means. The debate is addressed through a growing body of theory that seeks to explain globalisation on a conceptual level. However, theoretical accounts differ considerably in both their causal explanation of globalisation and their fundamental views on education and society.

Much of the expansion of education over the past half-century has taken place in the context of international aid and development programmes that sought to use education to promote economic growth and improve standards of living, particularly in former European colonies. The period following World War II marked a turning point in this respect; many European colonies won independence; the United Nations was founded with a mandate to promote 'economic and social progress and development'; and US President Harry Truman (1949) promised 'a bold new program for making the benefits of our scientific advances and industrial progress available for the improvement and growth of underdeveloped areas'. Within two decades, government agencies devoted specifically to international development had been founded in the United States, the United Kingdom and other high-income, industrialised economies.

This new field of social practice was supported by a new body of theory and research. In relation to education the work of economist Jacob Mincer (1958) and his theory of human capital were particularly influential. Essentially, Mincer argued that investments in education and training increased individuals' abilities to become economically productive, and that this would yield an economic return in similar ways to other types of investment, such as investments in bonds or shares. This provided a strong rationale for international aid and development projects that provided access to education. W.W. Rostow (1960), an influential academic and political adviser, argued that investments in education, combined with infrastructure and democratic governance, would put countries on a 'take-off' path that would create economic growth, industrialisation, and higher standards of living. While decades of investment in education have not materialised in economic growth and industrialisation, it has played a significant role in expanding enrolment in education and in embedding the widespread belief that schooling is a functional necessity for development and progress.

However, more recently the rationale for educational expansion has shifted away from economic growth and instead been defended in terms of human rights and ethical principles that are universal: applicable to all people regardless of cultural contexts or individual circumstances. This thinking underlies the EFA movement (see Chapter 11) and the United Nations' Millennium Development Goals, both of which commit to providing primary schooling for all children by the year 2015. The expansion of formal schooling is presented not as an investment, but rather as the realisation of a universal ethical principle.

Meyer et al. (1997) associate these universal beliefs and the associated expansion of educational enrolment with the diffusion of 'world culture' values: individualism, egalitarianism, democracy and a vision of social progress. They argue that such values are embodied in international organisations (e.g. the United Nations), which express them in their declarations and other official documents (e.g. the Universal Declaration of Human Rights). When national governments create policies, they look to these declarations as 'policy scripts' and borrow ideas, language and underlying world culture values. Thus, the remarkable similarity of schooling around the world is explained as a convergence on a common set of cultural beliefs and values.

However, others have taken exception to the 'world culture' approach to education, arguing that it ignores the conflict that accompanies educational expansion, and that schooling in local contexts takes on substantially different meanings. Anderson-Levitt

(2003) points out that on the local level the expansion of schooling is deeply contested; she presents anthropological evidence that, rather than converging, education systems may be diverging to increasingly localised models. In an alternative to the 'world culture' approach, Dale (2000) explains increasing similarity in education through what he terms a 'Globally Structured Educational Agenda'. This perspective explains the expansion of schooling through the global political economy – a combination of the world economic system and political institutions (e.g. national governments and international organisations) that accompany it. As a capitalist economic system continually seeks economic growth, institutions promote normative cultural values (e.g. the notion of education as a human right) that facilitate its expansion. This expansion results in a convergence of educational policy and practice around the world.

The 2010 documentary *Schooling the World* explores mass schooling in India's remote Himalayan region of Ladakh. It makes the argument that schooling is a way of undermining traditional cultures and incorporating children into the global economic system, all under the guise of egalitarianism, progress and human rights. The film shows how modern schooling prevents students from speaking the indigenous Ladakhi language, uproots traditional, sustainable agricultural practices, brands many students as failures, and ultimately equates success with obtaining employment overseas. Echoing the assertion by Bowles and Gintis (1976) that the 'hidden curriculum' prepares students to follow order and obey authority, the film shows how schooling is used to expand modern capitalist society.

Thus, explanations for the global expansion of education vary from universal ethical arguments to critiques of the global capitalist economic system. Depending on one's stance on these theoretical conceptualisations, the global expansion of education takes on fundamentally different meanings and has radically different ethical implications. The next section examines some aspects of the globalisation of education using the concept of the 'knowledge economy' as a case study.

Globalisation, education and the knowledge economy

The effects of the globalisation of education are manifested in new articulations of the economic importance of education and a sense of increased competition between national systems of education. This trend is epitomised in policymaking that conceptualises education in the context of a global 'knowledge economy' in which countries compete with one another, and in a new emphasis on the results of international tests that measure and compare educational achievement in different countries. In 1968, Peter Drucker coined the term 'knowledge economy' to describe an increase in economic activity that centres on the exchange of knowledge and information. While industrial economics creates value from the production of material goods, the knowledge economy does so through the creation and application of new types of knowledge. Examples of 'knowledge industries' that create and apply new types of knowledge include computer software development, financial services and medical research.

The prospect of a knowledge economy creates both economic challenges and opportunities for national governments, particularly in the field of education (see Chapter 13). On the one hand, 'knowledge work' can be performed virtually anywhere on earth, meaning that educated 'knowledge workers' can obtain skilled employment virtually anywhere on earth. The rise of the Indian computer software industry provides an example of this phenomenon; with the development of the internet multinational companies have increasingly outsourced skilled work to Indian software engineers, resulting in improved pay and career prospects for well-educated individuals in India. On the other hand, increased labour competition leads to downward pressures on wages; skilled workers around the world are increasingly trying to undercut one another in a global 'race to the bottom' (Brown and Lauder, 2006).

As countries' economic well-being and standards of living are increasingly tied to their citizens' ability to compete in the global knowledge economy, national governments must be seen to prioritise and advance educational achievement. Thus, the concept of the knowledge economy creates a new emphasis on education, albeit one that focuses on a relatively narrow conceptualisation of educational performance and achievement. At both international and national levels, official documents associate the knowledge economy with a greater emphasis on flexible, individualised instruction, learning technology in education, and 'learning to learn' (Robertson, 2005).

This link between educational achievement and economic outcomes has resulted in an increased interest in tests that compare and rank countries' educational achievement. The first international achievement test was designed by the International Association for the Evaluation of Educational Achievement (IEA) with the support of UNESCO in 1960. Administered to approximately ten thousand students in 12 countries, the test made international comparisons in four subjects (reading comprehension, mathematics, science and geography) possible for the first time. In following years, similar tests were repeated intermittently until the IEA introduced in 1995 the Trends in Mathematics and Science Studies (TIMSS), which has since been repeated every four years.

The Programme for International Student Assessment (PISA), designed and administered by the Organisation for Economic Co-operation and Development (OECD), is similar to TIMSS in many respects. However, rather than measuring 'curriculum mastery', PISA focuses on applied knowledge, requiring students to solve problems that simulate the 'skills required for effective functioning in everyday life' (OECD, 2000: 9). It is divided into three subject areas: scientific literacy, mathematical literacy and reading literacy, with the use of 'literacy' emphasising the practical focus of the test. Since 2000, PISA has been administered every three years and is taken by 15-year-olds.

Both TIMSS and PISA have ignited debates on educational policy and practice, as politicians and researchers seek to learn best practices from other countries. Often, the results of these tests have been used to invoke the notion of an 'achievement crisis' that urgently necessitates educational reform. Reflecting what Grek (2009) calls the 'PISA effect', results have been referenced in educational policy debates in the United States (Whitehouse, 2009), Japan (Takayama, 2006), and the United Kingdom. For example, in an article in the *Times Educational Supplement*, Michael Gove, the Secretary of State for Education in England and Wales, calls the 2009 PISA results a 'spur to action' and claims that they show that schools are 'failing to fully develop the potential of many of our children' (Gove, 2010). However, Gove also claims that PISA 'provides clear pointers to how we can reform our schools system to make it one of the best in the world' and continues to cite qualities of high-achieving countries: Finland (ranked very highly on all subjects) provides teacher autonomy; Hong Kong and Singapore (also highly ranked) promote competition between schools through standardised tests.

However, the examples that Gove chooses are selectively handpicked to support and legitimise existing policy preferences, specifically those underpinned by the neoliberal principles of competition and deregulation (see Chapter 1). In fact, in examining the set of countries, one might reach an entirely opposite set of conclusions: Finland (Gove's example of teacher autonomy) has virtually no competition between schools and very few standardised tests; Singapore and Hong Kong (examples of competition) have relatively centralised education systems, contradicting Gove's argument for decentralisation. In addition, these countries have vast differences in their geographies, histories and economies: culturally homogenous Finland in Scandinavia and the diverse Asian city states of Hong Kong and Singapore have little in common with one another, let alone with the United Kingdom. Thus, rather than promoting 'policy dialogue' as the OECD (2000: 3) envisages, international achievement tests are more likely to legitimise existing policies that are grounded in both domestic and global political economy.

Increased emphasis on international achievement tests provides one answer to the increasing similarity of educational models around the world. As nations compete with one another in the knowledge economy, they adopt a common set of policies and practices that are believed to promote educational achievement and – by extension – economic success. Thus, the competitive pressures of the global knowledge economy result in increasing similarities among education systems around the world. However, this process is not neutral: the concept of a knowledge economy embeds values of individualism, competition and free trade. As it plays an increasing role in educational policy formation around the world, it also normalises and spreads these values and creates convergence in educational policy and practice.

Conclusion

While there is controversy surrounding the term 'globalisation', in the field of education, globalisation is associated with a number of clear trends. Over the last century a single model of education through state-provided formal schooling has spread to virtually every corner of the earth. Furthermore, there is considerable evidence that education systems are becoming more alike in policy and practice. However, there is debate over why this is happening and what it means: to some the expansion of mass education is a principle of universal human rights, while for others it is associated with power and capitalist expansion.

Many aspects of the globalisation of education can be seen in the concept of the knowledge economy and its economically rationalised view of education. In particular, international achievement tests such as TIMSS and PISA have received increasing attention from policymakers and practitioners alike, resulting in policies that cite achievement crises as a motivator for reform. However, in many cases these reforms are based upon existing policy preferences and political ideology rather than genuine policy dialogue. Furthermore, the growing prevalence of the knowledge economy as a factor in educational policymaking embeds and spreads values of individualism and competition.

For most readers, the notion that education is beneficial to societies and individuals as well as a basic human right is something that is taken for granted. However, literature on the globalisation of education gives good reason to critically question this assumption. It shows that the model of schooling that is now used throughout the globe is both historically and culturally specific, and attempts to universalise this model require careful consideration and critical analysis.

Summary points

- The globalisation of education is evident in the spread of formal schooling throughout the world and increasing similarity in educational policy and practice.
- Despite widespread evidence of convergence, the reason for this trend is widely contested and debated. Theoretical conceptualisations of globalisation hold fundamentally different views on education and society.
- The concept of the knowledge economy (i.e. economic activity centred on the production and exchange of knowledge and information) is increasingly important in policymaking in many countries.
- Competition between countries in the knowledge economy creates increased interest in international achievement tests such as TIMSS and PISA. However, their role in educational policymaking is questionable, as they are often used to legitimise beliefs and practices.

Questions for discussion

- Why do you think that educational systems around the world are so similar? What does this say about the processes of globalisation?
- What role do international achievement tests play in educational policymaking? Do you think they are a good thing?
- Read Michael Gove's online editorial in the *Times Educational Supplement* (see link below). Do you agree with his argument? What do you think he might be missing?
- View the trailer to the film *Schooling the World* (available at http://schoolingtheworld.org). Does it change your views on education and globalisation?

Recommended reading

Robertson, S.L. (2005) Re-imagining and Rescripting the Future of Education: Global knowledge economy discourses and the challenge to education systems. *Comparative Education* 41(2): 151–70.
An article that introduces the knowledge economy as it relates to education and international organisations.

Shields, R. (2012) *Globalization and International Education*. London: Continuum.
An introduction to globalisation and international education, covering many key topics and trends.

Spring, J. (2009) *Globalization of Education: An introduction*. New York: Routledge.
An introductory text on globalisation and education.

References

Anderson-Levitt, K.M. (2003) A World Culture of Schooling? In: K.M. Anderson-Levitt (ed.) *Local Meanings, Global Schooling: Anthropology and world culture theory*. New York: Palgrave Macmillan.

Benavot, A. and Riddle, P. (1988) The Expansion of Primary Education. 1870–1940: Trends and issues. *Sociology of Education* 61: 191–210.

Bowles, S. and Gintis, H. (1976) *Schooling in Capitalist America: Educational reform and the contradictions of economic life*. New York: Basic Books.

Brown, P. and Lauder, H. (2006) Globalisation, Knowledge and the Myth of the Magnet Economy. *Globalisation, Societies and Education* 4(1): 25–57.

Dale, R. (2000) Globalization and Education: Demonstrating a 'common world educational culture' or locating a 'globally structured educational agenda'? *Educational Theory* 50(4): 427–48.

Drucker, P. (1968) *The Age of Discontinuity: Guidelines to our changing society*. New York: Harper and Row.

Friedman, T.L. (2006) *The World is Flat: A brief history of the twenty-first century*. New York: Farrar, Straus and Giroux.

Giddens, A. (1999) *Runaway World: How globalisation is reshaping our lives*. London: Profile Books.

Gove, M. (2010) PISA slip should put a rocket under our world-class ambitions and drive us to win the education space race. *Times Educational Supplement*, 17 December, p. 3. Available online at http://www.tes.co.uk/article.aspx?storycode=6066185 (accessed 10 September 2012).

Grek, S. (2009) Governing by Numbers: The PISA 'effect' in Europe. *Journal of Education Policy* 24(1): 23–37.

Meyer, J.W., Boli, J., Thomas, G.M. and Ramirez, F. (1997) World Society and the Nation State. *American Journal of Sociology* 103(1): 144–81.

Mincer, J. (1958) Investment in Human Capital and Personal Income Distribution. *Journal of Political Economy* 66: 281–382.

Mullikottu-Veettil, M. and Bray, M. (2004) The Decentralisation of Education in Kerala State, India: Rhetoric and reality. *International Review of Education* 50: 223–43.

OECD (2000) *Measuring Student Knowledge and Skills: The PISA 2000 assessment of reading, mathematical and scientific literacy*. Paris: OECD.

Ritzer, G. (2011) *The McDonaldization of Society* (6th edn). Thousand Oaks, CA: Pine Forge Press.

Robertson, S.L. (2005) Re-imagining and Rescripting the Future of Education: Global knowledge economy discourses and the challenge to education systems. *Comparative Education* 41(2): 151–70.

Rostow, W.W. (1960) *The Stages of Economic Growth: A non-communist manifesto*. Cambridge: Cambridge University Press.

Schooling the World (2011) *Schooling the World: The white man's last burden*. Available online at http://schoolingtheworld.org (accessed 12 September 2012).

Steiner-Khamsi, G. (2004) Globalization in Education: Real or imagined? In: G. Steiner-Khamsi (ed.) *The Global Politics of Educational Borrowing and Lending*. New York: Teachers College Press, pp. 1–6.

Stiglitz, J.E. (2002) *Globalization and Its Discontents*. New York: W.W. Norton.

Takayama, K. (2006) The Politics of International League Tables: PISA in Japan's achievement crisis debate. *Comparative Education* 44(4): 387–407.

Truman, H. (1949) Inaugural Address. Available online at http://www.bartleby.com/124/pres53.html (accessed 28 April 2012).

UNESCO (2011) *The Hidden Crisis: Armed conflict and education*. Paris: UNESCO.

The White House (2009) Educate to Innovate. Available online at http://www.whitehouse.gov/issues/education/educate-innovate (accessed 31 January 2012).

Chapter 11

Education for All and the role of multilateralism

Elaine Lam

Introduction

In 2011, 67 million children around the world were not attending school (UNESCO, 2011). Education can improve quality of life, economic outcomes and reduce poverty. As such, this staggering number of out-of-school children is a risk to economic growth and stability. The increasing interconnectedness of our world means that global issues are local concerns. Stelmach (2011: 32) notes the world economic crisis has only reinforced our interdependence and we need to 'consider the impact of local decisions as well as a collective response to challenges'. Indeed, the financial crisis has a significant impact on those living in poverty, resulting in 'innocent bystanders' (Bermingham *et al.*, 2009) of a problem created by a powerful centre. However, there has also never been a greater need for governments to consider the priorities beyond their own territories with the ripple effect of increasing security and stability concerns, such as the events of the Arab spring in 2011.

As governments struggle to manage levels of debt and budget deficits, '(t)here has never been a greater need to make the case that aid is being used effectively to achieve results' (Bermingham *et al.*, 2009: 130). As well, this is an opportune time to reflect on the role of foreign aid and consider ways to improve the relationship between education and development. Certainly, as argued by Clarke (2011: 479), 'Education is a fundamental human right – a vital resource in overcoming poverty and inequality globally. All children have the right to quality basic education, the bedrock for a productive life'. While there is agreement among scholars of the importance of education, the ways in which education is used as a development tool is sometimes questionable.

This chapter provides an overview of the complex relationship between education and development, challenges faced by developing countries, the problematic nature of aid, and describes global initiatives to support development goals.

Definitions

Development is defined as the state of being developed: that is, having a relatively high level of industrialization and standard of living (Merriam-Webster Online, 2012). Education is one aspect among many in the process of development. Sustainable development requires a multi-sectoral approach involving finance, economy, industry, culture, health and infrastructure to reduce poverty, hunger, disease, illiteracy and debt; the chapter will focus on the role of education.

The development of a nation state usually involves several key 'actors', significant groups or individuals. Five groups will be covered:

- Multilaterals and international agencies develop policies and frameworks on a global scale, such as the United Nations (UN), the Organisation for Economic Co-operation and Development (OECD), the Asian Development Bank and other regional organizations.
- Bilateral donors, such as the UK's Department for International Development (DfID), the United States Agency for International Development (USAID) and European, Chinese and Japanese agencies. When bilateral agencies work with a recipient country, they are known as 'country partnerships'.
- Local governments, which play an instrumental role in developing infrastructure, strategic plans and resources to support education initiatives.
- Non-government organizations (NGOs) that are typically known as charities operating in international contexts.
- Civil service organizations (CSOs) which arise out of the local needs such as employee unions and support groups.

Countries in the process of growing a modern industrial economy are considered 'developing countries'. Single quotation marks are used around 'developing countries' because the phrase is contentious; other terms such as 'transitional states' are sometimes used. The term developing countries is often preferred over Third World, which implies a hierarchical view. The phrase developing countries is consistent with current literature. It is essential to note that the poverty and debt in developing countries are frequently a result of colonization, unequal trade and policies by international organizations such as the World Bank (see Chapter 6). Sachs (1989) gives a historical account of international debt.

Stereotypically, developing countries refer to those in the south, such as countries in Africa and South America, although this is a very limited picture and can include countries in Asia, Eastern Europe, the Caribbean and the South Pacific. Further, there are minority people groups in rich industrialized countries such as travellers' groups in Western Europe, indigenous peoples in North America, Australia and New Zealand, and racialized groups in North America that suffer from poverty and underachievement. Although much more attention needs to be paid to marginalized groups in industrialized countries (see Chapter 6), this chapter is limited to the challenges facing developing countries, particularly as it relates to aid. It is essential to note that educational progress in developing countries varies widely. For example, across the African continent country-level statistics illustrate variance, with less than 20 per cent literacy rates in Niger and Burkina Faso to over 80 per cent in Mauritius, the Seychelles, South Africa and Zimbabwe (Seetanah, 2009).

Education issues in developing countries

Some of the issues faced by developing countries will be described in order to provide a brief overview of key challenges. To begin, remnants of colonization can be felt in many developing countries through the use of a dated colonial curriculum. For example, although the 11plus selection examination has long been eradicated in most of England, it still exists in former colonies and deters students who may be less successful from continuing their secondary schooling, much to the detriment of education completion goals. George and Lewis (2011) explain the resistance to historically entrenched colonial curricula, which includes opposition from parents and school officials: 'Some of those in positions of power are likely to have been educated in the colonial model and may find it difficult to understand why that which has "worked" in the past should be changed' (George and Lewis, 2011: 728).

Some developing countries still participate in Oxbridge GCSE and A-Level examinations or American SATs. While these have a strong currency in the global market, this foreign curriculum originally designed for English/Welsh or American pupils bears little or no relevance to the lives of children in developing countries. While it may be argued that pupils should follow a curriculum that carries international currency, George and Lewis (2011) argue that this approach forestalls acceptance of local knowledge. Foreign curriculum content may be inappropriate and should be removed from the lives of children who live in poverty, hunger, conflict and child labour. Relevant, hands-on learning is essential, particularly in communities where the importance and role of education is not clear. Children should also be taught in their home language to greatly increase opportunities for learning.

Another major obstacle to achieving education goals is the challenge associated with girls' access to schooling. There is a clear case for educating girls as they are able to make better decisions at home and work, and if they become mothers, they are able to protect their children from illnesses such as HIV/AIDS (Clarke, 2011). However, girls' attainment of education can be a complicated social matter that results in social loss: 'While on the one hand, education makes it possible for women to explore their own interests and exercise their potential, on the other hand, in doing so, they may threaten traditional family and/or community values' (Stelmach, 2011: 37).

Achieving gender equity also requires addressing a community's economic, social and cultural issues. For specific examples of successful interventions in Yemen and Burkina Faso, two countries which have experienced growth in girls' education, see Clarke (2011).

One of the most prominent challenges for developing countries is responding to emergency situations that arise as a result of natural disasters, conflict (war, genocide, mass exodus) and health crises such as HIV/AIDS. Even in industrialized countries, the impacts of such emergencies are widely felt. As a result of weakened infrastructure, governance and technology, mobilization of response efforts are often insufficient given the overwhelming humanitarian demands. Further, girls who are caught in violent civil conflict are twice as adversely affected as boys and doubled efforts are required to draw girls back to school (Clarke, 2011). One salient example of the challenges of education in emergencies is Dadaab, the world's largest refugee camp at the Kenya–Somalia border. Originally built to host 90,000 refugees, it now contains nearly 400,000 people (CARE website, 2012). According to UNICEF (2011), only a third of the 150,000 school-age children at the Dadaab camp have access to education facilities. Providing educational opportunities for these children living in unstable and poor conditions is an enormous challenge.

HIV/AIDS is the foremost example of a global pandemic that continues to plague developing countries in reaching their education goals. While there have been some improvements to the quality of life of people living with HIV/AIDS in industrialized countries, the devastating impact of infections is strongly felt in developing countries. Even with progress towards expanding access to antiretroviral treatments, there are over 14.8 million AIDS-related orphans in sub-Saharan Africa (AVERT website, 2012). The impact of HIV/AIDS continues to be one of the most serious problems and threatens to reverse gains made by global education initiatives.

The issues facing developing countries described above may be magnified for rural areas where resources are scarce and time-honoured traditions are culturally maintained. Liu's (2004) work on Chinese rural parents describes their relief when their children expressed intent to quit school because education was simply a financial burden. Further, the World Bank (2000) concludes that truancy is common in countries where poverty is ubiquitous. Resources are often limited for rural areas as they are geographically isolated and community needs are overlooked. There are some innovative solutions including video compact discs, computer mediated communication, mobile teaching vans, independent study, telephone hot lines, summer seminars and residential institutes (Stelmach, 2011). However, high infrastructure, utilities and teaching costs are obstacles to implementing these technologies.

While education in developing countries faces unique challenges from those of industrialized nations, it is useful to remember that implementing large-scale change in education systems shares common, universal challenges. For example, education systems in most countries are designed on values and beliefs held by the dominant social and economic class (Goodard, 2010). Minority and marginalized groups have difficulty seeking recognition in both industrialized and developing countries. Second, the role of teachers is critical to the success of any country's system, and their ability to instruct students is dependent on: 'motivation, qualification, experience, training, aptitude and a host of other factors, not the least of these being the environment and management structures within which they perform their role' (Anjum and Iqbal, 2012: 31). In addition, all education systems face issues regarding the quality of teaching and learning. For developing countries, any increase to access and enrolment must be sustained with improvements in quality and teaching, particularly in areas where sending children to school is not a high priority.

The problematic nature of aid

When donor countries honour their aid commitments it can reap benefits, such as supplementing government budgets, increasing investment and providing hard resources to cover school building costs and supplies (Asiedu and Nandwa, 2007). However, not all funding agreements are kept. Sceptics assert that aid leads to corruption and deters private sector investment (Easterley, 2003). This section will cover three criticisms of aid: uncoordinated efforts, top-down approaches and the tension of local decision making and best practices.

One of the strongest criticisms of aid is that it is often uncoordinated. Development agencies frequently design their own projects, deliver services using their own staff and carry out their own monitoring reports, resulting in duplicated efforts in countries where education officials are strapped for time and resources (Riddell, 2008). Further, duplicated efforts and high transactional activities result in limited innovation, strategic thinking and creativity to focus on what the recipient country truly needs. Often the lack of coordination is a result of a fear of misuse of donor funds, particularly as there is increased visibility by the media (Bermingham *et al.*, 2009). There is also little incentive to work together because of individual organizational targets, pressures to satisfy account-ability requirements and getting projects completed quickly (OECD, 2008a).

Another criticism of aid is its top-down approach. Aid can be negatively viewed as a way of controlling or exerting dominance on key regions for political reasons. Bermingham *et al.* (2009) note that throughout most of history, the provision of aid was driven by geopolitical interests beginning with reconstruction efforts by Allied forces post-World War II. Although the 'global' aid agenda was apparently built by consensus, the participation of researchers, governments and NGO personnel from developing countries in creating initiatives such as the Jomtien Education for All (EFA) Declaration was 'minor, if not minimal' (King, 2007: 381). Conditions imposed by multilateral agen-cies, such as those that require changes to governance, often result in a tension between governments and external agencies as they struggle for control.

The tension of local decision making and best practices is an ongoing issue, particularly as the governments of developing countries are encouraged to lead on education initia-tives. On the one hand, foreign agencies desire accountability and expect value for money. They often have experience of what has worked in other contexts and an under-standing of the latest trends. It is understandable that external agencies would like to 'borrow' good ideas that have resulted in positive outcomes in other nation states. On the other hand, local governments, education leaders, teachers and students understand their own needs and can influence their communities on the level of participation in education projects. While 'best practices' may be based on other programme and project experi-ence, it is essential to remember that 'borrowing' successful approaches and customizing them for the unique context is a very difficult process (Riddell, 2008). 'Education bor-rowing' or promoting 'best practices' in place of local solutions must be cautioned against as national cultures, learning environments and political governance are dynamic and unique for each education system. Supporting local solutions that are aligned with national policies, cultures, context and stakeholder needs will facilitate successful imple-mentation and may result in better outcomes for communities. Ownership of local solu-tions is easier to promote over foreign initiatives and strongly supports sustainable development. After all, national governments and policies will continue to prevail long after agency staff complete projects and return home.

Global initiatives

There are several high-level initiatives to support goals to provide school-aged children with opportunities to obtain primary and secondary education. Designed within multilat-eral forums, these initiatives are outlined in two phases: goal setting and implementation.

Goal setting (1990–2001)

The EFA initiative states global education goals to address the problem of out-of-school children and forms the backdrop of other initiatives outlined in this chapter. In 1990, the leaders of the world met in Thailand and pledged to provide education for all of the world's children by the year 2000, an ambitious goal that was reaffirmed during the World Education Forum in Senegal ten years later. The current target-year for EFA is 2015. The project has six goals, including free universal primary education (ensuring access and enrolment for all school aged children) and learning and life skills for youth and adult literacy (UNESCO, 2007).

As the new millennium approached, the world's leaders drafted a list of goals for the purpose of development called the Millennium Development Goals (MDGs) which included goals relating to primary education and gender equality. Although EFA and MDGs are widely accepted, they have faced criticism for lack of funding. While some MDGs relate to education, the focus of most education aid work has exclusively targeted EFA due to sector specificity.

Implementation (2002–ongoing)

In order to respond to the required levels of funding to reach EFA goals, 22 bilateral agencies and international partners developed the Fast Track Initiative (FTI) in 2002 for the purpose of achieving universal primary completion by 2015. FTI provides implementation and funding support while encouraging strategic planning, ownership and coordination of the education sector by local governments. Governments of low-income countries submit applications, including a national poverty reduction strategy and education sector plan. Upon successful endorsement, the catalytic fund provides support to ensure there is implementation of plans and that benchmark indicators are monitored (Global Partnership for Education, 2004). As of 2011, 43 developing countries were members of the EFA FTI. Clarke (2011) notes evidence that shows the positive impact of EFA FTI on girls' education through support for interventions such as using media channels to communicate the benefits of education to parents and communities. Additionally, families were provided with financial support to cover school fees and quotas for girls' enrolment were introduced. For more information on successful EFA FTI gender interventions see Clarke (2011).

The success of FTI is also due to a number of agreements and progression in the ways that aid is delivered. In 2005, representatives from over 100 countries, international organizations and CSOs pledged towards improving aid effectiveness through the Paris Declaration. It entails an agreement to develop further partnerships between governments and donors through harmonizing and aligning objectives, systems and procedures. Uncoordinated aid efforts can result in cumbersome processes for children receiving interventions, duplicated efforts and competing agendas. Five objectives were developed which can be measured through 12 indicators:

- Ownership: Partner countries exercise effective leadership over their development policies and strategies, and coordinate development actions.
- Alignment: Donors base their overall support on partner countries' national development strategies, institutions and procedures.
- Harmonization: Donors' actions are more harmonized, transparent and collectively effective.
- Managing for results: Managing resources and improving decision making for results.
- Mutual accountability: Donors and partners are accountable for development results (OECD, 2008b).

The transfer of ownership of governments as key players was later reinstated in 2008 through the Accra Agenda for Action which affirmed the need for developing countries to increase their role in discussions through strengthening their capacity to lead and manage development. This increases the onus on developing countries to take ownership of aid activities. Donors and international agencies also pledged to broaden country-level policy discussions, use developing country systems as much as possible and to deepen engagement with CSOs. For more information on the other pledges developed to facilitate action towards aid effectiveness see OECD (2008b).

While the Accra Agenda has notably pushed for implementation of the Paris Declaration to reach objectives and provides a policy framework to increase coordination and aid effectiveness, there are two criticisms. First, bilateral and multilateral donors are not provided with incentives to work together. Independently governed, each donor has its own set of priorities and political context. Bermingham *et al.* (2009: 137) note the lack of institutional incentives is a 'critical impediment'. Second, while the five Paris objectives form the basis for 12 indicators to measure progress, there is no specific tool to monitor improvements (Collins, 2009). The lack of robust measurement tools puts these important commitments at risk.

However, there is some progress on the Paris objectives through programmes such as FTI, particularly in the core areas of sound and operational education sector strategies, results-oriented performance assessment frameworks and coordinated technical cooperation through local donor groups (FTI Secretariat, 2009). The success of FTI in reaching EFA and Paris/Accra objectives can be linked to the use of direct budget support as well as Sector-Wide Approaches (SWAp), a novel way of increasing aid effectiveness. A SWAp is nationally owned education sector policy and strategy with a performance monitoring system that measures progress, based on broad stakeholder consultation. Formalized government-led aid coordination and dialogue are carried out, as well as an agreed process on how to coordinate reporting, budgeting, financial management and expenditure plans to ensure the SWAp is appropriately funded (OECD, 2005).

Scholars such as Riddell (2008) agree that a sector-wide approach to education is a strong model for governance and a worthwhile exercise. Preliminary data show that SWAps are beginning to deliver through growth in access, improved morale from direct transaction of funds to schools, timely payment of teachers' salaries, greater cohesion in the system and increased ownership of education goals (Riddell 2008).

However there is still a long way to go to develop sustainable education systems and reach national goals; in particular drop-out and repetition rates have not yet improved (Riddell, 2008). Further, Bermingham *et al.* (2009) argue that many countries struggle to establish SWAps that are acceptable to all stakeholders, due to capacity issues and government openness to discussion.

Conclusion and implications for education studies

The relationship between education and development is complex:

> [T]he challenge ... is to start imagining a more radical future in which we seek more purposefully to build bridges with other disciplines, engage with new methodological tools and encourage fresh voices but above all else communicate more clearly what we do and do not know about the wonderful complexity of the education-development relationship.

> (McGrath, 2010: 542)

Education in developing countries is a vast topic which encompasses both political and economic spheres. By studying systems beyond those at home, one is able to deepen understanding of the factors that impact the implementation of education initiatives such as context, funding, cultural notions and governance. By critically examining the issues faced by developing countries, there is an opportunity to reflect on taken-for-granted notions of schooling. Studying education in developing countries also allows us to reflect upon our own education systems and to analyse the purposes of education. Additionally, knowledge of education in other countries helps teachers develop a global perspective and understand the types of systems their newcomer pupils may be coming from. As mentioned at the beginning of this chapter, several groups share commonalities with those in developing countries such as ethnic populations in western nations that suffer from similar underachievement and marginalization. Goodard (2010) notes that education leaders have a responsibility to advocate for change to address the needs of minorities to reduce the risk of immense loss of human and social capital. It may be useful to consider the needs of UK minority pupils and to reflect on ways to address curriculum and pedagogical needs. In doing so, there is hope that education is able to achieve one of its roles – to promote peace, equality and access for all children.

Summary points

- The world financial crisis and stability issues provide an opportunity to improve on aid effectiveness and reflect on the role of education and development.
- Key issues facing education in developing countries include appropriateness of curriculum content, girls' education, emergency situations and rural education.
- There are common challenges for both industrialized and developing countries such as marginalization of minorities, the critical role of teachers and teaching quality.
- Aid is problematic and there is criticism of uncoordinated donor activities, top–down approach and tension between local decision making and 'best practices'.
- Borrowing 'best practices' is difficult given the unique context and dynamic environments of developing countries. Ownership of local solutions strongly supports sustainable development.
- EFA goals were developed to support learning opportunities for out-of-school children.
- Several initiatives have been developed to implement EFA such as the FTI, Paris Declaration and Accra Agenda. SWAps also show promising results.
- By studying education in other countries, there is an opportunity to reflect upon our own systems and understand the landscape of global education.

Questions for discussion

- How can we improve the provision of education aid?
- Why is education in developing countries sometimes viewed as irrelevant by parents and communities?
- As a future teacher/educator, what can you do to support global education efforts?
- Will EFA still be required by 2015, or will these goals be reached? Why or why not?

Recommended reading

Clarke, P. (2011) The Status of Girls' Education in Education for All Fast Track Initiative Partner Countries. *Prospects* 41: 479–90.
Describes issues related to girls' education and outlines successful interventions.

Harber, C. (2008) Perpetuating Violence: Schooling as an international problem. *Educational Studies* 34(5): 457–68.
Provides a discussion of the role of education as promoting peace and conversely perpetuating conflict.

White, H. (2007) Evaluating Aid Impact: Approaches and findings. In: S.Lahiri (ed.) *Theory and Practice of Foreign Aid*. Oxford: Elsevier.
Analyses case studies on aid evaluation from Ghana, Bangladesh and Kenya.

References

Anjum, M. and Iqbal, M. (2012) Identification of Problems Faced by Heads of Teacher Education Institutions in Achieving New Millennium Goals. *International Journal of Social Sciences and Education* 2(1): 30–42.

Asiedu, E. and Nandwa, B. (2007) On the Impact of Foreign Aid in Education on Growth: How relevant is the heterogeneity of aid flows and the heterogeneity of aid recipients? *Review of World Economics* 143(4): 631–49.

AVERT (2012) *AIDS Virus Education and Research (AVERT) website*. Available online at http://www.avert.org/aids-orphans.htm (accessed 16 April 2012).

BBC News (2009) [*Interview*] *with Ngozi Okonjo-Iweala, 11 Mar 2009*. Available online at http://news.bbc.co.uk/2/hi/business/7937674.stm (accessed 16 April 2012).

Bermingham, D., Christensen, O. and Mahn, T. (2009) Aid Effectiveness in Education: Why it matters. *Prospects* 39: 129–45.

CARE (2012) *Cooperative for Assistance and Relief Everywhere (CARE) website. Dadaab Refugee Camps: Update on the crisis in the Horn of Africa*. Available online at http://www.care.org/careswork/emergencies/dadaab/ (accessed 16 April 2012).

Clarke, P. (2011) The Status of Girls' Education in Education for All Fast Track Initiative Partner Countries. *Prospects* 41: 479–90.

Collins, L. (2009) Progress from Specificity: How to monitor the Paris Declaration in the Malawi education sector. *Prospects* 39: 163–83.

Easterley, W. (2003) Can Foreign Aid Buy Growth? *Journal of Economic Perspectives* 17(3): 23–48.

FTI Secretariat (2009) *Making Aid More Effective by 2010: 2008 survey on monitoring the Paris declaration indicators in selected FTI countries*. Available online at http://www.globalpartnership.org/media/library/FTI_Aid_Effectiveness_Report_42009.pdf (accessed 16 April 2012).

George, J. and Lewis, T. (2011) Exploring the Global/Local Boundary in Education in Developing Countries: The case of the Caribbean. *Compare* 41(6): 721–34.

Global Partnership for Education (2004) *Education for All Fast Track Initiative Framework*. Available online at http://www.educationfasttrack.org/media/library/FrameworkNOV04.pdf (accessed 16 April 2012).

Goodard, J. (2010) Toward Glocality: Facilitating leadership in an age of diversity. *Journal of School Leadership* 20(1): 37–56.

King, K. (2007) Multilateral Agencies in the Construction of the Global Agenda on Education. *Comparative Education* 43(3): 377–91.

Liu, F. (2004) Basic Education in China's Rural Areas: A legal obligation or an individual choice? *International Journal of Educational Development* 24: 5–21.

McGrath, S. (2010) Education and Development: Thirty years of continuity and change. *International Journal of Educational Development* 30: 537–43.

Merriam-Webster Online (2012) Merriam-Webster Online Dictionary. Available online at http://www.m-w.com (accessed 16 April 2012).

OECD (2005) *Budget Support, Sector Wide Approaches and Capacity Development in Public Financial Management*. DAC Guidelines and Reference Series, Harmonising Donor Practices for Effective Aid Delivery, Vol. 2. Paris: OECD.

OECD (2008a) *Incentives for Aid Effectiveness in Donor Agencies: Good practice and self-assessment tool*. Paris: OECD DAC.

OECD (2008b) *The Paris Declaration on Aid Effectiveness and Accra Agenda for Action*. Available online at http://www.oecd.org/dataoecd/30/63/43911948.pdf (accessed 16 April 2012).

Riddell, A. (2008) Issues and Challenges Raised by Development Agencies in Implementing the New Modalities of Aid to Education. *Prospects* 38: 363–76.

Sachs, J. (1989) *Developing Country Debt and the World Economy*. Cambridge, MA: National Bureau of Economic Research.

Seetanah, B. (2009) The Economic Importance of Education: Evidence from Africa using dynamic panel data analysis. *Journal of Applied Economics* 12(1): 137–57.

Stelmach, B. (2011) A Synthesis of International Rural Education Issues and Responses. *Rural Education* 32(2): 32–42.

UNESCO (2007) *United Nations Education Scientific and Cultural Organization website*. Paris: UNESCO. Available online at http://www.unesco.org/new/en/education/themes/leading-the-international-agenda/education-for-all/ (accessed 16 April 2012).

UNESCO (2011) *Global Monitoring Report: The hidden crisis - Armed conflict and education*. Paris: UNESCO.

UNICEF (2011) *United Nations Children's Fund Website. Field Stories*. Available online at http://www.unicef.org.au/Discover/Field-Stories/September/Back-to-school-in-Kenya.aspx (accessed 16 April 2012).

World Bank (2000) *Effective Schooling in Rural Africa. Report 3: Case study briefs on rural schooling*. Washington DC: Human Development Network.

Chapter 12

European school and university systems

Convergence and difference

David Coulby

Introduction

Europe as a whole is tending to come together politically, economically and culturally. Within the social sciences, not least in Education Studies, Europe is increasingly being used as the unit of analysis and description, rather than that of individual states. Europe may be seen and analysed as an educational space (Novoa and Lawn, 2002). This coming together of Europe is happening in a complex and conflicted way. Furthermore, any convergence in matters of education is at least matched by areas of stubborn isolationism as states and more local levels seek to retain control over educational institutions and practices.

This chapter describes and explains three trends:

- the trend towards European unification;
- the move towards conversion in matters of educational policy and practice;
- areas of radical difference between education systems in Europe.

The trend towards European unification

The trend towards European unification is complex because it involves two main international bodies, the European Union (EU) and the North Atlantic Treaty Organisation (NATO), as well as many less important organisations. The nature of these two bodies in terms of membership and policy is also complex and fractured, raising the vexed question of which states actually belong to Europe. This section examines these issues by considering firstly the EU and then NATO.

The EU, at the time of writing, consists of 27 member states: Belgium, the Netherlands, Luxembourg, Germany, France, Italy, Ireland, Denmark, the United Kingdom (UK), Spain, Portugal, Greece, Finland, Sweden, Austria, Poland, Hungary, the Czech Republic, Slovakia, Cyprus, Slovenia, Latvia, Estonia, Lithuania, Malta, Romania and Bulgaria. Croatia acceded in July 2012. Turkey has been agreed membership in principle, but controversially no timetable has yet been agreed. Other countries, including those of former Yugoslavia and of the southern Mediterranean littoral, have expressed interest in eventual membership.

EU membership then does not include the whole of Europe. Norway, perhaps on the basis of confidence in its own oil wealth, and Switzerland, on the basis of banking wealth and the tangible gains of the policy of neutrality during the twentieth century, have consciously opted not to be members. Some of the European mini-states, with advantageous tax and banking regimes, remain beyond EU control: Liechtenstein and Monaco. The movement of the EU to the east, following the fall of communism in Eastern Europe in 1989 and the break-up of the Soviet Union in 1991, has been painfully slow. The EU could hardly be said to have raced to embrace and assist the new democracies. The more impoverished and politically suspect states of former Yugoslavia remain beyond the pale. The question of the eventual entry of other former Soviet states (apart from the three Baltic countries) remains to be addressed, Ukraine, Belarus and indeed Russia itself.

Even within itself the EU is divided with some states subscribing to some policies, for example on immigration, and some states not. This is referred to as the multi-track Europe. Critically there is no unified policy on foreign affairs and defence (considered in the discussion of NATO below) or on the common currency. Previously regarded as the most potent symbol of European unification and the greatest achievement of the EU, the euro, is progressively becoming the currency of most EU states, though Sweden and Denmark, as well as the UK, have notably retained their own currencies. While the euro has become a preferred international currency for those states which, for economic or often political reasons, wish to avoid using the dollar, the crisis of 2011–12 has cast the future of the common currency in doubt. With Ireland, Spain and Italy all facing financial crisis and Greece on the brink of bankruptcy, the political will of the rich northern states, and especially Germany, to subsidise the entire Eurozone remains in doubt. The UK's reluctance to join the Eurozone remains significant. The UK has the second largest population and the second largest gross domestic product (wealth) of any of the EU countries (the first in both cases is Germany). London has by far Europe's largest financial sector. It is a United Nations (UN) Security Council state and a highly significant member of NATO. Opinion polls in the UK continually suggest an overwhelming majority against euro membership. This represents an apparent vote of no confidence in the common currency and perhaps even the European project as a whole.

Beyond the endangered euro the successes of the EU are open to question. It has singly failed to achieve a unified foreign policy (Sheehan, 2010). Most recently this was evident in the split that emerged over the desirability of the 2003 invasion of Iraq (Chandrasekaran, 2008). An even more fatal division occurred over policy with regard to the break-up of former Yugoslavia. Here, historically conditioned policies by Germany over the early recognition of Croatia and, most fatally, by the UK's inability, under the Conservative Government, to take a critical stance against Serbia, played a significant part in the initiation and prolongation of the bloodshed. It was only decisive action by the United States of America (USA) over Bosnia and, with the UK, over Kosovo, that averted the strong threat of genocide in Europe (Simms, 2001). The role of education in generating and perpetuating these conflicts has been significant. The treatment of minorities by states throughout Europe, Northern Ireland as well as Serbia, can test the boundaries between education and warfare (Coulby and Jones, 2001).

The EU's main policy and the one that absorbs nearly half of its not inconsiderable budget is the common agricultural policy (CAP). This policy provides subsidies for inefficient (in terms of world competition) farmers, especially in France and the other Mediterranean countries. One of its effects is to make it difficult for non-subsidised farmers in the majority world to compete to export food to the lucrative European market. It is one of the major areas of the EU's non-compliance with the terms of the World Trade

Organisation (WTO). There has been strong pressure from both the European Commission itself and from the states of northern Europe to reduce or abolish the CAP. An important deal between France and Germany in Nice in 2002 guaranteed the continuation of the CAP, as well as probably presaging the wider breach in the EU that subsequently emerged over Iraq. Whether the CAP can survive international hostility, the opposition of the UK and the pressure of the new member states, where agriculture is an important economic dimension, remains to be seen.

To cavil at waste, ineffectiveness and divisiveness within the EU is, in one way, to miss the point. The EU emerged as part of the post–World War II settlement in Europe. It provided a mechanism for the peaceful coexistence of France and Germany. The alliance between these two states remains the cornerstone of the EU to this day. The EU has undoubtedly played a major role in preserving peace between states in Europe for nearly 70 years. The other major international organisation in Europe, NATO, has played an even more active role in the preservation of European peace.

NATO does not have the same membership as the EU. The USA, still the world's only superpower, is a member of NATO, as is Canada. Many of the EU countries belong to NATO but not all. Ireland and Austria are not part of NATO. Norway belongs to NATO but not the EU. France, one of Europe's two nuclear powers, although currently a full member of NATO, has had an uneasy relationship with the organisation, especially with its perceived Anglo-American leadership. Turkey, persistently kept at arm's length by the EU, is a full member of NATO. It has borders with Iraq and the former Soviet Union.

Turkey has a rapidly expanding population which is already at the same level as Germany's. It has two mega cities, Ankara and Istanbul; the latter may be seen to be one of the most important cities in the history of Europe as a whole (Mansel, 1997). Istanbul controls the entrance to the Black Sea. Turkey is a democracy, though with a looming military presence. It is a secular state, though the influence of Islam is on the increase, not least in politics and education (Mango, 2004). It has a rapidly developing and vibrant economy based in part on trade with Eastern Europe and the Turkic states of the former Soviet Union (the now independent countries of Kazakhstan, Turkmenistan, Uzbekistan, Tajikistan and Kyrgyzstan). It has a significant Kurdish population in eastern Anatolia which for a long time it preferred to deal with militarily rather than politically. It has an uneasy relationship with Greece, its neighbour and co-member of NATO, which periodically flames up into military standoffs. It is in military occupation of the northern part of EU member Cyprus. There are significant Turkish minorities in many cities of the EU, in Belgium and the Netherlands as well as Germany. Geographically, it is perceived to be split between two continents with Istanbul (Constantinople, Byzantium, I Polis) on the European side of the straits and the vast bulk of Anatolia on the Asian side. It is not hard to see that Turkey presents the EU with a sequence of challenges. The crude rejections of a timetable for Turkish membership by France's President Chirac in 2002, repeated by Sarkozy in 2007, represent perhaps an inability to come to terms with Islam and with people of a darker complexion rather than a sustained political evaluation. Whether the EU and Turkey can come to an accommodation will be a severe test of the commitment to internationalism, democracy and interculturalism by both parties. The current signs are that Turkey is likely to reject the rejection and walk away from Europe in order to consolidate its rapidly rising profile in the Near East and the Turkic lands.

Many states in the EU, especially France, see NATO as an organisation whose time has past. The Cold War is over and the UK and USA have pulled back from their military camps in Germany. Such states would like to see it gradually superseded by a European Defence Force. Given the commitment of the UK to NATO and given the partiality of many states, not least those of Eastern Europe, to having their integrity guaranteed by the military might of the USA, this is unlikely to happen in the near future. Against this, economic pressures are leading to much closer military cooperation between Europe's two most powerful countries, France and the UK. It is within this context, then, that progress towards European unification remains complex and contested.

Convergence in educational policy and practice

It is the explicit policy of the EU (European Commission, 1996, 2002), as well as less powerful organisations such as the Council of Europe, to shift to greater convergence between the European states in terms of education. An example of this in action would be the inclusion of a 'European theme' in school and university curricula at all levels. The EU has energetically advocated and financed this policy. It has been adopted by states with varying degrees of enthusiasm. It conflicts with the nationalist versions of history and culture so often promoted by European curricular systems. Despite protracted efforts, Germany and Poland still cannot agree a school version of their shared history. The states of Spain cannot even agree a school version of national history, as between Castile and Catalonia, to take but one example (Tremlett, 2006). In Cyprus the Turkish invasion of 1974 and its aftermath remains an important and separate curriculum subject. In this context it is likely to take a considerable time for states to accept a version of European history and culture which matches the EU's agenda of progress towards civilisation, harmony and unity.

Actual areas of convergence have occurred more as a common response to changes in the wider political and economic climate than as a result of centralist EU policy. An important example here would be the shift towards English as the first foreign language for all education systems in Europe. There are minor reservations on this generalisation, not least in France, but it conveys the wider picture. Spain and Portugal abandoned French in favour of English as part of their liberalisation in the 1970s. The eastern European and former Soviet Baltic States enthusiastically relegated Russian and adopted English in 1989 and 1991, respectively. The adoption of English in many states has been wholesale and successful. English is effectively the second language of the Netherlands. Courses at university level taught in English are to be found in, for example, Finland, Denmark and Spain. In most European countries there is a vigorous industry providing supplementary, evening and vacation courses in English. The EU has not advocated this trend, preferring to stress a three-language policy and to advocate the lesser-spoken languages of the Union. Nor is the EU likely to acknowledge English as its common language. There is an unofficial policy of three big languages, English, German and French. Meanwhile much of the Union's demonised bureaucracy is actually a translation factory, ensuring that documentation is available in all the recognised languages.

The spread of English throughout European education systems is far from a matter for Anglo-Saxon self-satisfaction. The spread of English represents one component of cultural imperialism which is accompanying globalisation. In educational terms it may put in jeopardy not the lesser official languages of the Union, which will be well protected by their states, but rather the minority languages of the European nations, for example, Catalan, Friesian, Breton, Vlach, Welsh and Sami. Fortunately many states, including France, Spain and the UK, have belatedly come to see the importance of their national languages. Nevertheless, some European languages such as Gaelic, Sami and Livonian appear to be on the brink of extinction.

Still at school level, another area of convergence has been the increase in the number of years of compulsory schooling. In some states this results from continuing schooling to an older age; in others it results from an earlier start with schooling gradually replacing kindergarten. The emerging pattern is for schooling to continue to the age of 18 either as a result of state compulsion or economic necessity. This leads to the key school examination at or around this age: licenció, Abitur, baccalaureate, licence, A-levels. The key characteristic of this exam is that, by simply passing or by achieving a specific grade, it allows entrance to a place at university. In most states, though not really in Germany, the better the performance in this exam the higher the status of the university and the degree programme which the student can access.

It is at university level that there is the greatest amount of actual and potential convergence. Across Europe before and after 1991 there has been a great increase in higher education both in terms of student numbers and in terms of the range of subjects which can be studied to degree level. New universities and other higher educational institutions (*hogeschools*) have been opened. Older universities have expanded. New courses in social and technical sciences have proliferated and more areas of vocational work have been brought to university level, not least the education of teachers. Research and higher degrees have also flourished with universities developing specialist areas of knowledge which they then go on to teach at undergraduate level. In this way universities are key players in the emerging knowledge economy. They tend to be prioritised by the state to the extent to which it is engaged in this knowledge economy: both Finland and the UK being well advanced in this respect. University education, from being the privilege of the elite 60 years ago is becoming the expectation of the majority.

The final area of convergence also concerns higher education, in this case with regard to the duration and pattern of study. Given the expenditure necessitated by university expansion, it is not surprising that the far-reaching changes being advocated by the proponents of harmonisation concern particularly the length and level of the first and second degrees. These were the key structural policies accepted by the signatories to the Bologna Declaration (European Ministers in Charge of Higher Education, 1999). In this Declaration the Ministers accepted a model of higher education which involves a three-year undergraduate degree, followed by a two-year masters degree. This is sometimes referred to as the BA-MA model and is, to some extent, derived from the structure of degrees in England and the USA. However, the attractiveness of this model for the Ministers of Education was not some fond positive view of English universities. Far from it: English universities offer the shortest and therefore the cheapest undergraduate degrees in Europe. Some European countries, such as the Netherlands, had already been looking for ways to shorten the amount of time students spent on their first degrees. The Bologna Declaration facilitates and legitimises this process. As well as harmonisation, the process is driven by the much less lofty ideal of reducing the cost to the state of each graduate.

Obviously the implementation of these changes is happening differentially within the 27 countries and beyond (Drew *et al.*, 2008). The UK Secretary of State signed the Declaration knowing that little change would be needed in universities in England, though the implications for Scotland may be more far-reaching. Italy initially appeared to have found the changes to the structure of the degree courses straightforward. A law of 1999 specified for a three-year *laurea* to be followed by a two-year *laurea specialistica*. The implementation of this scheme is, however, proving problematic as universities and students both see the shortening of the degree as a diminution of status. In the Netherlands politicians would have welcomed the Declaration because it allowed them to push through the shortening of the first degree which had proved a far from popular policy. Unlike the UK which transformed all its polytechnics into universities under the 1992 Education Act, the Netherlands has so far not addressed the issue of the bipartite education system. Despite changes in title, the *hogeschools* have not become universities. The bipartite system remains also in Scandinavia, Belgium, Greece and Germany.

The continuation of bipartite higher education in so many European states could be seen to represent both the strength of entrenched university interests and the persistence of an elitist structure. To this extent the post-1992 changes in the UK might be seen as egalitarian as well as widening participation. But this is not the case. In practice the universities in the UK are organised in a highly hierarchical way with Oxford, Cambridge and London at the top and the large urban ex-polytechnics at the bottom. This is reflected in both student choice and arcane funding arrangements which favour the elite universities. The focus of the chapter now shifts from convergence to differences in European education.

Differences between European education systems

The first section of this chapter highlighted some of the ways in which the UK is an anomaly in Europe. This is also the case with regard to education. The UK has far more private schooling than other European countries, seven per cent of the cohort attending such schools. This schooling has a status which is unusual in other countries and it is linked to the elite universities (about half of all Oxford and Cambridge students come from private schools) in a way which would be unthinkable elsewhere (see Chapter 4). In the UK, especially in England, as far as the rich and the powerful are concerned, the publicly provided school system is for other people's children. This partly explains its chronic lack of funding and the way that it has been treated as the guinea pig for the wilder side of policy experimentation by both political parties since at least 1987 (see Chapter 1).

The extent to which religious institutions are involved in the control and curricular content of schools and universities differs widely across Europe (Zambeta, 2008). In France there are a few private, religious schools, but that is the total extent of religious involvement in the education system of a state that prides itself on the integrity of its laity. By contrast in the Netherlands, Belgium and the UK there are distinct religious schooling systems up to and including university level. These systems also differentiate in terms of the actual religions and denominations. In the UK there are state schools; there are also Church of England (Protestant) and Catholic schools. Both these denominations are represented in sufficient numbers to constitute a separate system. There are also a few Jewish, Islamic and Greek Orthodox schools (see Chapter 7). Gloucestershire University, like many smaller higher education institutions, is a Church of England university. The extent to which religion penetrates the school curriculum also differs between countries. Not all systems have a daily act of collective worship, though this is compulsory in the UK which also boasts at least one school which teaches biblical rather than Darwinian theories of evolution. In Greece, not only is Greek Orthodox religion a compulsory subject, all teachers in public schools are meant to be followers of this religion. In Europe, religious education mainly means education in or about Christianity. Attitudes to Islamic Turkey may well be far from benign in such a context. The ultimate response to Turkey's EU-entry bid will be a severe test for the intercultural toleration and celebration ostensibly espoused by the EU states.

It is probably in terms of curricular content that the greatest differences exist between European systems at school level. These result from the historical role that states have played in 'nation-building'. In all states in Europe, though much more in Greece, Latvia, Romania and the UK and much less in Norway and Finland, the teaching of history, national language and social and cultural subjects is infused with nationalism (Coulby, 2000). History in the school curriculum is all too often the story (legend, myth) of the heroic struggle of the nation to escape foreign oppression; of the glorious unifications of all parts of the nation under one monarch/republic; of the spread of the nation's civilisation to all other parts of a benighted world. The teaching of literature and culture can be equally triumphalist as schools celebrate the richness of the nation's cultural products and activities and either ignore or denigrate those of other nations. Schools in Norway teach children to be citizens of Norway and the world, schools in England teach children to be citizens of England, confident that that means 'of the world'; schools in Latvia teach children to be citizens of Latvia in contradistinction to the world. These are fundamental differences and contribute hugely to the contrasting national identities that are found in Europe. National and nationalist curricular systems at school level remain the most intractable divergence in education between European states.

Selection of pupils at secondary level according to their perceived abilities is a practice which is perhaps dying out in Europe, but only slowly. Bipartite and tripartite secondary education systems remain in some regions and some states. In most of the German Länder selection at secondary level continues to be the largely uncontested norm with middle class children attending the Gymnasium and progressing via the Abitur to university. There are usually two further types of school in subservience to the Gymnasium. In Transylvania there are grammar schools and non-grammar. Here the pattern is complicated by the fact that both tiers exist as Romanian speaking and Hungarian speaking (in some cities German speaking also). In the UK some local education authorities such as Kent and Wiltshire retain secondary selection, despite the fact that the evidence has been incontestable for decades that school performance overall is better in non-selective systems. In the Netherlands secondary stratification is more by curriculum than institutions. There, in secondary schools, pupils may be following three distinct curricula, each with its own exams and destination in higher education or the workplace. Progress towards the common school, taken for granted in France as well as the USA, remains slow, reflecting the vested political interests of middle class parents wishing to continue elite and socially exclusive secondary schooling for their children.

One of the benevolent effects of looking at education from an international or even a comparative perspective may be that it provides a shock with regard to anomalous practice in one's own system. This may well be the case for students in the UK with regard to the education of children and young people perceived to have special needs (Daniels and Garner, 1999). The whole industry of detailed categorisation (labelling) and separate, special provision (segregation) is absent in countries such as Italy and Norway. All children are educated together in the least restrictive environment with the maximum of social and curricular integration. The glacial progress towards inclusion in the UK reflects a society which too readily rejects and segregates children on the basis of perceived difference. The process tends to be self-perpetuating as those educated in non-special schools fail to develop the attitudes and skills which would allow them to integrate with those whom they perceive to be needy.

The differential access to higher education resulting from the extent of provision of university places was highlighted in the previous section. Given the increasing scope of the knowledge economy, the appetite of young people and their parents for university education and wider international trends (the USA and South Korea already approach a participation level of 60 per cent of the age cohort in higher education) this is likely to be an area of educational provision where differences will gradually reduce over time.

Conclusion

It may be that convergence within European education systems, as also perhaps at the political level of the continent as a whole, is largely illusory. Where it does occur, as in the spread of English as a second language, it is the result of wider economic and political forces, rather than of centralist Europeanisation policies.

Summary points

- European convergence is a slow process.
- The EU and NATO have different memberships.
- European schools and universities are not converging rapidly, either in their structure or their curriculum material.
- There is a slightly greater convergence at university level.
- Curricula remain inscribed by nationalism and, in many cases, religion.
- English as a first foreign language is one area of congruence, but this is not as the result of a centralised policy.

Questions for discussion

- In what areas of the school and university curriculum is convergence between European countries actually desirable?
- Is the unification of Europe a positive policy objective? If so, how can it be assisted by educational policies?

Recommended reading

The World Yearbook of Education series provides good coverage of current issues in international education. There is usually a good deal of material on Europe. The titles listed below are relevant to the topics of this volume.

Brown, A. and Davis, N. (eds) (2004) *World Yearbook of Education 2004: Digital Technology, Communities and Education*. London: RoutledgeFalmer.

Coulby, D. and Zambeta, E. (eds) (2005) *World Yearbook of Education 2005: Education, Globalisation and Nationalism*. London: RoutledgeFalmer.

References

Chandrasekaran, R. (2008) *Imperial Life in the Emerald City: Inside Baghdad's green zone*. London: Bloomsbury.

Coulby, D. (2000) *Beyond the National Curriculum: Curricular centralism and cultural diversity in Europe and the USA*. London and New York: RoutledgeFalmer.

Coulby, D. and Jones, C. (2001) *Education and Warfare in Europe*. Aldershot: Ashgate.

Daniels, H. and Garner, P. (eds) (1999) *World Yearbook of Education 1999: Inclusive Education*, series edited by D.Coulby and C.Jones. London: Kogan Page.

Drew, S., McCaig, C., Marsden, D., Haughton, P., McBride, J., Willis, B., and Wolstenholme, C. (2008) *Trans-national Education and Higher Education Institutions: Exploring patterns of HE institutional activity*. London: DIUS.

European Commission (1996) *Teaching and Learning: Towards the learning society*. Brussels: European Commission.

European Commission (2002) *A New Impetus for European Youth, White Paper*. Luxembourg: Office for Official Publications of the European Communities.

European Ministers in Charge of Higher Education (1999) *The Bologna Declaration: The European higher education area*. Bologna.

Mango, A. (2004) *The Turks Today*. London: John Murray.

Mansel, P. (1997) *Constantinople: City of the world's desire, 1453–1924*. London: Penguin Books.

Novoa, A. and Lawn, M. (eds) (2002) *Fabricating Europe: The formation of an education space*. Dordrecht, Boston, London: Kluwer Academic Publishers.

Sheehan, J. (2010) *The Monopoly of Violence: Why Europeans hate going to war*. London: Faber and Faber.

Simms, B. (2001) *Unfinest Hour: Britain and the destruction of Bosnia*. London: Penguin.

Tremlett, G. (2006) *Ghosts of Spain: Travels through a country's hidden past*. London: Faber and Faber.

Zambeta, E. (2008) Religion, Modernity and Social Rights in European Education. *Intercultural Education* 19(4): 297–305.

Chapter 13

Information technology and learning in the global knowledge economy

Graham Downes and Stephanie Brown

Introduction

> The 21st Century, it's changing. Technology is moving really rapidly and if [our pupils] were not computer literate they would be disadvantaged. From an employment point of view I don't know many businesses that function without ICT. I think it's an essential tool.

This teacher's observations resonate with many of our intuitive, commonsense perceptions of Information Communication Technology (ICT) in schools and society. A surface narrative suggests children are growing up in a digital world; they are motivated when using digital technologies and this is no bad thing given the global, digital economy we are living in. However, this narrative contains a number of problematical elements that become apparent when ICT is integrated into the classroom.

The tension between narrative and action is highlighted by Robertson's (2007) observations of 'Andy', a history teacher. A confident user of technology and keen to harness the motivating potential of it, Andy began to deliver lessons in the school's computer suite. However, rather than enhancing his teaching, Andy observed a shift in his practice, away from the history subject discourse to an IT technical discourse; established teacher/pupil relationships were disrupted and the nature of the knowledge also appeared to be transformed. Robertson suggests that a formula is constructed in education policy of 'learner + technology = transformed learner', disguising the tensions created by introducing digital technologies into existing classrooms. Robertson identifies problems with this policy: both technology and learner are homogenised, ignoring diversity in the user experience and types of technology; there is no unifying idea regarding the benefits of using ICT; the social space is transformed by ICT, often removing the teacher from the equation.

Prensky (2001) has argued that this is simply a case of the new replacing the old, with 'digital immigrants' (Andy) being unable to understand how the young 'digital natives' think and operate. There are frameworks that attempt to list the ways in which ICT enhances the learning of young people. For example, Fisher *et al.* (2006) identified areas of 'purposeful' classroom-based activity relating to the use of digital technologies. Paradoxically, such frameworks do not provide a unifying perspective on how ICT should be used within the classroom. As a result, it is difficult to define the exact nature and purpose of ICT as a subject: what constitutes ICT, what it is for and whether it is even a subject.

This chapter explains the complex interrelationship between culture, politics and economics. Drawing on the work of Jessop (2002), it argues that ICT is a social practice that has emerged from economic necessity and political discourse. ICT is born of the knowledge economy 'imaginary', an idea that has the force to transform as well as describe existing social practices, and which is politically constructed.

Theoretical background

Discourse

'Discourse' describes the complex relationship between language, ideas and actions. Epistemological debate has traditionally centred around the division of knowledge into the subjective (existing inside our heads) and objective (existing externally). Structuralists argue that we make meaning subjectively through language systems. Although objects exist, we project values and meaning onto them through such systems. For example, a red light has little meaning on its own, but when put next to a green and amber light it means stop. Such signs are open to interpretation and reinterpretation. They rely on a consensus to exist.

Structural approaches highlight the significance of words and symbols in formulating our 'commonsense' views of the world (Hawkes, 1977). However, others have highlighted the importance of the object in the way we make meaning. Bhaskar argues that systems, or words and signs, can only maintain their integrity if they are consistent with the objects that they refer to (Scott, 2005). Those who examine the interaction between culture, politics and economics generally accept this approach to meaning making: the material world affects the way we develop language structures. But language structures create our perceptions of the world, and ultimately our actions. Such a perspective necessarily means that, while we can claim that some things are true (a wall is solid), we cannot talk about truths as complete, as we do not all perceive the world in the same way. Discourses may differ in their depiction of the material world, even though they are consistent with it. One of the main methods used to analyse the impact of language on our everyday lives is called 'critical discourse analysis'.

Marxist political economy

Marxism portrays the world as highly structured, and events within it as predetermined by material and economic factors; within capitalist societies these factors work in contradictory ways. Jessop (2002) attempts to develop this approach to include the discursive factors outlined in the previous section. He posits that economic forces have a tendency to push our understanding of the world in a certain direction. Although capitalism itself is a general term that covers a variety of activities, Jessop observes that all such activities have certain constants. Specifically, capitalist societies require people to be locked into a process of accumulating capital through competition and the realisation of profit. Some people control this process (capitalists) while others realise the process (workers). He argues that the development and continued existence of the capitalist mode of production is not something that has happened organically; in order to expand the accumulation of capital, the system requires extra economic support from the state. The conflation of politics and economics is often referred to as 'political economy'.

Hegemony and imaginaries

Lacan's concept of 'mirror identity' proposed that all relationships are predicated on an imagined sense of the self in the world (Bracher, 1994). Social commentators such as Anderson (1991) argue that these imaginary relationships define societies and nations. A state can therefore be formulated as 'an imagined political community – and imagined as both inherently limited and sovereign' (Anderson, 1991: 6); the way we imagine that our society is integral in achieving compliance and informing social actions. Social realities are sites of contestation: the social sphere is too complex and overdetermined to establish absolute 'truths'. Instead, what exist are truth claims which Jessop (2002) refers to as 'imaginaries'. This is not to say imaginaries are untrue; in order to establish themselves as social realities it is necessary that they contain characteristics that connect with social groups' existing perceptions (Jessop et al., 2008).

However, as discussed earlier, no idea can offer a complete account of the social world. Within the structuring of a state, we can see differing rhetorics that vie to establish a coherent social reality. Gramsci (Jessop, 2002) referred to the dominance of certain rhetorics as 'hegemony'. Hegemony does not exist solely among politicians; all of us accept hegemonic discourses at some level. Consider the example of globalisation. Many eminent economists have written about the concept; most of us accept that globalisation exists and that it informs organisational discourse such as competitiveness and the need for 'high tech' industries. Yet examples of activities are apparent in our daily lives where there is no evidence of globalisation (Chang, 2011).

Both perspectives are credible, but most of us accept globalisation as a dominant force in our lives. Thus, one idea has achieved discursive dominance over the other. The example is reductive and does not illustrate the complex ways in which imaginaries interact. Rather than being mutually exclusive, as the example suggests, competing imaginaries often coexist within societies that are pluralistic and full of compromises. These compromises are characterised by 'assemblages' which can be described as a developing unity, linking together heterogeneous elements (Deleuze and Guattari, 2010). Imaginaries coexist in complex structures, bounded by similarities but defined by difference.

The knowledge economy as an imaginary

The idea of the knowledge economy can be traced back to a group of intellectuals who argued that capitalist societies were evolving to become knowledge based (Bell, 2000). These ideas were developed by Manuel Castells (2010) and his notion of the 'networked society'. Castells argued that, rather than being a commodity in its own right, knowledge is a critical factor in the production process and that new technologies lead to radically new 'networked' formations of production. These ideas were adopted by the Organisation for Economic Cooperation and Development (OECD). Originally in the guise of the 'information society', the idea evolved into the 'knowledge economy' through the work of economists such as Romer (2007) who argued that it was the rearranging of resources that created value. Thus, knowledge became central to the processes of production and capital accumulation.

Therefore, we can make the following assertions about the existence of ICT in education:

1. It is a social practice.
2. Capitalist formations affect its nature.
3. Specific imaginaries affect its form.

The 'knowledge economy' is a significant imaginary in relation to ICT and education. It is the reconceptualisation of knowledge within this imaginary that gives it the capability to fundamentally affect change within education systems. As Osborne (2004: 430) observes 'such a transformation (to a knowledge based economy) would entail more than a shift from one educational ideology to another, but a shift in our very conception as to what knowledge is and to what knowledge is for'. However, what is less clear is what 'knowledge' actually looks like in this transformed economy. As Robertson (forthcoming: 9) observes, 'knowledge, it would seem, is everywhere and nowhere'. It is thus empty, ambiguous, difficult to pin down, but simultaneously seductive and a powerful idea. After all, knowledge is typically viewed as a good thing: it is difficult to say otherwise. Yet the knowledge economy is neither predetermined nor necessarily preferable. Rather, it has emerged through a tortuous route to a place of dominance; i.e. it is hegemonic.

There ensued a process of instrumentalisation that had the effect of materialising and stabilising the idea within nation states (Robertson, 2007). Central to this was the emergence of human capital theory. If knowledge is critical to the economy, it follows that those with appropriate knowledge will be able to create value and improve productivity. Knowledge and economic growth become inextricably linked to individual knowledge, and education becomes central to economic discourses.

In this new economy, schools were conceived as essential to the production of knowledgeable subjects, accommodating individuals who actively produced new knowledge rather than passive recipients of existing knowledge. Organisations such as OECD became increasingly involved in developing education policy internationally. An example of a significant change in OECD policy was the 'Schooling for Tomorrow' programme, which developed a toolbox to improve decision making at a national and sub-national level (OECD, 2000). Three pairs of scenarios were developed as possible responses to learning in a knowledge economy: the status quo; re-schooling; and de-schooling.

The status quo scenario was a description of schools as they currently exist. The document made clear that change was required to meet the needs of the knowledge economy. Therefore, the status quo was unsustainable. Re-schooling explored the possibility of schools reinventing themselves in a way that privileged the learner. The de-schooling scenario examined the possibility that states could do away with schools altogether. In these final two scenarios ICT plays a crucial role, either as a way of personalising existing education, or replacing schools with distance learning. Although OECD tended to favour re-schooling, the necessary case for educational change had been made.

The interpretation of the knowledge economy in UK education policy

The knowledge economy imaginary altered the conceptualisation of knowledge in global discourses. However, for the knowledge economy to take effect it needed to be implemented through specific government policies: the government adopts key ideas from the imaginary and translates them into policy. This is then implemented through specific projects; these projects are called 'translation projects'. That said, it should be noted that the way in which an imaginary is translated is context dependent – the UK has translated the knowledge economy in a different way from other countries; as a result, UK translation projects take a different form from other OECD countries.

The 1997 the New Labour Government proposed a technologically foregrounded education system within the National Grid for Learning, a translation project designed to put the knowledge economy imaginary into practice. Connection to the internet was seen as an 'essential prerequisite for the new post-industrial information age'

(Selwyn, 1999: 55). New Labour's eagerness to establish itself as a modernising party provided the impetus for a national interest in education technology. The rhetoric emphasised that a workforce equipped with appropriate skills was needed for Britain to respond to the challenges of globalisation. Education had to provide the workforce and schools would need to be properly equipped to accomplish this. The political discourse constructed the child as a consumer of information: a future worker oblivious to the world of technology and in need of specific training. Language used in speeches and policy documentation suggested that power was centred upon policymakers and institutions; the discourse afforded no recognition or value to skills acquired by children in their leisure time.

The way in which language is used in policy formation is profound because, as described in the section on discourse, it creates our perceptions of the world and organises our actions. Fairclough (2000) argues that the way New Labour used language was particularly important; the pedantry involved in selecting specific terminology helps to craft a discourse that controls, moulds and manages public perception. The language was persuasive and presented information as absolute, offering no alternative. Consider this foreword by David Blunkett in a New Labour green paper from 1998:

> Jobs are changing and with them the skills needed for the world of tomorrow. In our hearts we know we have no choice but to prepare for this new age, in which the key to success will be the education, knowledge and skills of our people.
>
> (DfEE, 1998: 1)

'We have no choice': the words speak for themselves. The examination of other key policy documents demonstrates how discourse is utilised to reconceptualise education: 'technology has revolutionised the way we work and is now set to transform education. Children cannot be effective in tomorrow's world if they are trained in yesterday's skills' (DfEE, 1997: 2).

The language is passive with education portrayed as old and out of date. Furthermore, technology is given agency; the concept is reified to become something capable of instigating a transformation. What is omitted from the rhetoric is possibly of greater importance than that which is included. As this quote from the white paper *Our Competitive Future* demonstrates 'In the increasingly global economy of today we cannot compete in the old way. Capital is mobile, technology can migrate quickly and goods can be made in low cost countries' (DTI, 1998).

Again, the voice is passive but, as Fairclough (2000) shows, technology and capital are once again given agency through the use of metaphor. However, as neither technology nor capital has the ability to move independently, it is necessary for social actors, such as multinational corporations, to bring about change. These actors are omitted from the discourse, yet they provide the most powerful voice within it.

In October 1997 the DfEE released a document entitled *Connecting the Learning Society* in which the Learning Grid was introduced. Plans were made for schools to be connected to the internet free of charge, stating that every school should be connected to the 'superhighway' by 2002 (DfEE, 1997: 1). This brought a new demand upon teachers, half a million of whom would be retrained, and by 1999 training teachers would have to prove competency in basic ICT skills in order to gain qualified teacher status. Financing the grid was to be both a public and private partnership, with its maintenance relying mainly upon commercial companies (Selwyn, 1999: 56). The government subsequently provided other initiatives such as eLearning credits that provided ring-fenced funding for schools to increase their ICT software and hardware. The knowledge economy imaginary had arrived at the doorstep of education, and education had no choice but to let it in.

New Labour proposed that the Learning Grid would reach fruition within three years and the interim period was spent selling 'the grid' to education, constructing a discourse in which it was conceptualised as inevitable. By 2005 the knowledge economy imaginary had shaped discourses surrounding knowledge and the role of ICT in education; expectations were managed and the hard sell was no longer necessary. The release of *Fulfilling the Potential* is a translation project that presented a more diluted language structure in its documentation: 'Looking ahead to 2006 and beyond, this paper invites schools to develop the use of ICT in the context of our broader strategies for primary and secondary education and for school workforce reform' (DfES, 2005: 1).

While no longer explicit in its existence, the knowledge economy imaginary had provided a foundation from which to work; without this foundation eLearning could not exist, and there would be no translation project. The imaginary continues to organise society today, and society is less resistant to its dominance.

The discursive shift regarding education and ICT provided a convergence of bodies that developed into new assemblages. A new type of 'technological skill' was foregrounded and this, in turn, developed a new public–private relationship. Schools were required to train future workers in the technologically-based skills that were required by business, and businesses provided the software and hardware to make this happen (Buckingham, 2007: 17). Not only was technical skill represented as unquestionably beneficial, it was also the glue bonding the new partnership together. The government fulfilled their duty of removing the barriers to ICT use within education; education then provided a homogeneous group of learners who were eager to use the new skills: future employment and national economic success were virtually guaranteed. The ICT, school and consumer assemblage was not coincidental; in 1998 the Department for Trade and Industry (DTI) encouraged all businesses to invest in their staff and support employees to continually develop skills and qualifications (DTI, 1998). Education and business had to work collaboratively for the good of the economy.

As with any assemblage there are tensions that result from the different contributing elements. By providing ring-fenced funding, specifically eLearning credits, the government 'pump-primed' the educational software industry (Buckingham, 2007: 9). Education provides a stable market that can be relied upon to purchase the products and packages; education is used to legitimise and market products to the wider consumer community (Buckingham, 2007). Voucher schemes such as 'Computers for Schools' run by Tesco appear benevolent, but are not entirely: in return for donating some of their profits to providing ICT for schools, Tesco receives loyal customers and a positive brand identity (ibid.). Using schools for capital gain is not limited to multinational companies: many education technology packages, particularly those that are internet based, collect and sell user data.

Additionally, while teachers acknowledge the spatio-temporal transformation that the internet can bring to research projects, this opens up schools to direct marketing through the use of search engines (Buckingham, 2007). The education technology market has expanded two-dimensionally. First, schools are judged upon the ICT that they consume: more advanced technology is seen as being synonymous with a more advanced education. Second, dedicated funding credits represent a commercial opportunity for technological companies.

Rather than education being the consumers of ICT, the ICT discourse has consumed education. The public/private relationship is unbalanced: education is used as a legitimising vehicle, but educationalists play a minor part in the discursive relationships. Power is seated in the hands of private businesses that develop specialised, complex and often overpriced packages that educationalists feel obliged to embrace for the good of the students' education. The capitalist based market provides assumptions that predicate ICT use within the classroom environment: ICT transforms learning, ICT motivates learners and ICT makes learning better. Yet teachers find the discourse surrounding the benefits for using technology for teaching and specific learning outcomes to be fragmented; they are unclear how to implement ICT and how to incorporate it within the learning environment. Children are taught predominantly the same curriculum as that introduced in 1988, but, where afforded by software packages and teacher creativity, with an ICT twist.

Conclusion

While it seems to offer opportunities for teachers to be creative and contemporary with their teaching, technology puts limitations on practice. For example, to allow the whole class to access the internet, students and teachers are required to leave their 'usual' bases and to converge in the ICT suite. The spatial change structures learning in an unconventional manner; children often sit with their backs to the teacher within a labyrinth of tables in which the teacher finds it virtually impossible to monitor learning. Additionally, the homogenised groupings of technology and learners fail to account for either the different possibilities ICT packages can offer or the previous experiences of the learners. ICT packages allow teachers to vary the degree of complexity regarding children's subject knowledge, but offer no variety to the technological complexity of the learners' experience. Learning via ICT can prove to be a rigid experience; children become adept at navigating specific packages that are rarely transferable between key stages or of use outside of the school walls.

While many of today's adults who work and thrive in technologically-bound roles received little or no ICT training at school, today's children are considered to be at an advantage because of their ICT foregrounded education. Teachers incorporate, where possible, complex computer packages for the good of the children's future while simultaneously grappling with 'the learner + technology = transformed learner' model provided by government imaginaries.

The introduction of technology into the classroom transforms its spatial territory and creates a disparate experience of ICT, which is quite different from the imagined 'equal access for all' that the New Labour Government initially intended. Because of the disparate and confused interrelationship between politics and the economy, translation of discourses into the classroom practice is problematic. Referring back to the opening quote, and considering Andy's actions, the framing of the ICT discourse is evident. Both perceive an absolute need to incorporate ICT into their teaching. However, in Andy's case, the disruptive nature of the discourse upon existing spaces creates confusion, and while the benefits are perceived to be fundamentally good, they are largely undefinable.

Summary points

- Capitalist formations and the state play significant roles in the formation of language.
- ICT can be seen as a social practice. It is constructed through language and convention.
- Imaginaries are powerful discursive structures that have the ability to disrupt and reorganise conventional ideas.
- The knowledge economy has had significant impact in shaping ICT as social practice in schools.
- The knowledge economy is an imaginary that can be identified within assemblages at a multinational and national level.
- The knowledge economy has been translated into practice through government initiatives and projects, the policy documents of which contain powerful and persuasive rhetoric.

Questions for discussion

- Think about your perceptions of knowledge. How has this been shaped by the knowledge economy?
- What challenges do teachers face when using ICT in the classroom?
- How might classrooms need to change to meet the demands of new technologies?

Recommended reading

Sutherland, R., Robertson, S. and John, P. (eds) (2009) *Improving Classroom Learning with ICT*. Abingdon: Routledge.
This book examines the ways in which ICT can be used in the classroom; the authors explain why the process of integrating ICT is not straightforward.

References

Anderson, B. (1991) *Imagined Communities* (2nd edn). London: Verso.
Bell, D. (2000). *The End of Ideology: On the exhaustion of political ideas in the fifties: with 'The resumption of history in the new century'*. Cambridge, MA: Harvard University Press.
Bracher, M. (1994) *Lacanian Theory of Discourse: Subject, structure, and society*. New York: New York University Press.
Buckingham, D. (2007) *Beyond Technology: Children's learning in the age of digital culture*. Cambridge: Polity.
Castells, M. (2010) *The Rise of the Network Society*. Chichester: Wiley-Blackwell.
Chang, H.-J. (2011) *23 Things They Didn't Tell You about Capitalism*. London: Bloomsbury Press.
DfEE (1997) *National Grid for Learning: The government's consultation paper*. London: DfEE.
DfEE (1998) *The Learning Age: A renaissance for a new Britain*. London: DfEE.
DfES (2005) *Fulfilling the Potential: Transforming teaching and learning through ICT in schools*. Nottingham: DfES Publications.
DTI (1998) *Our Competitive Future: Building the knowledge driven economy*. London: DTI.
Deleuze, G. and Guattari, F. (2010) *A Thousand Plateaus: Capitalism and schizophrenia*. London: Continuum.
Fairclough, N. (2000) *New Labour, New Language?* London: Routledge.
Fisher, T., Higgins, C. and Loveless, A. (2006) *Teachers Learning with Digital Technologies: A review of research and projects*. Bristol: Futurelab.
Hawkes, T. (1977) *Structuralism and Semiotics*. Berkeley, CA: University of California Press.
Jessop, B. (2002) *The Future of the Capitalist State*. Cambridge: Polity.

Jessop, B., Fairclough, N. and Wodak, R. (2008) *Education and the Knowledge-based Economy in Europe.* Rotterdam: Sense Publishers.

OECD (2000) *Schooling for . Paris Tomorrow Toolbox*: OECD.

Osborne, T. (2004). On Mediators: Intellectuals and the ideas trade in the knowledge society. *Economy and Society* 33(4): 430–47.

Prensky, M. (2001) Digital Natives, Digital Immigrants. Available online at http://www.marcprensky. com/writing/prensky%20-%20digital%20natives,%20digital%20immigrants%20-%20part1.pdf (accessed 29 April 2012).

Robertson, S. (2007) *Aliens in the Classroom 2: When technology meets classroom life.* Bristol: Centre for Globalisation, Education and Societies.

Robertson, S. L. (forthcoming). Untangling Theories and Hegemonic Projects in Researching Education and the Knowledge Economy. In: A. Reid, P. Hart and C. Russell (eds) *The Sage Companion to Research in Education.* London: Sage.

Romer, P. (2007) Economic Growth. In: D. Henderson (ed.) *The Concise Encyclopedia of Economics.* Indianapolis, IN: Liberty Fund.

Scott, D. (2005) Critical Realism and Empirical Research Methods in Education. *Journal of Philosophy of Education* 39(4): 633–46.

Selwyn, N. (1999) 'Gilding the Grid': The Marketing of the National Grid for Learning. *British Journal of Sociology of Education* 20(1): 55–68.

Chapter 14

Developing a futures perspective in the classroom

David Hicks

Introduction

Why do teachers need to think about future events and trends? How can we help young people think more critically and creatively about the future? This chapter sets out to answer questions such as these and in particular explores:

- the rationale for students acquiring a futures perspective in their life and work;
- the field of futures studies and the conceptual framework this offers for educators;
- how futures related ideas and issues can make a significant contribution to good classroom practice.

Educational rationale

Living in a world of change

We live today in a world of rapid and turbulent change. Issues of wealth and poverty, peace and conflict, justice and injustice, environmental damage and protection affect both the local and global community (Worldwatch Institute, 2011). Research shows that students and teachers want to know more about such issues because they affect their lives today and will continue to do so in the future (DEA/Ipsos MORI, 2008, 2009).

It is as vital for young people to understand the temporal relationships between past, present and future as it is the spatial interrelationships between local, national and global (Hicks and Holden, 2007). If all education is in some way a preparation for the future, then when and where are students given the opportunity to explore possible futures for themselves and society more widely? While historians deal with time past and all teachers deal with the present, explicit exploration of the future is often still missing from the curriculum (Hicks, 2006). Figure 14.1 is a reminder that the curriculum itself necessarily contains both a spatial and a temporal dimension.

Thinking critically and creatively about the future

So why is it important to help young people think critically and creatively about the future? Here are eight important educational reasons.

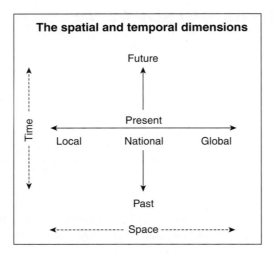

Figure 14.1 Curriculum dimensions

Student motivation

Student expectation about the future can affect behaviour in the present, e.g. that something is, or is not, worth working for. Clear images of desired personal goals can help stimulate motivation and achievement.

Anticipating change

Anticipatory skills and flexibility of mind are important in times of rapid change. Such skills enable students to deal more effectively with uncertainty and to initiate, rather than merely respond to, change.

Critical thinking

In weighing up information, considering trends and imagining alternatives, students will need to exercise reflective and critical thinking. This is often triggered by realising the contradictions between how the world is now and how one would like it to be.

Clarifying values

All images of the future are underpinned by differing value assumptions about human nature and society. In a democratic society students need to be able to begin to identify such value judgements before they can themselves make appropriate choices between alternatives.

Decision making

Becoming more aware of trends and events which are likely to influence one's future and investigating the possible consequences of one's actions on others in the future, lead to more thoughtful decision making in the present.

Creative imagination

One faculty that can contribute to, and which is particularly enhanced by, designing possible futures is that of the creative imagination. Both this *and* critical thinking are needed to envision a range of preferable futures from the personal to the global.

A better world

It is important in a democratic society that students develop their sense of vision particularly in relation to more just and sustainable futures. Such forward-looking thinking is an essential ingredient in both the preserving and improving of society.

Responsible citizenship

Critical participation in democratic life leads to the development of political skills and thus more active and responsible citizenship. Future generations are then more likely to benefit, rather than lose, from decisions made today.

These eight reasons are a reminder that, while the future is yet to come, it plays a vital part in our lives. Although the future hasn't happened, we nevertheless think about it, plan for it and should be concerned about it. As the today we inherit is yesterday's future, so we can play a part in shaping our future and the future of society – or leave it to others to do this, in which case we inhabit someone else's vision of the future. How might one therefore begin to think more critically and creatively about the future?

The field of futures studies

Futures studies as a field of academic enquiry emerged in the 1960s and embraces two dominant modes of knowledge: the technical, concerned with predicting the future and the humanist, concerned with developing a better society. It is the latter strand which is of particular interest to educators. Key texts in this field are Slaughter's *Knowledge Base of Futures Studies* (2005) and Bell's *Foundations of Futures Studies* (2010).

Bell (2010: 73) argues that the purpose of futures studies is to 'discover or invent, examine, evaluate and propose possible, probable and preferable futures'. He continues, 'futurists seek to know: what can or could be (the possible), what is likely to be (the probable), and what ought to be (the preferable)'. Dator (2005: xix) elaborates further:

> The future cannot be studied because the future does not exist. Futures studies does not…pretend to study the future. It studies ideas about the future … (which) often serve as the basis for actions in the present … Different groups often have very different images of the future. Men's images may differ from women's. Western images may differ from non-Western, and so on.
>
> One of the main tasks of futures studies is to identify and examine the major alternative futures which exist at any given time and place. The future cannot be predicted, but preferred futures can and should be envisioned, invented, implemented, continuously evaluated, revised, and re-envisioned. Thus, another major task of futures studies is to facilitate individuals and groups in formulating, implementing, and re-envisioning their preferred futures.

The field of futures studies is thus a rich and vital resource for teachers and educators which offers various frameworks for thinking about alternative futures which can be adapted for use at all levels in the classroom.

Education for the future

Educators who are concerned about this aspect of education talk about the need for a 'futures dimension' within the curriculum and the need for pupils to develop a 'futures perspective', i.e. the ability to think more critically and creatively about the future. The purpose of such a dimension in the curriculum is to help teachers and pupils to:

- develop a more future-orientated perspective on their own lives and events in the world;
- identify and envision alternative futures which are more just and sustainable;
- exercise critical thinking skills and the creative imagination more effectively;
- participate in more thoughtful and informed decision-making in the present;
- engage in active and responsible citizenship, both in the local, national and global community, and on behalf of present and future generations.

Young people and the future

Understanding how children and young people develop ideas about the future is crucial because it is from this formative period that adult perceptions emerge. This then affects what people feel is, and is not, worth working for, whether in relation to their own lives, their community or the wider world. Here are some of the things we know.

Early years

While it might be thought that younger children have little concept of the future, early years specialist Page (2000) found this not to be so. At ages 4–5, time is viewed in terms of the child's own activities, i.e. four sleeps rather than four days. They do not understand that time exists independently of themselves, but there is a growing sense of progression beginning with notions of 'before' and 'after' and moving on to 'yesterday' and 'tomorrow'. The 'future' means being older or things changing. There is a growing awareness of issues such as the environment, war, places and events in the news. Thinking about the future involves imaginative fantasy which gives a great sense of control and freedom over the future. While this may seem unrealistic from an adult point of view, it is a vital developmental stage. Young children are developing positive feelings about their place in the future and their role in its creation.

Primary level

While different levels of ability are found in conceptualising the future at ages 7–8, this is when a more 'adult' understanding of time begins to appear. Research by Hicks and Holden (2007) shows the emergence of an ability to think ahead and the realisation that the future may be something to work towards, as well as something to be concerned about. Reality and fantasy may still sit side by side and children sometimes fear that their own area may be subject to violence and conflict seen in other places on TV. There is a growing awareness of social and environmental issues and children are generally optimistic that the future will be better both for themselves and others.

Secondary level

As they grow older young people's concerns for the future tend to reflect current national and global issues and events although these may change over time (Holden, 2007). In personal terms secondary students are often concerned about getting a good job, having a good life and doing well at school. In relation to the future of their local community, issues such as crime and violence, employment, and environmental threats are important concerns. In terms of the global future there is often concern about the environment, conflict and inequality. Pessimism appears to increase with age and many secondary students feel that they have not learnt enough about these issues at school.

Youth futures

A survey by UCAS and Forum for the Future (2007) invited university applicants in the UK to say what they felt life would be like in 2031, in twenty-five years' time when respondents would be in their forties and at the height of their careers. Some of the main findings were:

- Respondents expect the world they'll be living in to be technologically advanced, but environmentally impoverished.
- Three-quarters believe lifestyles will need to change radically for civilisation to survive into the twenty-second century.
- Compared to their parents at the same age, 42 per cent see themselves as more worried about the future.
- Most (69 per cent) believe that individuals are responsible for the change required for civilisation to continue.
- Women are less optimistic about the future than men, feel more change is necessary and are more prepared to contribute to that change.

What would one need to know and what skills would one need to have therefore in order to think more critically and creatively about the future? Here are nine key concepts which should underpin all subject areas of the curriculum and which highlight the key elements of futures thinking and a futures-orientated school (Hicks, 2006).

Some key concepts

State of the world

The state of the world continues to give cause for concern. Issues to do with sustainability, wealth and poverty, peace and conflict, and human rights, all have a major impact both locally and globally. Students need to know about the causes of such problems, how they will affect their lives now and in the future, and the action needed to help resolve them.

Managing change

In periods of rapid social and technological change, the past cannot provide an accurate guide to the future. Anticipation and adaptability, foresight and flexibility, innovation and intuition, become increasingly essential tools for survival. Students need to develop such skills in order to become more adaptable and pro-active towards change.

Views of the future

People's views of the future may vary greatly depending, for example, on age, gender, class and culture, as well as their attitudes to change, the environment and technology. Students need to be aware of how views of the future thus differ and the ways in which this affects people's priorities in the present.

Alternative futures

At any point in time a range of different futures is possible. It is useful to distinguish between probable futures, i.e. those which seem *likely* to come about, and preferable futures, i.e. those one feels *should* come about. Students need to explore a range of probable and preferable futures, from the personal and local to the global.

Hopes and fears

Hopes and fears for the future often influence decision-making in the present. Fears can lead to the avoidance of problems rather than their resolution. Clarifying hopes for the future can enhance motivation in the present and thus positive action for change. Students need to explore their own hopes and fears for the future and learn to work creatively with them.

Past, present and future

Interdependence exists across both space and time. Past, present and future are inextricably connected. We are directly linked back in time by the oldest members of the community and forward nearly a century by those born today. Students need to explore these links and to gain a sense of both continuity and change as well as of responsibility for the future.

Visions for the future

The early years of a new century provide a valuable opportunity for reviewing the state of society. What needs to be left behind and what taken forward? In particular, what visions of a better future are needed to motivate active and responsible citizenship in the present? Students therefore need to develop their skills of envisioning and use of the creative imagination.

Future generations

Economists, philosophers and international lawyers increasingly recognise the rights of future generations. It has been suggested that no generation should inherit less human and natural wealth than the one that preceded it. Students need to discuss the rights of future generations and what the responsibility to uphold these may involve.

Sustainable futures

Current consumerist lifestyles on this planet are increasingly seen as unsustainable. A sustainable society would prioritise concern for the environment, the poorest members of the community, and the needs of future generations. Students need to understand how this applies to their everyday lives and possible future employment.

Good practice

Hutchinson (1996) has shown that school textbooks often fail to give any consideration to the future and that both comics and computer games tend to offer violent and uncritical technological views of the future. It is not surprising therefore that young people often have stereotypical views of the future themselves. Most movies that are about the future, for example, are apocalyptic and violent. What, therefore, does good practice, which helps young people interrogate the images offered them by society, look like. Here are some examples.

Trends shaping the future

A significant trend of any sort may well have an influence on the future. This might be to do with traffic increase, population growth or global warming, for example. Any trend over time may increase, decline or remain stable. Trends do not predict the future but they do indicate important social, economic, political and environmental shifts that are going on. One useful source on global trends is the annual Worldwatch Institute report *Vital Signs: The trends which are shaping our future* (2012).

Some current trends include:

- world nuclear generation stagnates;
- wind power growth continues to break records;
- glacial melt and ocean warming drive sea level upwards;
- global output stagnant;
- global chronic hunger rises;
- educational attainment worldwide on the rise.

Which of these trends will have a local impact in your community? Will that trend bring benefits or disadvantages locally? What will they be? Will some people benefit or suffer more than others? What action is being taken to support or diminish this trend locally, nationally and globally?

Probable futures

One of the most useful distinctions that futurists make is that between probable and preferable futures. Probable futures are all those which one thinks are most *likely* to come about. This can relate to your own personal future, e.g. I will be studying at university for the next three years; the local future, e.g. it's likely that traffic congestion will continue to get worse; the global future, e.g. climate change means more floods are likely in the UK. It is important and useful to think about probable futures because these are the futures we are most likely to have to deal with. Civil servants, local government departments, town planners, business and industry are all concerned with probable futures, asking questions such as: How many hospital beds will we need in the near future? How can we meet the public demand for more organic foods? Do coastal sea defences need improving at this place? We are constantly planning for probable futures. This does not mean, however, that people necessarily agree on what the future will probably be like.

Preferable futures

Preferable futures are all those which one would most *wish* to come about. They arise out of our deepest hopes, aspirations and dreams, for ourselves, for others and the planet. They may also relate to one's political and spiritual beliefs about how one would like the world to be. This can relate to your own personal future, e.g. I would like to become a really good teacher; the local future, e.g. we really need to reduce the amount of traffic in the town centre in order to make this a better place for shoppers; the global future, e.g. what needs to be done in order to help create a more, rather than less, sustainable future. Politicians, non-governmental organisations, town planners, business and industry are also concerned with preferable futures. They have a vision of what, for them, the future ought to be like and they work towards achieving this. People therefore do not necessarily agree on what a preferable future for society would look like, although they may well be clear about the preferred future for their own personal life.

In some research (Hicks, 2006) undergraduates were asked to write about what the main features of their preferable future for society would be. None had been asked this question before. Here are the features they came up with in order of importance (see Table 14.1).

It is likely that the last four features would rank higher now as these issues have been very much in the news in the last few years since this research was carried out. What would your key features be?

Table 14.1 Students' preferred futures 2020

	%
Green – clean air and water, trees, wildlife, flowers	79
Convivial – cooperative, relaxed, happy, caring, laughter	74
Transport – no cars, no pollution, public transport, bikes	55
Peaceful – absence of violent conflict, security, global harmony	53
Equity – no poverty, fair shares for all, no hunger	38
Justice – equal rights of people and planet, no discrimination	36
Community – local, small, friendly, simpler, sense of community	36
Education – for all, ongoing for life, holistic, community	30
Energy – lower consumption, renewable and clean resources	26
Work – for all, satisfying, shared, shorter hours	23
Healthy – better health care, alternative, longer life	19
Food – organic farming, locally grown, balanced diet	15

Timelines

An excellent way of exploring probable and preferable futures is through the use of timelines as shown in Figure 14.2 below.

The simplest form of timeline is just a straight line with today's date at the left-hand side and some future date at the other. The line is then annotated with key words, dates, cartoons, icons to indicate the changes that seem appropriate, recorded in sequential order. You may, for example, have used timelines in history to record past events which are already known.

This timeline is more complex in that it is designed to record both probable and preferable futures, as well as recent and current trends that may shape those futures. Where the lines intersect is the present. What is mapped on the timeline and what its overall time frame is depends on the context in which it is used. For younger children a horizon of a year would be sufficient, for older pupils it could be a decade or longer. It also depends on the subject matter.

First, one invites students to note down briefly important current trends which seem relevant to the topic in question. If this was 'climate change in the UK' it might include recent floods, extreme weather, glaciers melting, IPCC (Intergovernmental Panel on Climate Change) reports. Second, students should complete the probable timeline. Given these recent events and current trends what is most likely to happen over the next, say, twenty years? Key words, icons, cartoons, etc. are used to illustrate this. Last, the preferable line is completed. Given the probable future, what would students prefer to see happening? Timelines should then be displayed so everyone can see them. Do the probable futures have any common features? Do the preferred futures have any common features? With many topics there will be a gap between what students expect and what they hope for. This should then lead on to an exploration of who else shares elements of such a preferable future and is working to help bring this about.

Vision and action

It is important to note that people's image of the future varies depending on their age, gender and culture as these all deeply affect our views of the world. What may appear

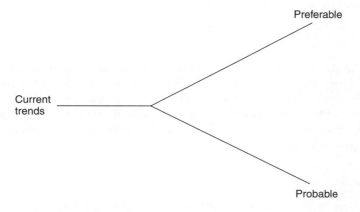

Figure 14.2 Using timelines

'normal' in Europe and North America may look quite different elsewhere, and this applies as much to the future as the present. However, some futures are clearly preferable to others, presumably most people would prefer a less rather than a more violent future. Similarly many people would prefer a more equitable and just future rather than an inequitable and unjust one. For many educators today the crucial question is what does a more sustainable future look like? (Hicks, 2012) (see Chapter 15). Past generations have always had their visions of a better future and many of the things we take for granted we only have because our ancestors struggled to create a better world for their children and grandchildren. We inherit both their successes and their failures.

At the start of this chapter reference was made to the major issues facing world society today, issues which will continue to challenge us for much of the century. Thinking about the future should not therefore occur in a vacuum. It should, as Dator (2005) argues, help individuals and groups formulate and implement their preferred futures. This could relate to your own personal and professional life, organisations in the community, the school you may teach in, the work of a voluntary group or an activist organisation (Hicks, 2006). In particular we need to be able to envision clearly what a more sustainable future would look like. However, Meadows *et al.* (2005: 272) point out that:

> We should say immediately, for the sake of sceptics … we do not believe vision makes anything happen. Vision without action is useless. But without action vision is directionless and feeble. Vision is absolutely necessary to guide and motivate. More than that, vision, when widely shared and firmly kept in sight, does bring into being new systems.

Taking responsibility for oneself and others in the local and global community is a vital life skill which requires critical and creative thinking about both present and future. Geographers have been amongst the first to embrace the need for a futures dimension in the curriculum (Hicks, 2007) which is equally important in Personal, Social and Health Education, in Citizenship, Religious Education and other subjects too. Being able to take a more critical futures-orientated perspective on life allows us to learn from our mistakes, individually and as a species, so that future generations will benefit, rather than suffer, from our endeavours here in the present.

Conclusion

This chapter has set out the rationale for a more futures-orientated curriculum which will help students to think critically and creatively about the sort of society that they would like to live in. It highlights the importance and value of the international field of futures studies as a source of key concepts and insights which can fruitfully be adapted for classroom use. Examples have also been given of practical ideas which can be adapted for use with different age groups in the classroom.

Summary points

- All education requires more critical and creative thinking about the future.
- Up until recently this has been a neglected dimension of the curriculum.

- The international field of futures studies provides a vital source for ideas.
- A number of key concepts are identified to aid in curriculum planning.
- Understanding probable and preferable futures is a vital educational task.

Questions for discussion

- What argument would you use in order to persuade colleagues of the need for a futures perspective in the curriculum?
- What would be the key features of your preferred future: a) for a school; b) for your community?
- Which of the resources listed below do you find most useful and why?

Recommended reading

Gidley, J. and Inayatullah, S. (eds) (2002) *Youth Futures: Comparative research and transformative visions.* Westport, CT: Praeger.
An authoritative and wide ranging source which looks at what young people in different parts of the world feel about their future.

Hicks, D. (2006) *Lessons for the Future: The missing dimension in education.* Victoria, BC: Trafford Publications.
A thought provoking book about the need for a clearer futures perspective in the classroom drawing on innovative work by both teachers and students.

Hicks, D. and Holden, C. (2007) Remembering the Future: What do children think? *Environmental Education Research* 13(4): 501–12.
A useful overview and review of the research on children's views of the future.

Teaching for a Better World (2011). Available online at http:// www.teaching4abetterworld.co.uk (accessed 12 March 2012).
See the detailed Teaching Unit – Preparing for the Future.

Turney, J. (2010) *The Rough Guide to the Future.* London: Rough Guides.
Sets out 'the hopes, fears and best predictions of 50 of the world's leading futurologists and scientists'.

References

Bell, W. (2010) *Foundations of Futures Studies*, 2 vols. New Brunswick, NJ: TransactionPublishers.

Dator, J. (2005) 'Foreword'. In: R. Slaughter (ed.) *The Knowledge Base of Futures Studies.* Vol. 1: Foundations. [CD-ROM] Brisbane, QLD: Foresight International.

DEA/Ipsos MORI (2008) *Young People's Experiences of Global Learning.* London: DEA (renamed Think Global).

DEA/Ipsos MORI (2009) *Teachers' Attitudes to Global Learning.* London: DEA (renamed Think Global).

Hicks, D. (2006) *Lessons for the Future: The missing dimension in education.* Victoria, BC: Trafford Publications. Available online at http://www.trafford.com/Bookstore/BookDetail.aspx?Book=184438 (accessed 12 March 2012).

Hicks, D. (2007) Lessons for the Future: A geographical contribution. *Geography* 92(3): 179–88.

Hicks, D. (2012) *Sustainable Schools, Sustainable Futures: A resource for teachers.* Godalming: Worldwide Fund for Nature. Available online at http://wwf.org.uk/futures (accessed 10 September 2012).

Hicks, D. and Holden, C. (2007) Remembering the Future: What do children think? *Environmental Education Research* 13(4): 501–12.

Holden, C. (2007) Young People's Concerns. In: D. Hicks and C. Holden (eds) *Teaching the Global Dimension.* London: Routledge.

Hutchinson, F. (1996) *Educating beyond Violent Futures.* London: Routledge.

Meadows, D., Randers, J. and Meadows, D. (2005) *Limits to Growth: The 30-year update.* London: Earthscan.

Page, J. (2000) *Reframing the Early Childhood Curriculum: Educational imperatives for the future.* London: RoutledgeFalmer.

Slaughter, R. (ed.) (2005) *Knowledge Base of Futures Studies.* [Professional Edition CD-ROM] Brisbane, QLD: Foresight Institute.

UCAS/Forum for the Future (2007) *The Future Leaders Survey 2006/07.* Available online at http://www.forumforthefuture.org/sites/default/files/project/downloads/futureleaders0708.pdf (accessed 12 March 2012).

Worldwatch Institute (2011) *Vital Signs 2011: The trends that are shaping our future.* Washington, DC: Worldwatch Institute. Available online at http://www.worldwatch.org/bookstore/publication/vital-signs-2012 (accessed 1 March 2012).

Chapter 15

Education for sustainability

David Hicks

Introduction

Why is it that teachers need to know about issues to do with the environment and human well-being? How can we help young people understand the need for a more sustainable future? This chapter sets out to answer questions such as these and, in particular, explores:

- the rationale for a curriculum which explores issues of sustainability;
- debates about the meaning and nature of sustainability/unsustainability;
- educational initiatives illustrating good practice in education for sustainability.

Put at its most simple any human activity is sustainable if it can continue fairly indefinitely without causing harm to people or the planet. Alternatively, any human activity which results in ongoing harm to people or planet is the opposite – unsustainable.

Educational rationale

Unsustainable times

One of the key events of the twentieth century was the 1992 UN Conference on Environment and Development, attended by world leaders and activists from all over the world. This event, which became known as the first Earth Summit, recognised that human activity was increasingly threatening the environment or biosphere – that narrow zone of earth, air and water, on which all life (plants, creatures, humans) depends. It also recognised that issues of development, i.e. global wealth and poverty, were threatening people's life chances in both rich and poor countries. The welfare of planet and people, issues of environment and development, were thus recognised as being inextricably related. One of the terms often used to describe these concerns is 'sustainable development'.

The UN also recognised that education, at all levels, had a crucial part to play in the exploration and resolution of such issues. Among the terms used to describe this concern are education for sustainability, education for sustainable development and learning for sustainability. So important is this matter that the UN declared 2005–14 to be the Decade of Education for Sustainable Development (2011).

Creating sustainable futures

Here are six important educational reasons for an education for sustainability which builds on the futures rationale in Chapter 14 on page 134.

The biosphere

Over the last two centuries the rich countries of the world have used the biosphere as an apparently endless source of raw materials and a sink for all our wastes. The impact on the environment has often been detrimental. Students therefore need to know why and how this came about and ways in which this situation can be resolved sustainably.

Human well-being

Over the last two centuries the rich countries of the world have also used their power to exploit and consume more than their fair share of the earth's resources. Students therefore need to explore and understand the ways in which these processes have led to extremes of wealth and poverty and ways in which this situation can be resolved sustainably.

Limits to growth

This prolonged exploitation of the earth's resources with its stress on constant economic growth has led to a rampant consumerism in the rich world which is threatening our future. Students therefore need to understand the limits to growth that exist in a finite world and the ways in which one can live more sustainably and harmoniously on this planet.

A new vision

All of this requires a new vision of both society and the future, locally and globally. Such a participatory vision needs to weave together all the varying elements of a more sustainable future. Students, therefore, need to develop the skills of practical envisioning and action for change that can lead to a variety of more sustainable futures.

Holistic thinking

Many of the problems we face today are the result of a mechanistic world view which means that we constantly break things down into their separate parts and too often ignore the ways in which they are related. Students therefore need to develop a more holistic or ecological view of their communities and the world through using the skills of 'joined-up thinking'.

Action for change

A number of key global issues, such as climate change, peak oil and the limits to growth, will ensure that the twenty-first century is very different from today. Students, therefore, need to know about existing initiatives, both large and small, that will inspire both hope and action for change from which more sustainable communities can emerge.

Some debates

Economics v. ecology

The problem that underlies all global dilemmas is the question of how we can move from largely unsustainable ways of living towards a more sustainable society. This, however, is where the views of economists and ecologists collide. Put at its simplest, economists tend to believe that there are no limits to growth, while ecologists recognise the finiteness of the Earth's natural systems.

In the current global recession economists and politicians continue to argue that the only thing that can save the world is increased consumption and economic growth (Lawson, 2009). Yet world fisheries are on the verge of collapse, oil production may have already peaked and climate change increasingly brings new hazards. The assumption that economic activity is somehow independent from the biosphere has never been true. Growth, that is making an economy bigger, is not the same as sustainable development, which should aim to improve both human and environmental well-being (McKibben, 2009).

Ecologists and others have long argued that: (i) technological solutions on their own will not bring about a sustainable society; (ii) exponential growth can lead to sudden catastrophes, both economic and environmental; (iii) problems cannot be dealt with in isolation, but only when seen as part of an organic whole. Taking the biosphere as their model ecologists insist that there are clear limits to growth and that humans need to learn to live within these limits. As a result of such concerns various authorities are arguing for a different view of economics, for example, *The New Economics: A bigger picture* (Boyle and Simms, 2009) and *Prosperity without Growth: Economics for a finite planet* (Jackson, 2009).

Impact of neoliberalism

Neoliberalism is the political belief system which underpins the current western world view. Among its core beliefs is the notion that human nature is basically competitive and that this is how the world works (Gray, 2009). What follows from this is the notion of 'economic rationality': that competition between people, institutions and countries will bring material benefits to all. Governments should therefore not interfere with the process of the free market. This view also affects the way in which education is viewed and organised (Apple, 2006).

By contrast a welfare-state view of society stresses the importance of cooperation and responsibility for the welfare of others, especially the less fortunate. This view argues that the state has a key role to play in promoting the welfare of all in society. This would involve legislation ensuring state support for those in genuine need, which protected the environment and promoted sustainable development. Whereas neoliberalism leaves it to individuals and businesses to promote sustainability, if they think it profitable, a welfare state view stresses the need for governments to take the lead and to actively encourage initiatives which will help create a more sustainable society (see Chapter 1).

Contested meanings

The Brundtland Report (1987: 79) described sustainable development as 'development that meets the needs of the present without compromising the ability of future generations to meet their own needs'. While a useful starting point, critics might argue that neoliberal models of sustainable development focus narrowly on economic growth as a measure of progress and discount other costs. Thus actually: (i) some people benefit at the expense of others; (ii) people benefit at the expense of the environment (iii) people today benefit at the expense of future generations. This is patently unsustainable. A more radical notion of sustainability would emphasise: (i) *human well-being*: increased levels of social and economic well-being for all, especially the least advantaged; (ii) *environmental value*: increased emphasis on the need to protect the biosphere on which all life depends; (iii) *future generations*: should inherit at least as much wealth, natural and human, as we ourselves inherited.

The Earth Summit revealed major tensions between rich and poor countries which saw the problems and solutions in quite different ways. Thus governments of rich countries often want poorer countries to take a more responsible attitude towards the environment. Poorer countries often see this as a luxury and want richer governments to help them eradicate poverty. Many poorer countries see imperialism and the strategies of the International Monetary Fund as largely responsible for unsustainable development. They resent the suggestion that they shouldn't exploit their natural resources for their own benefit. They also see the corporate neocolonialism of transnational corporations as a major factor in supporting unsustainable global practices.

Although sustainable development is part of international policy language, its meaning is still widely contested due to fundamental ideological differences. When you come across the terms 'sustainable growth' and 'sustainable development' do not take them at face value. Read carefully between the lines to decide which version of sustainability is being promoted.

The long transition

All of these concerns matter because issues such as climate change and peak oil will create a future that will be very different from today, because we now know that climate change has arisen from use of the fossil fuels that provide the energy we need (Henson, 2011). The resulting global warming has led to increased floods, drought and extreme weather conditions which impact on agriculture, food prices and every aspect of daily life. The poor, who have contributed least to global warming, suffer most. Climate change is here to stay (Oreskes and Conway, 2010). The term 'peak oil' refers to the fact that world oil supply (a finite resource) is about to peak and decline during this century. We are thus at the beginning of a major social and cultural major transition as a result of the unsustainable practices of the rich world over the last 200 years. Working towards a more sustainable future is no longer a luxury but an urgent necessity (Heinberg, 2005). Many groups in the UK and around the world are involved in exciting action for change in their local communities (Hopkins, 2008) and educators and schools also have a crucial role to play in this (Hicks, 2009, 2010, 2011).

Education for sustainability

A four-dimensional model

One of the best models of sustainability is that put forward by UNESCO (2010) in *Teaching and Learning for a Sustainable Future*. It points out that a holistic or multidimensional notion of sustainability must encompass the ecological, economic, social and political dimensions of life. The *ecological* dimension requires care and protection of the biosphere as our essential life support system. The *economic* dimension requires a society in which jobs and income are protected but not to the detriment of the environment. The *social* dimension requires a society in which peace and equity are valued and present.

The *political* dimension requires a democratic society in which both power and decision-making are participatory in nature. Models such as this highlight the interconnectedness of all human experience and the ways in which the welfare of people and the welfare of the planet are inextricably intertwined.

Sustainable schools

The role of education for sustainability in the curriculum was clearly set out in the *National Framework for Sustainable Schools*.

> Sustainable development is a way of thinking about how we organise our lives and work – including our education system – so that we don't destroy our most precious resource, the planet. From over-fishing to global warming, our way of life is placing increasing burden on the planet, which cannot be sustained. Things which were once taken for granted such as a secure supply of energy or a stable climate do not look so permanent now. We need to help people in all parts of the world to find solutions that improve their quality of life without storing up problems for the future, or impacting unfairly on other people's lives. Sustainable development means much more than recycling bottles or giving money to charity. It is about thinking and working in a profoundly different way.
>
> (DCSF, 2007)

While the 2010 Conservative/Liberal Democrat Coalition Government liked to down-play the initiatives of previous governments, the guidelines on education for sustainability which emanated from the Department of Children Schools and Families are invaluable. The National Framework suggests that issues of sustainability can be explored through 'eight doorways': food and drink, energy and water, travel and traffic, purchasing and waste, buildings and grounds, inclusion and participation, local well-being, the global dimension. These doorways highlight the fact that rather than issues of sustainability being another add-on they are integral to the concerns of everyday life.

Good practice

Good practice in relation to education for sustainability should take place in the classroom, the whole school and the local community. It often begins in small ways and grows into a holistic endeavour involving children, teachers, management and ancillary staff. The eight doorways are a reminder that much of the curriculum can be approached in a way which highlights issues of sustainability. Where does our food and drink come from? What impact does its creation have on other people and the environment? How much energy and water do we use each day? Where do they come from and what impact does this have on others and the environment? Once some of the basic concepts of education for sustainability are understood they can become woven into the fabric of everyday teaching. Children know that electricity comes at the press of a switch and water at the touch of a tap but, if they are not taught to ask questions about the why and how of this, they will become yet another generation committed to unsustainable practices.

Food and farming 2050: A classroom activity

Figure 15.1 is a classroom activity, taken from *Sustainable Schools, Sustainable Futures* (Hicks, 2012), which encourages pupils to explore and debate a scenario illustrating possible aspects of a more sustainable food future. Each pupil needs a copy of the scenario and the accompanying questions.

✓   A scenario is a picture of a possible future, it is not a prediction, and is used to prompt discussion and debate.
✓   Pupils work in small groups. First they individually note down their own responses to the questions below and then work to create composite small group responses.
✓   Groups then take it in turns to share their response with the rest of the class. Either the group responses or a composite class response to each question should be put up for display.

Look carefully at the scenario of what a more sustainable food future might look like. Imagine you are visiting this future with a group of friends to gather information about it. You can look around to see how things are different and also listen to what people are saying about life in this future.

1.   What are the first three things you notice about this future?
2.   How is this future different from today?
3.   What are people doing and saying that is different?
4.   What are the advantages of living in this future?
5.   What questions do you have about this future?

This activity is an example of how one of the 'doorways' to sustainability can be explored. It would not, of course, stand alone but be embedded in a wider project on sustainable food and farming.

Awards for Sustainable Energy: A case study

The Ashden Awards for Sustainable Energy (2011) are given each year to organisations including schools that demonstrate inspiring sustainable energy solutions. This brief study highlights some aspects of what one award-winning school did.

Ashley Primary School, Walton-on-Thames

Following an expedition to see the effects of climate change in the Antarctic, the head teacher of Ashley Primary School in Walton-on-Thames initiated an ambitious programme of sustainable energy work in the school, with active support from the governing body. Pupils are actively engaged in efforts to reduce energy consumption at school and at home, and participate in the promotion of the energy activities through film and case study material.

•   Pupils monitor electricity consumption in each building using data provided by eco-Driver. This data can be viewed half hourly, daily, weekly and monthly, so that pupils can see the impact of their actions through their use of the system.

Figure 15.1 Food and farming 2050

Reproduced with permission of World Wide Fund for Nature UK.

- The three school buildings are set weekly electricity consumption targets with a collective target of less than 100 kWh per day. Energy monitors share the data every Friday and the pupils are financially rewarded if targets are met. The School Council decides how the money is spent.
- 71 staff, governors' and pupils' families have joined a Carbon Countdown Challenge to use less than 100 kWh of electricity per week in their homes.
- Fluorescent lamps in the old school building are being replaced by more efficient T5 versions, installed in existing fittings using an adaptor. Efficient IT equipment has been chosen and wasteful appliances eliminated.
- Light sensors with an over-ride facility have been installed in the cloakrooms and toilets of the new building. This building has solar tubes in classrooms, corridors and cloakrooms to bring daylight into dark areas.
- A 35 kW biomass boiler has been installed in the original school building which burns wood pellets sourced locally. Double glazing has reduced heat loss from the building.
- There is a 4.2 kWp photovoltaic array on the roof of the new teaching block, along with a bank of eight solar thermal evacuated tubes (11 kW).
- £154,000 has been spent on sustainable energy measures, over half from the school's own resources and the rest from grants.
- An impressive 51 per cent reduction in electricity use and 18 per cent reduction in gas use occurred between 2007 and 2008, saving about 14 tonnes/year CO_2. Use continues to fall. There have been similar reductions in some of the Carbon Challenge homes.
- There are plans for energy efficiency, passive solar heating, natural lighting, a green roof and PV array in a £3 million new school build.

Sustainable Schools: Some research findings

Jackson (2007) *Leading Sustainable Schools: What the research tells us*. Nottingham: National College for School Leadership.

What sort of leadership is found in schools committed to learning for sustainability? Here are some of the findings from a pioneering piece of research into the characteristics of such leaders and their schools.

> From this study, it is evident that leaders who develop sustainability within their school do so with a passion and conviction, underpinned by personal values. There is a philosophical... dimension to why these leaders engage with sustainability... We found sustainable school leaders place sustainability at the heart of their school, providing an ethos which pervades all aspects of the school and its external relationships.
>
> Successful schools are often inward looking, focused on attainment and good management, and the survey indicates that most school leaders place the global dimension relatively low on their priorities. However, sustainable schools look outwards to engage with their local communities and have a global perspective. This wider, more inclusive vision is also seen in the strong pupil voice and involvement of pupils in decision-making that we found in many of the case study schools.

From the case studies, schools are using sustainability to deliver the National Curriculum in ways that are relevant and real to the students, leading to high levels of attainment or value-added progress. The survey results indicate that pupils are key in developing sustainability and there are several supporting comments endorsing their role in driving this agenda in schools.

The emerging model of green, or sustainable, school leadership builds on what we already know of effective school leaders, but has distinct additional characteristics based on the personal values of leaders who choose to embrace sustainable development. These include fostering participation in decision-making, an outward orientation looking beyond the school gates and an optimistic world view.

Distributed leadership seems to be the model best fitted to fostering sustainability in schools, with different aspects of sustainable development being led by different members of the school community. By sharing out the tasks many are enabled to participate in the overall strategy, reducing the burden on the head teacher and more deeply embedding sustainability across the school.

The key qualities of a sustainable school leader are that they are optimistic and outward looking. These leaders are conscious of the place of the school in the local and global community... These leaders have an integrated, systemic understanding of the world and their place in it and can communicate this to others. They understand the interconnectedness of society, the environment and individuals within these contexts.

Education for Sustainable Development: An Ofsted report

Ofsted (2009) *Education for Sustainable Development: Improving schools – improving lives.* London: Ofsted.

What do official reports from the Office for Standards in Education have to say about good practice in education for sustainability? This report arose out of visits to schools over a three-year period to evaluate how effectively they developed pupils' understanding of sustainability and whether education for sustainable development had any wider impact on improving the life of the school. Here are some of the report's key findings.

- Discussion with pupils showed that, over the three years of the survey, they developed a better understanding of the impact of their lifestyles on the sustainability of the environment.
- At the beginning of the survey, none of the schools were outstanding in its approach to sustainability. By the time of the third visit, all but one of the schools had improved by at least one inspection grade. One school had improved from satisfactory to outstanding.
- In the most successful schools, education for sustainability was an integral element of the curriculum and all pupils and staff contributed to improving the sustainability of their institution.
- Most of the head teachers found that, over the course of the survey, education for sustainability had been an important factor in improving teaching and learning more generally.

- Some school leaders identified links between particular pupils' involvement in sustainable activities and improvements in their attitudes and behaviour generally.
- Pupils responded particularly well to education for sustainability when it gave them the opportunity to take part in practical activities inside and outside the classroom and enabled them to research, plan and implement projects that made a clear difference to the school and the local community.
- A common characteristic of the lessons observed, across the full range of National Curriculum subjects seen during the survey, was the high level of engagement of the pupils in work they perceived as relevant to their lives and future well-being.
- The schools demonstrated how greater awareness of the need for sustainability can lead to reduced financial costs and better management of resources and estates.
- The knowledge and understanding that the pupils gained at school contributed to their leading more sustainable lives at home which, in turn, led their families to re-examine their lifestyles and use of resources.

Conclusion

This chapter has set out the rationale for and importance of an education that explores issues of sustainability throughout the school. It has looked at some of the debates that underlie notions of sustainability and the ways in which these are influenced by differing world views. Some key elements of education for sustainability have been set out and examples of good practice given in the classroom, as a whole-school endeavour, in relation to school leadership and school inspection. The chapter is best read in conjunction with Chapter 14 'Developing a futures perspective in the classroom'.

Summary points

- Any human activity causing ongoing harm to people or environment is unsustainable.
- Issues of environment (planet) and development (people) are key educational concerns.
- Ongoing ideological debates exist in relation to the meanings of sustainability.
- A four-dimensional model of education for sustainability recognises its holistic nature.
- Good practice embraces the classroom, the whole school, leadership and inspection.
- Education for sustainability in schools can improve learning, behaviour and inspection.

Questions for discussion

- Why do you think that issues of sustainability, local and global, should be at the heart of the curriculum today?
- How do you think your main subject and other subjects can contribute to education for sustainability?
- Which of the resources listed do you find most valuable and why?

Recommended reading

Clark, D. (2006) *The Rough Guide to Ethical Living*. London: Rough Guides.
An excellent primer on issues relating to sustainability, from low-carbon living and fair trade to responsible shopping and organic food.

Hicks, D. (2012) *Sustainable Schools, Sustainable Futures: A resource for teachers.* Godalming: World Wide Fund for Nature. Available online at http://wwf.org.uk/futures (accessed 10 September 2012).
A thought-provoking and practical book which contains sustainable scenarios for each of the eight doorways to sustainability.

Hopkins, R. (2011) *The Transition Companion: Making your community more resilient in uncertain times.* Dartington: Green Books.
A ground-breaking book which looks at how groups in the UK and elsewhere are tackling issues to do with climate change and peak oil in their own local communities.

Teaching for a Better World. Available online at http://www.teaching4abetterworld.co.uk (accessed 12 March 2012).
A website for teachers and students which explores the global dimension, a futures perspective and education for sustainability. Includes useful articles to download.

UNESCO (2010) *Teaching and Learning for a Sustainable Future.* Paris: UNESCO. Available online at http://www.unesco.org/education/tlsf/mods/theme_gs.html (accessed 12 March 2012).
A comprehensive educational resource which explores the key aspects of a more sustainable society.

References

Apple, M. (2006) *Educating the 'Right' Way: Markets, standards, God, and inequality* (2nd edn). London: RoutledgeFalmer.

Ashden Awards for Sustainable Energy (2011). Available online at http://www.ashdenawards.org/aboutus (accessed 12 March 2012).

Boyle, D. and Simms, A. (2009) *The New Economics: A bigger picture.* London: Earthscan.

Brundtland Report (1987) *Our Common Future.* Oxford: Oxford University Press.

DCSF (2007) *National Framework for Sustainable Schools.* London: DCSF. Available online at www.rm.com/_RMVirtual/Media/Downloads/National_Framework_Sustainable_Schools_poster.pdf (accessed 12 March 2012).

Gray, G. (2009) *False Dawn: The delusions of global capitalism.* London: Granta.

Heinberg, R. (2005) *The Party's Over: Oil, war and the fate of industrial societies.* Forest Row, East Sussex: Clairview Books.

Henson, R. (2011) *The Rough Guide to Climate Change* (3rd edn). London: Rough Guides.

Hicks, D. (2012) *Sustainable Schools, Sustainable Futures: A resource for teachers.* Godalming: World Wide Fund for Nature UK.

Hicks, D. (2011) A sustainable future: Four challenges for geographers. *Teaching Geography* 36(1): 9–11.

Hicks, D. (2010) The Long Transition: Educating for optimism and hope in troubled times. Available online at http://www.teaching4abetterworld.co.uk/docs/download13.pdf (accessed 12 March 2012).

Hicks, D. (2009) Naturally Resourceful: Could your school be a transition school? *Primary Geographer* 70: 19–21.

Hopkins, R. (2008) *The Transition Handbook: From oil dependency to local resilience.* Dartington: Green Books.

Jackson, L. (2007) *Leading Sustainable Schools: What the research tells us.* Nottingham: National College for School Leadership.

Jackson, T. (2009) *Prosperity without Growth: Economics for a finite planet.* London: Earthscan.

Lawson, N. (2009) *All Consuming: How shopping got us into this mess and how we can find a way out.* London: Penguin.

McKibben, B. (2009) *Deep Economy: Economics as if the world mattered.* Oxford: Oneworld.

Ofsted (2009) *Education for Sustainable Development.* London: Ofsted. Available online at http://www.ofsted.gov.uk/resources/education-for-sustainable-development-improving-schools-improving-lives (accessed 12 March 2012).

Oreskes, N. and Conway, E. (2010) *Merchants of Doubt: How a handful of scientists obscured the truth on issues from tobacco smoke to global warming.* London: Bloomsbury.

UN Decade for Education for Sustainable Development (2011). Available online at http://www.unesco.org/new/en/education/themes/leading-the-international-agenda/education-for-sustainable-development/ (accessed 12 March 2012).

UNESCO (2010) *Teaching and Learning for a Sustainable Future*. Paris: UNESCO. Available online at http://www.unesco.org/education/tlsf/mods/theme_gs.html (accessed 12 March 2012).

Section 3

Learning, knowledge and the curriculum

Chapter 16

Knowledge is a dangerous thing
Curriculum and education

Alan Howe and Dan Davies

Introduction

In this chapter we consider a concept that is central to education – the curriculum. After considering what is meant by the term 'curriculum', we will ask why a curriculum is deemed to be necessary and how it might come into existence. We discuss the role of the state, teachers and pupils in deciding on the content of the National Curriculum in England, while arguing that such a state-sponsored curriculum can be a dangerous thing. This argument can be illustrated by considering how a subject such as science has become part of the 'core' of that curriculum, and how it has retained that nominal status despite over a decade of emphasis on 'the basics' of literacy and numeracy. The case study will give us an opportunity to ask the questions:

- How is a curriculum written?
- Why does a curriculum change?
- How does assessment determine the nature of a curriculum?
- Is the notion of a curriculum useful?

We conclude by considering ways in which we can critically evaluate curricula.

What is meant by 'curriculum'?

In the following paragraphs we consider some of the ways in which people have conceptualized the curriculum and how differing views carry with them assumptions about teaching and learning.

Curriculum as a body of knowledge

One way of thinking about the curriculum is to see it as a 'body of knowledge'. As we shall see when we later discuss scientific knowledge, the question of whether 'true' knowledge exists has been discussed for a long time; a branch of philosophy – 'epistemology' – seeks to answer questions about what 'counts' as knowledge. One apparently straightforward view is to see knowledge as propositional – it tells us *that* $2 + 2 = 4$ or *that* fish can swim. A curriculum based on such a propositional view might contain a selection from all the factual information that humans claim to know. Imagine for a moment a website that contained every scrap of human knowledge and that you had been set the task of exploring that website with some children. Where would you start? How long would you need? What would you leave out? What would be the most important pages to highlight and revisit? For example, would 'photosynthesis' take priority over 'Darwinian evolutionary theory' or 'human reproduction'? Conceiving a curriculum in this way inevitably requires difficult decisions to be made. It suggests that some types of knowledge will be more important than others, some ideas more fundamental, some information unnecessary.

The supremacy of *subjects* as fundamental units of the school curriculum to impart knowledge was firmly established during the first half of the twentieth century, largely as a result of the dominance of a traditional view of knowledge, and of learning perpetuated by senior academics and politicians who themselves had experienced a knowledge-based curriculum and a school examinations system which reflected subject boundaries. The current Secretary of State for Education, Michael Gove, publically praised the views of American educationalist E. D. Hirsch who believes the underlying purpose of a curriculum is to provide children with the 'core knowledge' required to succeed: 'The only way to attain … high achievement with fairness to all students is through a structure … which builds knowledge cumulatively' (Hirsch, 2006: xi).

This view of curriculum calls into question the nature of the knowledge selected: does it have the status of 'universal truth' or 'working hypothesis'? It also suggests that its content can be transmitted from where it is stored (e.g. in the head of a teacher) to the learner. But what happens if there are 'faults' in that transmission process? Does it matter if each learner carries his or her own version of that knowledge in their heads, rather than the 'official' version the teacher sought to impart? This definition of curriculum is problematic.

Curriculum as a way to achieve a product

Alternatively, curriculum can be thought of as a set of experiences that will achieve a desired outcome. That outcome might be expressed in terms of aims, objectives or targets. If the target is for the learner to become literate and numerate then the curriculum will be directed towards that end. If the aim is for a learner to gain a set of qualifications, the curriculum will be focused on pupils passing the examinations. The fundamental problem with this approach is that the curriculum becomes linear (headed in a preordained direction), instrumental (concerned with achieving the aim without considering the value of the journey) and leads to a loss of freedom for the pupil and teacher. It also suffers from some of the same difficulties as the knowledge-based curriculum, since the designated outcomes to be achieved need to be selected from all the possible educational outcomes there might be. For example, should an outcome be that all 11-year-olds should know the names of the Kings and Queens of England since 1066? If so, of what use will this propositional knowledge be to them in their daily lives? Alternatively, a more utilitarian, skills-based output might be that all 11-year-olds are able to read fluently. Such an outcome might be widely supported, but how it could be reliably measured, and the experiences that need to be put in place in the primary curriculum to guarantee its achievement, are far from straightforward.

Curriculum as a process

Criticisms of the two ways of conceiving a curriculum outlined above have led to the development of a third alternative. Seeing the curriculum as a *process* promotes the notion that clear curriculum *principles* will be informed by ideas about human development and its potentials (Blenkin and Kelly, 1981). This view regards education as valuable in itself rather than as a means to an end: learners' needs shape the curriculum rather than *vice versa*. The strength of this approach, according to its proponents, is that it is fundamentally 'moral': principles will be based on the needs of learners to attain intrinsically worthwhile outcomes such as cognitive functioning and intellectual development. It is 'democratic' in that any changes or developments to the curriculum will need to be clearly linked to the attainment of these principles (Kelly, 2004).

Another advantage of the 'process' approach is that the whole of the educational experience can and should be included in the concept of curriculum – not just 'official knowledge'. Many educators have noted that much of what learners experience in schools is not published in any official subject or exam syllabus. The social relationships (e.g. between teacher and pupil) and organisational features (e.g. setting by ability) in schools communicate to learners very strong messages about their place in society. Shute (1993), taking an extreme view, refers to the 'tyranny' of the unwritten curriculum, where children learn that 'passive acceptance is preferable to active criticism' and that 'education consists of memorizing the provided Right Answers' (ibid.: 7). Bernstein (cited in Kelly, 2004: 89) offers a radical alternative that identifies three rights of learners: the right to individual enhancement; the right to be included; and the right to participate. These rights, he argues, should be fundamental curriculum principles.

This is a view of curriculum to which we subscribe, while acknowledging that it has faced sustained criticism over the last 30 years by proponents of the other two models on the grounds that it neither helps to define a standardised content for all learners (model 1) nor equips them with the skills needed for employment (model 2). Governments, while paying lip service to learners' needs and development, tend to shy away from the process model since its outcomes are difficult to measure, making national 'standards' impossible to define and the notion of 'value for money' irrelevant.

This brief discussion of 'definitions' can only hint at the complex debates, arguments and counter-arguments that whirl around the concept of curriculum.

Do we need a national curriculum?

If we define curriculum as the entire content of children's experience in schools then we cannot escape having one. However, for much of the twentieth century, teachers in schools in the UK managed without a *nationally prescribed* curriculum of any sort. This is not to say that local and national education officials endorsed an *ad hoc* approach to curriculum selection, rather that there was widespread recognition that the school community was in the best position to make judgements about their pupils' education. Between 1927 and 1944 the *Handbook of Suggestions for the Consideration of Teachers and Others Concerned with the Work of Public Elementary Schools* noted that 'it is not possible to lay down any rule as to the exact number of subjects which should be taken in an individual school' (Board of Education, 1927: 38). Changes in subject terminology – from arithmetic to mathematics, from nature study to science, from scripture to religious education – do, however, suggest that the school curriculum was attempting to become a more complete reflection of the important cultural activities of a modern Britain.

During the 1960s those involved in education began to question the nature of the curriculum, particularly that in primary schools, in two respects. First, it was proposed by champions of 'progressive' education that the curriculum should reflect a Piagetian view of the way that children acquire knowledge through exploration and discovery without reference to what were seen as artificially constructed subject boundaries. The influential Plowden Report (1967) claimed that:

> (in) the appraisal we have made of the curriculum, and of the methods which have proved to be the most fruitful... 'finding out' has proved to be better for children than 'being told' ... The third of the three Rs is no longer mere mechanical arithmetic, French has made its way into the primary school, nature study is becoming science... The gloomy forebodings of the decline of knowledge which would follow progressive methods have been discredited.
>
> (Plowden, 1967, para. 1233)

In 1967 young people too were commenting critically on the curriculum that they had received. School children were invited to submit their ideas to a newspaper competition with resulting entries published in a book, *The School that I'd Like* (Blishen, 1969). Blishen noted that young people wanted 'to discover how to be responsible for themselves and their own ideas', citing for example 'K., a boy, 17' who hoped that 'in the future schools will try to present material so the student will become deeply involved ... to this end there would be no such things as set 'lessons' and subject boundaries between subjects would be freely crossed' (ibid.: 7).

During the 1970s, Britain began an economic decline that led to low productivity, higher inflation and social unrest. The 'problems' were perceived as indicative of a declining society with significant blame directed towards poor teaching and schooling that had become unfit for purpose, partly as a result of the direction primary schools had taken on the recommendations of the Plowden Report. The then Labour Prime Minister, James Callaghan (1976), argued for society's right to have more influence in what was taught in schools through establishing a core curriculum of basic knowledge; his speech at Ruskin College in 1976 kick-started modern debate on education.

The rise (and fall?) of science in the primary curriculum

A central concern of the Callaghan government was the perceived 'sorry state' of science education, its performance deemed unacceptable in three respects: the unwillingness of young people to seek employment in technological industries; the high proportion of girls abandoning science; and the large quantity of empty places on university science and technology courses. The proposed solution to these problems was curriculum reform to ensure a clear focus on the needs of industry and the employability of young people. The rate of subsequent curriculum change seems in retrospect remarkably slow when compared to the hurried implementation of new initiatives in the recent past. Nine years after the debate began, science became the second subject to be compulsory in the school curriculum after the publication of the *Science 5-16* policy document. It began with the phrase: 'science should have a place in the education of all pupils of compulsory school age' (DES, 1985: 1). In 1988 the Education Reform Act built on this move towards compulsion by establishing a 'core national curriculum' of three subjects – English, mathematics and science.

This tale, of the elevation of primary school science from occasional 'nature study' to a statutory and core curriculum subject, shows in one way the necessity of a curriculum: if, in the view of government, teachers and schools cannot be relied upon to provide an education that is sufficient to meet national priorities, then legislation must enforce a curriculum as a means to that end. This principle has, until recently, been applied to the curriculum in England by successive governments over the last 25 years. However, since publication of *Excellence and Enjoyment: The Primary National Strategy* (DfES, 2003) there have been signs of a loosening of government control over curriculum, albeit accompanied by a more prescriptive approach to pedagogy, particularly in the teaching of reading. Schools have been encouraged to innovate around the edges of the National Curriculum, which it is recommended should take up no more than 60 per cent of the teaching week. More recently, the 2010 Coalition Government has promoted the establishment of free schools and advocated existing state schools leaving local authority control to become academies. Both categories are exempt from the National Curriculum (though not from its assessment and testing requirements). Recent attempts to renew the National Curriculum – for example the Rose Review (Rose, 2009) – have foundered, and the review initiated by the 2011 Education Act, postponed at the time of writing, was to prescribe a further 'slimming down' of subject content.

Science seems set to retain its core status in the primary National Curriculum, despite losing ground over the past decade or so, from around 20 per cent of curriculum time in the early 1990s to just 7 per cent in 2007 (Ofsted, 1999; Martin *et al.*, 2008). It was relegated by increased emphasis on literacy and numeracy to an 'afternoon' subject in many schools (Boyle and Bragg, 2005). An additional factor in the marginalisation of science has been primary schools' responses to the perceived loosening of government control over the curriculum. Troman *et al.* (2007: 558) suggests that, in the case of *Excellence and Enjoyment*, 'Teachers have interpreted the policy text in their own terms and were using it to justify preferred curriculum changes.' One of these changes was the move towards what many primary schools have called a 'creative curriculum', with the following features:

- cross-curricularity;
- a 'thematic approach' to most areas of the curriculum (apart from literacy and numeracy in some cases, which are perhaps regarded as being too 'important' or 'basic' to be included within topics);
- memorable, large-scale 'critical events' (Jeffrey, 2008) or 'provocations' used to initiate whole-school questioning and enquiry;
- suspension of timetable for themed weeks (Jeffrey, 2006);
- more curriculum time allocated to the arts (Woods, 2004);
- an emphasis upon skills, attributes and dispositions rather than knowledge;
- personalised learning with a focus upon the child;
- child-initiated activities.

In presenting their 'creative curriculum' to the community, school websites may claim that the curriculum has been developed by staff within the school to meet the needs of pupils within their local context. For some schools, a creative curriculum appears to signal a return to a 'topic-based approach' prevalent before the introduction of the National

Curriculum. Because few primary teachers have a science background, there is the danger that scientific learning becomes submerged within thematic work, and that arts-based versions of creativity leave little room for science to contribute to a 'creative curriculum'.

Curriculum and power

If a centrally-prescribed curriculum – or at least a testing regime based on that curriculum's content – is necessary to control what is taught in schools, the next matter to consider is who the authors of that curriculum should be. In a democratic society we would expect it to be unacceptable for unelected representatives to make key decisions about the education of our children. In setting up the National Curriculum for England and Wales in 1987, the then Secretary of State for Education, Kenneth Baker, appointed 'working parties' of 'experts' to advise and draft the curriculum but maintained, and exercised, the authority to accept, reject and change any proposal.

The idea that the curriculum might be constructed upon anything other than subjects was not seriously considered; working parties were appointed along traditional subject lines, reflecting the school curriculum of the previous centuries. The membership of these groups, while not claiming to be in any way representative of society in general, was drawn from some of the 'stakeholders' of the education system – subject experts, industrialists, those from commerce, schools and teacher training institutions. It could be argued that this membership epitomised the assertion that far from being rational entities, school subjects are 'in fact the creation of interest groups whose prime concern has been maintaining and extending their own status' (Kelly, 2004: 32). This can also be illustrated in the creation – after an initial joint 'science and technology' working group had failed to reach agreement – of a new and distinct subject named 'Design and Technology', unique in the developed world at the time. So the actual process of curriculum construction had a momentum towards subject separation (Coulby, 1990), with powerful groups in the ascendancy.

There were many education 'experts' who were not happy with the resulting National Curriculum. It has since gone through many changes to address some of the shortcomings of the day, and is currently being rewritten in response to perceived shortcomings revealed by international comparisons. The process, however, has at least been played out in the public domain; it has been possible to observe a democratic process at work as elected representatives seek to control and direct the education of our young people, negotiating a path between interested parties of subject associations, parents, business and commerce. However, in the reform of the National Curriculum initiated by the 2011 Education Act, the names of those responsible for redrafting subject programmes of study were, at the time of writing, secret! The fundamental concern for educators is that the state will not necessarily maintain a relatively 'benign' dominance over the school curriculum. It is not difficult to imagine an alternative future where an imposed hierarchy of subjects does not represent any kind of consensus. A curriculum that expresses explicit values at odds with those of minority or disempowered groups, that furthers national interests above those of global concerns, that promotes certain lifestyles and sexual orientation, and discredits others, is possible. Some argue that this is what we already have.

It is something of a paradox that in 2012 when the Secretary of State for Education was commissioning a review of the National Curriculum for England (Scotland, Wales and Northern Ireland determine their own curriculum) with the aim of making it more relevant and effective, he also drove through policies which permitted free schools and academies to set it aside, devise their own, or adopt a commercially produced one. One such commercial product is the International Primary Curriculum (IPC) (www.internationalprimarycurriculum.com). Developed in 2000 for the Shell Company Group of Schools, this curriculum was first promoted to mainstream primary schools in England in 2003 (Bunnell, 2010); according to the IPC website there are now 429 primary schools in the UK who have purchased and are operating this curriculum. This 'marketisation' of the curriculum is one facet of the free-market reform of education in England discussed in Chapter 1. It can be celebrated as an initiative likely to result in locally determined highly relevant curricula. Conversely, it can be a cause for concern – free markets can become dominated by a few wealthy and powerful providers of services or products. Curriculum authors would be accountable only to the market and there would be no requirement for their product to be balanced or unbiased.

Evaluating a curriculum

In moving on to consider how we might evaluate a curriculum, we continue our focus on the emergence of science as a core subject, because its 'epistemology' (or theory of knowledge) has changed fundamentally over the years, and is still the subject of debate.

It also seems appropriate to evaluate a curriculum against its stated aims. While these are missing from current web-based documentation, they were stated in the original order (DfEE/QCA, 1999) as follows:

- to establish an entitlement of access for all pupils;
- to establish standards, which in turn inform judgements about performance of pupils, teachers and school;
- to promote continuity and coherence in pupils' learning;
- to promote public understanding of the work of schools.

Leaving aside the first and last of these aims, which refer to the curriculum as a whole, we need to consider whether the 'standards' established for science (set down in four Attainment Targets, each with eight levels) are appropriate, and whether the Programmes of Study at Key Stages 1 to 4 (ages 5 to 16) do indeed promote continuity and coherence.

Overall, the science curriculum currently in place in England can be seen as representing a shifting balance between two differing strands of thought about the status of knowledge and its role in the education of children. The balance appears to have moved in recent years towards a postmodern view of 'how science works', although the very construction of the curriculum in terms of knowledge to be imparted suggests a traditional model. Evaluating this curriculum against its stated aims leads us to the following conclusions:

1. By laying down by statute what all pupils should be taught, the curriculum has arguably established an 'entitlement' (aim 1), although the teaching methods employed and the ways in which teachers interpret and represent the science written in the document will clearly affect that entitlement.

2. Through its prescription of level descriptors of attainment for scientific enquiry and the conceptual components, the curriculum certainly appears to have established standards (aim 2), although again the precise nature of assessment (whether externally set tests or ongoing teacher assessment, for example) will influence how such 'standards' are represented.

3. By specifying content and overlapping levels of attainment from Key Stages 1 to 4 the curriculum appears to have provided for continuity and coherence in pupils' learning (aim 3), though there is continuing evidence (e.g. Galton *et al.*, 1999) of discontinuity between primary and secondary learning in science.

4. Finally, it could be argued that by adopting a relatively traditional model of the science curriculum, which would not be unfamiliar to adults educated several decades ago, the National Curriculum for science promotes public understanding – or at least recognition – of what is happening in classrooms (aim 4).

Against its own aims, this curriculum appears to be relatively successful, although we might wish to question those aims in the first place.

Summary points

- There are various conceptions and definitions of 'curriculum', which reflect different epistemological assumptions.
- Politics, power and economics have influenced (and continue to influence) the development of the statutory curriculum in England.
- The National Curriculum is dominated by subjects; particular domains of knowledge have assumed core status.
- A curriculum (such as science in the National Curriculum) can be evaluated in terms of the views of knowledge that it represents and against its own stated aims.

Questions for discussion

- Why might a curriculum be viewed as being 'dangerous'?
- The Secretary of State for Education said before his appointment in 2009 'Whether on GM (genetic modification), or MMR (measles, mumps and rubella vaccination), fighting terrorism or fighting climate change, the better informed our citizens, the better the chance of having a public debate which is rooted in fact, testable propositions and good sense' (Gove, 2009:4). Does this suggest essential knowledge that all children should study in school science?

Recommended reading

Alexander, R. (ed.) (2010) *Children, their World, their Education: Final report and recommendations of the Cambridge Primary Review.* Abingdon: Routledge.
Chapters 13 and 14 offer historical, comparative and critical perspectives on the National Curriculum in England.

Kelly, A.V. (2006) *The Curriculum: Theory and practice* (6th edn). London: Sage Publications.
This provides a powerful analysis of different views of curriculum and argues for a process model of curriculum based on notions of human development.

References

Blenkin, G.M. and Kelly, A.V. (1981) *Primary Curriculum*. London: Sage Publications.

Blishen, E. (1969) *The School That I'd Like*. London: Penguin.

Board of Education (1927) *Handbook of Suggestions for the Consideration of Teachers and Others Concerned with the Work of Public Elementary Schools*. London: Board of Education.

Boyle, B. and Bragg, J. (2005) No Science Today – The demise of primary science. *Curriculum Journal* 16(4): 423–37.

Bunnell, T. (2010) The Momentum behind the International Primary Curriculum in Schools in England. *Journal of Curriculum Studies* 42(4): 471–86.

Callaghan, J. (1976) *Towards a National Debate* [speech] at a foundation stone-laying ceremony at Ruskin College, Oxford, 18 October 1976.

Coulby, D. (1990) The Construction and Implementation of the Primary Core Curriculum. In: D. Coulby and S. Ward (eds) *The Primary Core National Curriculum: Policy into practice*. London: Cassell.

Department for Education and Employment (DfEE)/QCA (1999) *The National Curriculum: Handbook for primary teachers in England*. London: DfEE/QCA. Available online at http://www.21stcenturyscience. org/data/files/c21-evaln-rpt-feb07-10101.pdf (accessed 15 November 2007).

Department for Education and Science (DES) (1985) *Science 5–16*. London: HMSO.

Department for Education and Skills (DfES) (2003) *Excellence and Enjoyment – the Primary National Strategy*. London: DFES.

Galton, M., Gray, J. and Rudduck, J. (1999) *The Impact of School Transitions and Transfers on Pupil Progress and Attainment: Research report RR131*. Nottingham: DfEE.

Gove, M. (2009) *What Is Education For?* [Speech] by Michael Gove MP to the Royal Society of Arts, 30 June 2009. Available online at http://www.thersa.org/__data/assets/pdf_file/0009/213021/ Gove-speech-to-RSA.pdf (accessed 16 April 2012).

Hirsch, E.D. (2006) *The Knowledge Deficit*. New York: Houghton Mifflin Harcourt.

Jeffrey, R. (2006) Creative Teaching and Learning: Towards a common discourse and practice. *Cambridge Journal of Education* 36(3): 399–414.

Jeffrey, B. (2008) Creative Learning Identities *Education 3–13* 36(3, August): 253–63.

Kelly, A.V. (2004) *The Curriculum: Theory and practice*. London: Sage Publications.

Martin, M.O., Mullis, I.V.S. and Foy, P. (eds) (2008) *TIMSS 2007 International Science Report: Findings from IEA's trends in international mathematics and science study at the fourth and eighth grades*. Boston: TIMSS and PIRLS International Study Center.

Ofsted (1999) *A Review of Primary Schools in England, 1994–1998*. London: The Stationery Office.

Plowden, B. (1967) *Children and their Primary Schools: A Report of the Central Advisory Council for Education*. London: HMSO.

Rose, J. (ed.) (2009) *Independent Review of the Primary Curriculum: Final report*. Nottingham: DCSF Publications.

Shute, C. (1993) *Compulsory Schooling Disease: How children absorb fascist values*. Nottingham: Educational Heretics Press.

Troman, G., Jeffrey, B. and Raggl, A. (2007) Creativity and Performativity Policies in Primary School Cultures. *Journal of Education Policy* 22(5, September): 549–72.

Woods, P. (2004) *Creative Teaching and Learning: Historical, political and institutional perspectives*, Creativity in Education Seminar Series. Exeter: Economic and Social Research Council (ESRC).

Chapter 17

Young children learning

The importance of play

Viki Bennett and Nicki Henderson

Introduction

Learning for young children is a naturally creative and rewarding experience. This chapter explores the repertoire of strategies that young children employ in their learning. Drawing on the findings of key theorists, the first section explains young children's learning under these headings:

- investigation
- movement
- schema
- repetition
- communication.

Children learn best when they feel secure and motivated, particularly when they play. The second section shows the orchestrating nature of play in learning across the different strategies. Each is illustrated by an observation of children – a 'scenario'. Principles of effective practice in early-years education are included.

Investigation

Young children have a natural desire to investigate the world around them. Research by Pascal and Bertram (2006: 59) demonstrates that 'from birth, children have a strong exploratory drive through which they experiment, explore, interact with and make sense of their world'. Investigation involves first-hand discovery and children use all of their senses to increase their knowledge and understanding. They examine and look closely, handle and take things apart, put things in their mouths to taste and test, and seek out the potential for making and responding to sound.

Scenario 1 – In a puddle

India (3 years, 7 months) is jumping in the puddles. She investigates the movement of the water by varying the style of her jump. She feels the water on her legs, her hands and sometimes on her face. She can hear the splash every time she lands and she can see the water travelling outwards and upwards. This active investigation enables her to find out more about water and the impact that her own body can make on it.

Piaget (1896–1980) was an early developmental psychologist who explained that children learn and develop as they investigate new and familiar aspects of their environment. He defined stages of cognitive development and ages at which these occur. Piaget's theories have dominated the discourse about children's learning and development, although subsequent thinking has disputed the assigning of milestones to chronological ages.

India is investigating familiar and unfamiliar aspects of water. As she encounters a new phenomenon – stamping hard enough to force water up to her face – she seeks to understand the experience. Piaget suggests that when this happens a 'disequilibrium' occurs, which the child can resolve through cognitive adaptation. Adaptation to the disequilibrium takes two forms:

1. Assimilation – the child incorporates the new phenomenon into her current understanding of the world. India already knew that water travelled in lots of directions. Her discovery that water can reach her face by the force of stamping feet would lead her to 'assimilate' this into her existing knowledge of water.
2. Accommodation – the child makes changes to her previous understanding of the world. For example, Jessie had established that all words that began with 'ch' sounded the same at the beginning: 'church, chicken, children'. When her brother Christopher was born she had to adjust her knowledge and recognise the consonant cluster could also make a different sound.

Bruner (1915–) developed Piaget's ideas and proposes 'learning as discovery': children's independent exploration helps them to understand and remember crucial concepts. Laevers (2005: 8) advises that it is essential for adults to foster children's exploratory drive by 'giving them room for experimentation (and) letting them decide upon the way an activity is performed'. Similarly, Nutbrown *et al.*, (2008: 112) recognise 'the necessity of allowing learners to discover the world through an activity rather through direct instruction'. They suggest that children shouldn't be 'given answers to satisfy their curiosity but encouraged to arrive at them for themselves'.

In order to investigate, young children need opportunities to explore a wide range of materials at their own pace. They are entitled to have their ideas valued and extended by supportive and interested adults.

Movement

Children love to move and be physical. Even before birth they learn by being active and interactive. During the foetal period this becomes apparent to the mother who feels the developing baby moving in response to her voice, her body movements and other environmental stimuli. David and Powell (2007: 15) suggest that children's 'ability to investigate increases as they become physically more able'. Piaget recognised that the foundation of young children's learning is dependent upon their early sensory and motor experiences. He argued that children, particularly from birth to 2 years, find out about the world through their 'motor activity'; he called this critical time 'the sensorimotor stage'. More recent research confirms the power of movement as a tool for learning. Maude (2003: 211) declares it to be 'the main medium of exploration for the young child'.

Movement is made up of both gross and fine motor actions and involves children exploring and manipulating their environment. It allows them to take control, feel confident, build a sense of self, take risks and to recognise cause and effect.

Scenario 2 – Height and speed

> Harry (4 years, 2 months) is sitting on a see-saw with his friend, Alice. He propels himself from the floor using his legs and enjoys the effect of the upward movement on his body, particularly the jolt as Alice reaches the ground. He notices that the speed and height of his travel is controlled by the force of his leg push and experiments with this. He recognises that Alice's movement and his own are connected. Harry is having fun and is happy with the physical risk that this activity involves. He can decide to increase the height and speed each time and is therefore becoming more confident as he does so.

Harry is moving his body with skill and control and is making sense of a range of physical processes. He is using movement to hypothesise, try out, draw conclusions and demonstrate new understanding.

Children need to be with adults who respect and promote physical learning. Research described by Doherty and Bailey (2003) demonstrates that movement experiences are of fundamental importance in each child's development and education: children 'would rather take part in physical activities than any other endeavour' (ibid.: 2). Young children need to have frequent opportunities to move and have access to space, stimulating materials and equipment. The *Early Years Foundation Framework* (DfE, 2012) promotes physical development as a prime area of learning and development which requires 'opportunities for young children to be active and interactive; and to develop their co-ordination, control, and movement' (ibid.: 5).

Schema

Children engage in actions and behaviours that may seem to adults to be random and lacking in purpose: lining up and connecting small toys, wrapping objects, carrying items from place to place and hiding themselves under coverings. Piaget (1962) calls these repeated patterns 'schema'. He describes them as 'coordinated systems of movements and perceptions, which constitute any elementary behaviour capable of being repeated and applied to new situations' (ibid.: 274). He suggests that children explore the world by trying out schema on everything they meet in the environment. At first explorations will be action-based and generalised: all objects can be bitten. But as they are repeated, learning becomes more thought-based: apples are good to bite, but stones are not. In this way schema are instrumental in facilitating new learning at certain crucial stages.

His hypothesis has been developed by later theorists. Athey (2007) defines schema as 'patterns of behaviours and thinking in children that exist underneath the surface features of various contents, contexts and specific experiences'. She observes that more than one schema may be present at any one time and, building on Piaget's original work, names and groups them according to the behaviour: dynamic vertical schema, circular direction and rotation, going over or under and enveloping and containing. Bruce (2005a) suggests that schema continue from childhood into adulthood and can influence lifelong interests and learning.

Scenario 3 – Dropping the boat

> Alfie (9 months) is sitting in his high chair. He drops his toy boat to the floor and looks down at it. His mother picks it up and gives it back to him saying 'here you

are'. Alfie drops the boat again and the sequence is repeated a number of times. Both Alfie and his mother smile and giggle throughout.

Scenario 4 – Musical circles

Aiden is 3, years 9 months. Recently the practitioners in the early years setting have noticed him regularly painting circular patterns. He repeats this circular movement when using his crayons and stirring his ice-cream. When dancing to his favourite music he loves to swirl round and round with his arms outstretched.

Alfie displays an early schematic behavioural pattern often seen in babies. He is captivated by the way an object moves up and down. Athey names this behaviour 'a dynamic vertical schema'. Aiden is fascinated by the round–and–round movement which Athey describes as 'a rotation schema'. He is exploring circular movements in different contexts. Bruce (2005b) suggests that the importance of schema is that they provide a mechanism for analysing 'where the leaner is' and helping predict other situations that will be of interest to the child. To kindle Aiden's learning further, his interest in rotation can be drawn upon to develop deeper understanding. A trip to a fair or theme park, dancing with streamers and ribbons, playing with hoops and wheels will enhance his language, social and physical development and knowledge and understanding of the world.

Repetition

Young children relish the opportunity for repetition and through it steer their learning and gain satisfaction. Neuroscientific research in the 1990s reveals the power of repetition on the human brain, and is important in studying how young children learn. The brain is a network of physical pathways made up of neurons, axons and dendrites. Pathways are strengthened by repetition of a certain behaviour or action. Put simply, the tracks that come to be used most often are developed because of the increased level of energy and muscle activity. Conversely, tracks that are not used or used less will atrophy and eventually disappear. The overwhelming majority of these connections are formed in the first few years: 'Everything a baby sees, hears, tastes, touches and smells influences the way the brain gets hooked up' (Gopnik *et al.*, 2001: 181). From birth children are active participants in their own brain development and the repetitive experiences that they select at this time are crucial in constructing and consolidating meaning.

Scenario 5 – Goal kicks

Luke (2 years, 9 months) is playing with a collection of balls. He is practising his favourite activity of aiming the balls at the goal. He holds each ball with both hands out in front of him and as he drops and attempts to kick it into the goal. When successful and he shows how pleased he is by exclaiming 'yes!' He repeats these actions with all the balls and gathers them back to play the game again, continuing for 30 minutes. He chooses to play this game regularly for the next six weeks during which his ability to aim and kick improves.

Luke is practising and consolidating, motivated to repeat this game by the rewarding experience of a goal. Laevers (2005) concludes that children learn best when they are deeply involved and satisfied by an activity. He recognises persistence and precision as key signals of involvement and suggests that the amount of energy and concentration invested contributes to successful learning. Luke will draw on this experience and find that the elements of repetition – enjoyment, trial and error, persistence, concentration and energy – are valid strategies to apply to any learning situation. Claxton (1999) recommends cultivating effective habits and attitudes for lifelong learning in order to develop 'learning power'. He identifies four key aspects of learning: resilience, resourcefulness, reflectiveness and reciprocity. Luke's resilience and self-belief is essential to this learning experience.

Scenario 6 – Repeated patterns

Molly (5 years, 2 months) is listening to her favourite story. She turns the pages and recognises her favourite character. She anticipates and predicts events by pointing at the pictures and making statements. She notices when two pages are turned at once, and that the pattern of the story is different from previous readings. She joins in with the repetitive phrases and, on completion, asks her father for the story to be read again.

Molly has become familiar with book conventions and is able to choose stories that particularly interest and excite her. She knows how to open and handle the book, is familiar with the story structure, recognises individual specific events and understands the relationship between the spoken and written word. This repeated experience, in a safe and secure environment, has helped her to develop confidence, preference, satisfaction, and will enable her to transfer these skills into new situations.

In order to facilitate repetition children need time and space to return to their chosen activities. However, children's learning will only *deepen* and *flourish* if adults recognise that when a concept or skill has been mastered, the levels of complexity and challenge need to be increased. This is in line with Bruner's (1977) view of learning as a spiral: children should have opportunities to revisit the same concept over time but at more sophisticated levels. For example most children enjoy riding on wheeled vehicles and as they ride on a range of surfaces they learn about the differences in speed and effort required to make the vehicle move over them. These early experiences should be revisited and built upon later in a more complex exploration of friction, using materials and vocabulary that are developmentally appropriate. Bruner (1977) states that 'any subject can be taught to any child at any age in some form that is honest' (ibid.: ix). This theory is a prompt for practitioners to plan according to children's current understandings:

Practitioners must consider the individual needs, interests, and stage of development of each child in their care, and must use this information to plan a challenging and enjoyable experience for each child in all of the areas of learning and development'.
(DfE, 2012: 6)

Communication

Communication is at the heart of young children's learning. From birth, they are highly skilful and effective at conveying and receiving messages from those around them. They achieve this by using an increasing range of verbal and non-verbal language strategies. These include speaking and listening; body language such as facial expression, eye contact and gesture; representation such as the written word, mathematical and musical notation, role-play, dance and picture.

Vygotsky (1978) suggests that children learn best when they are able to use language to clarify their thoughts. Children engage in 'egocentric speech' – a spoken commentary on what they are doing or have done. He proposes that as children grow older the 'egocentric speech' disappears and becomes internalised as inner speech, or thought. Bruner (1977) describes language as a 'tool of thought'. His research confirms that 'inner speech' enables children to consolidate and apply knowledge. In addition Vygotsky recognised the importance of children interacting with adults and more experienced others who listen, question, describe, model and demonstrate. With appropriate language and support, a child can move beyond the edge of his or her capability to a new level of understanding, the Zone of Proximal Development. Building upon this notion Bruner (1986) recommends 'scaffolding' as a teaching strategy – the supportive process of advising, encouraging, and facilitating.

Scenario 7 – Chickens and eggs

Annabelle (5 years, 7 months) is helping her childminder to feed the chickens. As they approach the hen house Annabelle speculates about the number of eggs that will have been laid today stating, 'I think there will be six'. 'What makes you think that?' asks the childminder. Annabelle replies 'There were six yesterday so there will be six today'. 'Good thinking! I wonder why there have been six every day?'

In this exchange the childminder is encouraging Annabelle to verbalise her language for thinking. She is helping her to identify patterns and to draw conclusions. She is affirming Annabelle's reasoning by showing a genuine interest in what she thinks. As the conversation continues the childminder may choose to introduce new and specific language appropriate to the activity, such as half-dozen, dozen, broody, cluck, peck and scratch.

Research continues to confirm that children's learning is most effective when adults offer opportunities for sustained dialogue and exploration. The EPPE project (Sylva et al., 2004) investigates the effects of preschool education and care on the development of children aged 3–7 years. It emphasises the quality of adult–child verbal interactions and recommends episodes of 'sustained shared thinking' with children:

Sustained shared thinking' occurs when two or more individuals 'work together' in an intellectual way to solve a problem, clarify a concept, evaluate an activity, extend a narrative etc. Both parties must contribute to the thinking and it must develop and extend the understanding. It was more likely to occur when children were interacting one-to-one with an adult or with a single peer partner and during focused group work. Adult 'modelling' skills or appropriate behaviour was often combined with sustained periods of shared thinking; open-ended questioning and modelling were also associated with better cognitive achievement.

(Sylva et al., 2004: 13)

The philosophy and pedagogy of the Reggio Emilia pre-schools in Northern Italy are internationally acclaimed. Reciprocal relationships are recognised as fundamental to children's learning. Value is placed on the interaction and mutual trust between teachers, children and parents: 'the interactive partners of the educational process' (Rinaldi, 1998: 118). This is facilitated through a 'pedagogy of listening', encapsulated in the following example.

Scenario 8 – Shadow bird

A group of children notice a shadow in the shape of a bird on the floor of the pre-school. Initially they are not aware that this is created by a mobile hanging in the window. They are fascinated by the movement of the shadow and use their hands and the available resources (tape and boxes) to try and 'stop the bird' and 'keep it from leaving'. The practitioner uses her skills in questioning and encouragement to elicit the children's thoughts and knowledge as they return to the shadow bird throughout the day. The activity also captures the imagination of a group of older children who use their previous understanding of the effects of the sun to suggest reasons why the 'shadow bird' keeps moving beyond the confines of the children's 'cage' creations. As the children talk, hypothesise and discover, the practitioner records the children's learning experiences by taking photographs and writing in detail what the children say and do. The practitioner is able to analyse this information to make suggestions about what the children know and think. This process of 'documentation' allows the children's learning to be made visible and crucially involves other teachers, parents and the children themselves.

Malaguzzi (1997), the founder of the Reggio Emilia approach to early years education, celebrates children's range of communication strategies as a 'hundred languages' and advocates this as a fundamental consideration for all those concerned with young children's learning. This is recognised through the introduction of 'expressive arts and design' as a specific area of learning in the *Statutory Framework for the Early Years Education* (DfE, 2012: 5) which calls for practitioners to provide children with 'opportunities and encouragement for sharing their thoughts, ideas and feelings through a variety of activities'.

Play

The importance of play in young children's learning is confirmed by extensive research and authoritative opinion. In play there is no risk of failure. Because young children naturally chose to play they create their own rules and goals and control materials, people and time. This enables their confidence and self-belief to flourish, which in turn contributes to a state of emotional security. The more secure children feel, the higher their level of cognitive operation. Vygotsky (1978: 2) states that, particularly in imaginative play, children are 'a head taller than themselves'; they operate at higher levels of thought and action than they would in any other context. For Bruce (2005b: 130) play is an 'integrating mechanism' that helps children' to consolidate, coordinate and get together what they know, feel and understand in ways which give them a sense of control over what is happening to them'. Play is the most effective context in which young children can pursue the learning mechanisms of this chapter: investigation, movement, schema, repetition and communication.

Scenario 9 – Log ladder

Jack (4 years, 1 month), Oliver (4 years, 11 months) and Susie (5 years, 10 months) are playing in the park with their grandfather and have collected some small logs. The children decide to lay the logs on the ground in a line. 'It looks like a ladder!' shouts Susie, 'I'm going to climb it!' She jumps over each log in turn and the other children do the same. They repeat the action again and again and, as Susie jumps, she starts to count out loud. Jack asks his grandfather to count his jumps which he is happy to do. After five minutes, Oliver withdraws from the ladder game and starts collecting leaves.

The children have created their own game using the skills of negotiation and problem-solving, adapting and refining the ladder layout as they play (repetition). They have established their own set of rules and eventually agreed how the play should proceed (communication). The game is based on physical movement and the children show their physical prowess by jumping over the logs successfully (movement). The enthusiasm for the game motivates Susie to add a new dimension to the play by introducing the language of number. She represents her knowledge by counting as she jumps and inspires the other children to count higher than they have felt confident to do before (communication).

Scenario 10 – Bridge building

Aaron (6 years, 1 month) and his class have been studying local bridges. Aaron has chosen to use the wooden bricks to build a suspension bridge for his red toy car to travel over. He places two chairs at roughly a metre distance apart and selects bricks of the same size to create a supporting stack adjacent to one of the chairs. He then selects flatter bricks and lays them on the chair seat, overlapping them onto the supporting stack, creating the beginnings of a road. He notices that the road is not level and carefully adds another brick to his stack to reconcile this. He builds a further two supporting stacks and carefully balances more flat bricks over them to continue the road. Throughout the play he handles the bricks with precision and steps back to view the stability of the structure.

Aaron's construction represents his knowledge of bridges (communication). He knows that the bridge needs to be level and that it has to be stable enough to allow his car to cross from one side of the gap to the other. He is familiar with brick play and has an ongoing vertical schema (repetition, schema). He is confident to make choices about the types of bricks he needs and, through a process of trial and error, tests the bricks and adjusts them in order that they fit his required purpose (investigation). Aaron displays high levels of concentration and precision as demonstrated in his ability to use his hands to make refined and deliberate adjustments (movement). Throughout the play Aaron shows resilience and determination. He is not distracted by the other children around him. He overcomes possible failures and is rewarded by the successful journey his red toy car makes.

Conclusion

Only through play are children able to utilise the full range of learning strategies. During play children are empowered, take control, take risks, overcome failure, consolidate skills and understanding, think creatively and imaginatively and, above all, learn positive attitudes about themselves as learners. 'Children learn by leading their own play and in taking part in play that is guided by adults' (*Statutory Framework for the Early Years Education* (DfE, 2012: 6).

Summary points

- Children are capable and competent learners.
- They learn at different rates and in different ways.
- They need the support of genuine, sensitive and knowledgeable adults.
- The early years are critical in children's learning and development.
- Learning depends on children's emotional security.
- Meaningful contexts are important.

Questions for discussion

- What are the benefits of observing schematic behaviour?
- Why is there no risk of failure for young children when they play?
- What value do you place on learning through activity rather than on direct instruction in your own learning?

Recommended reading

Else, P. (2009) *The Value of Play*. London: Continuum.
Offers a comprehensive overview of the importance and purpose of children's play and considers types of play.

Miller, L. and Pound, L. (eds) (2011) *Theories and Approaches to Learning in the Early Years (Critical Issues in the Early Years)*. London: Sage.
A collection of current critical interpretations of national and international early-years approaches.

Moyles, J. (ed.) (2007) *Early Years Foundations: Meeting the challenge*. Maidenhead: Open University Press, McGraw Hill Education.
By exploring the nature of how children learn through the perspective of the principles of the *Early Years Foundation Stage* the writers offer support to early years professionals to direct their thinking and provision.

Taylor, J. and Woods, M. (eds) (2005) *Early Childhood Studies: An holistic* approach (2nd edn). London: Hodder Arnold.
Provides an important overview of the holistic approach to understanding children's development and learning.

References

Athey, C. (2007) *Extending Thought in Young Children: A parent–teacher partnership* (2nd edn). London: Paul Chapman Publishing.
Bruce, T. (2005a) *Early Childhood Education* (3rd edn). London: Hodder Education.

Bruce, T. (2005b) Play Matters. In: L. Abbott and A. Langston (eds) *Birth to Three Matters: Supporting the framework of effective practice*. Maidenhead: Open University Press.

Bruner, J. (1977) *The Process of Education* (2nd edn). Cambridge, MA: Harvard University Press.

Bruner, J. (1986) *Actual Minds Possible Worlds*. Cambridge, MA: Harvard University Press.

Claxton, G. (1999) *Building Learning Power*. Bristol: Teaching and Learning.

David, T. and Powell, S. (2007) Beginning at the Beginning. In: J. Moyles (ed.) *Beginning Teaching, Beginning Learning* (3rd edn). Buckingham: Open University Press.

DfE (2012) *Statutory Framework for the Early Years Education*. London: DfE.

Doherty, J and Bailey, R. (2003) *Supporting Physical Development and Physical Education in the Early Years*. Buckingham: OUP.

Gopnik, A., Meltzoff, A. and Kuhl, P. (2001) *How Babies Think: The Science of Childhood*. London: Phoenix.

Laevers, F. (2005) *Deep-level-learning and the Experiential Approach in Early Childhood and Primary Education*. Available online at http://www.cego.be/sites/default/files/images/BO_D%26P_Deep-levelLearning.pdf (accessed 11 May, 2012).

Maude, P. (2003) How Do I Do This Better? From movement development into physical literacy. In: D. Whitebread (ed.) *Teaching and Learning in the Early Years* (2nd edn). London: RoutledgeFalmer.

Malaguzzi, T. (1977) No Way. The hundred is there. In: T. Filippini and V. Vecchi, (eds) *The Hundred Languages of Children: Narrative of the possible*. Reggio Emilia: Reggio Children.

Nutbrown, C., Clough, P. and Selbie, P. (2008) *Early Childhood Education: History, philosophy and experience*. London: Sage.

Pascal, C. and Bertram, T. (2006) Introducing Child Development. In: T. Bruce (ed.) *Early Childhood: A guide for students*. London: Sage.

Piaget, J. (1962) *Play. Dreams and imitation in childhood*. London: Routledge and Kegan Paul.

Rinaldi, C. (1998) Projected Curriculum Constructed through Documentation – progettazione. In: C. Edwards, L. Gandini and G. Forman (eds) *The Hundred Languages of Children: The Reggio Emilia approach – advanced reflections* (2nd edn). London: Ablex.

Sylva, K., Melhuish, E., Sammons, P., Siraj-Blatchford, I. and Taggart, B. (2004) *The Effective Provision of Pre-school Education (EPPE) Project, Technical Paper 12, Final Report*. London: DfES/Institute of Education, University of London.

Vygotsky, L. (1978) *Mind in Society*. Cambridge, MA: Harvard University Press.

Chapter 18

Affective teaching and the affective dimensions of learning

Janet Rose, Louise Gilbert and Hilary Smith

Introduction

This chapter considers the notion of the affective teacher and the affective dimensions of learning. It highlights the importance of emotions in the thinking process and draws attention to the significance of the pupil–teacher relationship in developing a positive emotional climate for learning. A new approach to supporting children's behaviour called 'emotion coaching' is explained, drawing on recent evidence from a research project undertaken at Bath Spa University. The integral nature of emotions in learning is analysed briefly within the broader context of social justice and citizenship and it is argued that educators should put well-being on an equal footing with academic knowledge and skills.

The affective dimensions of learning

Educators need to comprehend and understand the affective dimensions of learning for three reasons:

1. It is now understood that emotions fundamentally drive cognitive learning.
2. In order to generate successful learning, educators need to engage the affective dimensions of pupils' minds.
3. Emotional intelligence is of equal, if not greater, significance than academic intelligence.

Emotions and cognition

The traditional separation of cognition from emotions has now been superseded by evidence that thinking and reasoning, and emotional processing are fundamentally integrated at multiple levels in the brain. As Immordino-Yang and Damasio (2007) point out:

> Recent advances in neuroscience are highlighting connections between emotion, social functioning, and decision making that have the potential to revolutionize our understanding of the role of affect in education. In particular, the neurobiological evidence suggests that the aspects of cognition that we recruit most heavily in schools, namely learning, attention, memory, decision making, and social functioning, are both profoundly affected by and subsumed within the processes of emotion
>
> (ibid.: 3).

This research has shown that rational decision making is impossible without emotional processing or 'emotional thought'. A new area of neuroscience known as 'neuroeconomics' considers human behaviour as never purely rational but always built upon cumulative emotional experiences. Higher-level cognitive skills taught in schools such as reading and mathematics do not operate as 'rational, disembodied systems detached from emotion' but are instead grounded in emotional functions (Goswami, 2011: 28). Goleman's (1995) work has drawn attention to the 'emotional mind' as a powerful 'system of knowing' which feeds into and informs the operations of the rational mind. He notes that the 'thinking' brain grew out of the emotional brain and that 'there was an emotional brain long before there was a rational one' (Goleman, 1995: 10): we literally feel before we think. In turn, the rational mind can refine and sometimes veto the input of the impulsive emotional mind, but only if it learns to do this.

Affective learning

How and what we learn is, in part, controlled and mediated by our emotional capacity to engage with the physical and social world. Our emotions and relationships influence our motivation and give meaning to our knowledge formation. An individual's emotional response controls the value afforded to a new stimulus and directs the mind to appropriate stored knowledge relevant to the current situation or problem. The following illustrates this point:

> Why does a high school student solve a math problem, for example? The reasons range from the intrinsic reward of having found the solution, to getting a good grade, to avoiding punishment, to helping tutor a friend, to getting into a good college, to pleasing his/her parents or the teacher. All of these reasons have a powerful emotional component and relate both to pleasurable sensations and to survival within our culture.
>
> (Immordino-Yang and Damasio, 2007: 4)

If experiences are emotionally negative, they will affect our capacity to learn effectively or efficiently; therefore, 'models of classroom learning must incorporate the emotions in order to better understand the behaviour of learners' (Goswami, 2011: 28). As Blakemore and Frith (2005: 179) put it, 'a learner needs to be emotionally competent for optimal learning to occur'. To promote learning, educators need to engage the affective domain of their pupils' minds and attend to their affective needs to maximise success at school.

Emotional intelligence

The term 'emotional intelligence' was coined by Salovey and Meyer (1990: 10) who defined it as 'the ability to perceive accurately, appraise, and express emotion; and the ability to regulate emotions to promote emotional and intellectual growth'. One of the primary mechanisms for developing emotional intelligence is our capacity to contain our emotional instincts and moderate our behaviour by engaging our rational brain. In order to do this, we need to learn strategies for responding to negative stressful states. There are recognised social, cognitive and health advantages to having effective emotional regulation; it is linked to better emotional balance, rational thinking, faster processing, improved attention and concentration, more efficient immune systems and greater resilience. The capacity to recover from stressful events helps to develop a sense of 'self-efficacy' which Goleman (1995: 89) describes as 'the belief that one has mastery over the events of one's life and can meet challenges when they come up'. Success is now believed to be as much to do with socio-emotional and self-regulatory capacities as academic skills and knowledge. We can help this by developing a good relationship with pupils and understanding the role of attachment in children's well-being. It means being an *affective* teacher in order to be an *effective* teacher.

The affective teacher

Grootenboer (2010: 274) notes that 'it is widely recognised that a good education, at any level, focuses on the development of "the whole person"' and therefore 'good learning should be concerned with affective qualities'. Hence, 'what it means to be a "good" teacher is not only a mix of professional knowledge and skills, but also an ability to empathise and build relationships with the learner' (McNess *et al.*, 2003: 244). An affective teacher is one who:

1. recognises the importance of, and embraces the idea of, attachment-like relationships with pupils;
2. is a caring professional who operates an ethic of care;
3. creates a nurturing learning environment.

Attachment-like relationships

It is well understood that we learn through our relationships with others and that responsive, caring adult–child relationships are critical for children and young people. The theory of attachment was first proposed by Bowlby (1969) who described it as a 'lasting psychological connectedness between human beings' (ibid.: 194). The theory has been revised from Bowlby's original assertion that attachment ought to take place between mother and child to a broader perspective that acknowledges that multiple attachments can occur with any caregiver. Recognition of children's capacity to attach to others is formalised in the Key Person role, which is now a statutory requirement in the Early Years Foundation Stage for all early-years settings in England. However, Bergin and Bergin (2009) suggest that attachment relationships ought to exist between pupils and teachers of all ages. Secure attachments develop when adults sensitively tune into children's signals, interpret them accurately, are empathetic and responsive to their needs and support them appropriately. In essence, they provide a nurturing relationship that is openly communicative, accessible, engaged and cooperative.

Attachment theory is important for three reasons. First, a child's primary attachments (to caregivers) lay the foundations for socio-emotional well-being and the capacity to learn. Second, educators need to establish an attachment-like relationship with their pupils, particularly with challenging and vulnerable pupils. Third, secure attachment relationships correlate strongly with higher academic attainment, better self-regulation and social competence.

The importance of secure attachment to later cognitive, emotional and social development has been established by numerous studies, and attachment affects our adult lives.

Robson (2011) refers to research which shows how secure attachments have a positive impact on children's capacity to problem solve, to empathise, to have friends, to be competent in conflict resolution and be less likely to be a bully or to be bullied.

Perhaps of more significance is the evidence which reveals the compensatory role good relationships can provide to counteract poor attachments, highlighting the role of educators in providing additional attachments for children and young people in school. It is estimated that at least one third of children have an insecure attachment with at least one caregiver and teachers are likely to encounter insecurely attached children in their classroom. A warm, supportive teacher can predict better knowledge, test scores, academic motivation and cooperation, including peer relations and improved behaviour (Bergin and Bergin, 2009).

Teachers may not be able to provide the same kind of attachment that can occur between a child and their primary caregiver, and professional boundaries still need to exist. Attachment relationships become more difficult in secondary schools where pupils spend less time with a single teacher. Therefore, the more suitable term 'attachment-like relationships' is suggested. Nonetheless, while pupil–teacher relationships may not take on all the attributes of a primary caregiver relationship, it is still possible to develop nurturing classroom relationships.

A nurturing environment

Research on nurture groups in schools which operationalise Bowlby's attachment theory has shown the significance of attachment for academic attainment. Nurture groups were established in the 1970s and aimed to improve emotional and behavioural adjustment by working with small groups of vulnerable children in separate classrooms. Recently, a call has been made for the principles of nurture groups to be applied to mainstream classrooms, creating the idea of 'nurturing classrooms' with a balance of affection and teaching (MacKay et al., 2010). Nurturing relationships promote children's learning and behaviour, particularly for vulnerable or high-risk children, and help to satisfy children's innate need for a 'sense of belonging'. Education professionals can help to create this 'sense of belonging' by envisaging themselves and the classroom environment as a 'secure base' and a 'safe haven'.

A secure attachment with a teacher provides children with a secure base to venture from and to explore and learn from their environment; the safe haven provides a refuge when that environment causes distress. The pupil begins to negotiate the 'shifts between dependence, interdependence and independence' (Underdown, 2007: 48). Rather than creating dependency, attachment provides the child with a physical and psychological premise from which to learn with confidence and self-esteem. As Robson (2011: 32) argues, 'children's relationships are significant for their development of social understanding and their socio-emotional well-being which is so important to school success'. We need to generate a 'sense of belonging' in the classroom: to be caring professionals.

The caring professional and the ethic of care

Being a caring professional is more than just a feeling or an attribute: it is a 'moral act'. Affective teaching as a 'moral act' has been described as the 'ethic of care' and can be traced to the work of Noddings (1992) who viewed caring as a universal human concept and the foundation for making ethical decisions. Swick (2007: 98) claims that 'acts of caring ... provide the entire community with a philosophy of caring that helps to raise the quality of life for everyone', a view supported by Brooker (2010) who says that caring gives rise to 'ethical politics and to notions of social justice and equality' (ibid.: 183). Through nurturing relationships and by setting norms of caring behaviour, affective teachers show pupils how caring 'works'. Siraj–Blatchford (2007) shares this vision, claiming that practitioners should help to prepare children to participate and contribute to an inclusive global society and develop a 'cosmopolitan citizenship'. The affective teacher can help to ensure that such messages reflect a commitment to the welfare of others. As Bronfenbrenner (1979) suggests:

> No society can long sustain itself unless its members have learned the sensitivities, motivations, and skills involved in assisting and caring for other human beings since children who experience caring, supportive relationships are more caring themselves in every aspect of their lives.
>
> (ibid.: 53)

The research of Olsen and Wyett (2000) demonstrates that affective teachers who treat pupils with 'unconditional positive regard', who are empathetic and who understand and respond to their pupils' emotions have pupils who:

> score higher on measures of self-concept, have increased scores on intelligence measures, exhibit higher levels of thinking, make gains in creativity scores, do more problem solving, make greater gains on standardized math[s] and reading tests, are more involved in learning and present fewer discipline problems.
>
> (ibid.: 743)

The power of the affective teacher is at its most potent in supporting children's behaviour. In one study affective teaching produced 'a lower frequency of misbehaviour, including off-task behaviour, talking without permission, moving without permission and aggression' (Shechtman and Leichtentritt, 2004: 323). The remaining sections of this chapter explore how an affective approach to behaviour management has long-term potential for generating well-being and positive citizenship.

An affective approach to supporting children's behaviour

Almost every government's educational policy over the last century or so has attempted to address children's challenging behaviour and discipline in schools. Concerns range from low-level disruption in the classroom to violence and exclusion. The New Labour Government broadened the attention to wider issues such as children's well-being and mental health in the *Every Child Matters* agenda (DfES, 2004) (see Chapter 2). The term 'behaviour management' was replaced with 'learning behaviour' which recognised relationships and emotional connections as the key to student engagement and motivation (Ellis and Tod, 2009). This acknowledged the need to adopt more caring, protective and supportive approaches through the initiation and endorsement of programmes such as nurture groups, Behaviour4Learning and the promotion of 'emotional literacy' in schools.

But the 2010 Coalition Government narrowed the focus back to disciplinary issues and traditional, authoritarian approaches to behaviour control. It archived much of the previous New Labour Government's guidance on behaviour, implying that social and emotional well-being and emotional literacy were no longer an educational priority. In contrast, part of the 2011 Education Act is devoted to strengthening aspects of previous legislation in respect of teachers' statutory authority to discipline pupils for misbehaviour. This was reinforced by a guidance document: *Ensuring Good Behaviour in Schools* (DfE, 2012) which advised on how to frame a school behaviour policy. It redefines what constitutes 'reasonable force' that staff may use on pupils. Noted for its brevity, it uses terms such as 'discipline', 'misbehaviour' and 'punishment' which had fallen into disuse in recent years. It does not address the complexities of social and emotional needs, nor refer to emotional well-being as a route to supporting positive learning behaviour.

Indeed, official approaches signalled a return to narrow approaches based on the work of behaviourists. Behaviourism rests on the premise that behaviour can be controlled and modified via the reinforcement techniques of reward and punishment. Despite its critics, and considerable psychological advances in the understanding of children's motivation, self-concept, self-esteem and self-regulation, behaviourist principles are still evident in many behaviour policies in schools, with rewards and sanctions used as key tools for classroom control (Ellis and Tod, 2009).

This chapter has cited a solid base of research evidence which suggests that an affective approach to children's learning and behaviour facilitates academic achievement and social functioning. An approach that encapsulates affective principles of behaviour management is emotion coaching. It reflects the evidence of the most successful programmes for improving behaviour for learning focus on the emotional and social causes of difficult-to-manage behaviour and proactively teaches social and emotional competencies (Weare and Gray, 2003).

Case study: Emotion coaching

Emotion coaching is based on the work of John Gottman and his colleagues (Gottman *et al.,* 1997; Gottman and DeClaire, 1997) who emphasise the process of 'emotional regulation' rather than 'behaviour modification': a focus on the feelings which are ultimately driving the behaviour, instead of just the behaviour itself. Emotion coaching involves the development of 'meta-emotion', the 'organised set of feelings and cognitions about one's own emotions and the emotions of others' (Gottman and DeClaire, 1997: 7). Meta-emotion is essentially your personal views and beliefs about emotions, what they mean to you and how aware you are of them – an integral part of emotional intelligence. It includes how you value emotions, in what ways or contexts you think they ought to be expressed (or not!) and how you ought to respond to them. They are invariably influenced by the emotion display rules of your particular socio-cultural context.

Through emotion coaching educators can take advantage of opportune moments to teach appropriate behaviour. Emotion coaching (also known as 'meta-emotion philosophy') reflects the capacity to be both aware of our own, as well as children's and young people's emotions. Adults who are 'mind-minded', who tune into young children's thoughts and feelings, help to scaffold children's understanding of their own behaviour. Such an approach leads to emotional regulation, more competent problem solving, higher self-esteem, better academic success and more positive peer relations.

Emotion coaching comprises two key elements: empathy and guidance. These express themselves through various processes which adults undertake whenever 'emotional moments' occur. Emotional empathy involves recognising, labelling and validating a child's emotions, regardless of the behaviour, in order to promote self-awareness of emotions. The circumstances might also require setting limits on appropriate behaviour (such as stating clearly what is acceptable behaviour) and possible consequential action (such as implementing behaviour management procedures). But key to this process is guidance: engagement with the pupil in problem solving in order to support the ability to self-regulate and to seek alternative courses of action preventing future transgressions.

In this way, a pupil's safe haven/secure base and sense of acceptance is maintained, while the boundaries of inappropriate behaviour are communicated. The process is adaptable and responsive to children's developmental capabilities, with the adult scaffolding pro-social solutions where necessary. Gottman's research shows that emotion coaching has a positive impact on the stress response system, since the techniques of emotion coaching trigger the brain into helping the body to calm down, enabling the child to respond and adapt behaviour appropriately.

The 0–19 Melksham Resilience Project

This research project, based at Bath Spa University, evaluated the impact of adopting emotion coaching techniques into professional practice, particularly during behavioural incidents. Participating institutions included secondary and primary schools, a children's centre and a youth centre. Practitioners and parents were trained and supported to help embed emotion coaching into practice, and young people were trained in the techniques as part of a peer-mentoring programme. Preliminary findings were that emotion coaching:

- promotes children's and young people's self-awareness of their emotions and positive self-regulation of their behaviour;
- reduces incidences of exclusion, such as 'call outs' where pupils are removed from the classroom for disruptive behaviour;
- enables adults to communicate more effectively and consistently with children and young people in stressful situations, and helps to de-escalate volatile situations;
- promotes nurturing and emotionally supportive relationships which can provide optimal contexts for the promotion of resilience.

The impact of adopting emotion coaching in practice is illustrated by the case of a Year 8 girl who

> was being removed routinely from lessons – she was on the call-out register every day and she's not any more.

The practitioners talk of how emotion coaching has led to fewer *stand offs* as it helps the staff to

> talk pupils down from the edge.

The participating staff considered that the pupils

have trust with their teachers and it impacts on everything ... they have this resilience to think they can cope... they don't have to fly off the handle.

Improved relationships with parents were also recorded where parents became less antagonistic, more cooperative and more willing to listen.

It also had a positive impact on the staff as exemplified by one teacher:

These are the kids that drive you nuts but I'm now very aware that I switch something on and I'm going through those stages in a considered way. I can be calmer and then help the child to calm down.

The participants in the project emphasised how their ability to empathise with pupils and to validate their emotions was greatly increased, making them less dismissive and more able to build a rapport with pupils:

It makes the children feel more secure and gives them a vocabulary to talk about how they are feeling instead of just acting. This helps them to be more positive and happier.

Another declared:

I know now that empathy is an important part of teaching.

The 0–19 Melksham Resilience Project shows how emotion coaching not only can help to reduce negative behavioural incidents, but also help to develop nurturing relationships in which pupils can feel protected, comforted and secure with caring and trustworthy adults who support them in their emotional self-regulation. It is an integral aspect of the affective teacher and has implications far beyond the school.

Implications of affective teaching for society

Ecclestone and Hayes (2009) note that children's well-being is recognised as a 'hallmark of civilised societies' and a 'key outcome of learning in progressive societies' as well as being enshrined in the United Nations Convention of the Rights of the Child (ibid.: 371). Yet research suggests that children in the UK are amongst the least happy and more likely to experience the effects of negative well-being, such as low self-esteem, social exclusion, bullying, mental health problems, aggression and criminal activity when compared with other western, industrialised countries (UNICEF, 2011).

The literature on resilience highlights the importance of social relationships and social skills in counteracting adversity such as socio-economic disadvantage. Opportunities for individuals to experience social and emotional support, gain recognition of their strengths and capabilities and to develop positive social skills, promote feelings of competence and self-belief and supports positive planning for the future (Kumpfer *et al.*, 2010). Although temperament and other factors play a role in promoting children's capacity to adapt effectively, it is clear that educators can help to 'inoculate' children against the effects of adversity. Other resilience studies have also shown how a warm and supportive adult–child relationship can buffer the effects of poverty and can act as the greatest moderating effect on the behaviour of children from poor families (Jones and Schoon, 2008).

A network of supportive adults, who work together to help children and young people to build a repertoire of internal and external socio-emotional regulatory skills, provides the context for promoting resilience.

We have suggested how the process of nurturing relationships in educational contexts can be aided through emotion coaching strategies and that these can, in turn, support the development of resilience in young children. At the core of nurturing relationships is the process of fostering empathy which has important implications in promoting social justice. Hoffman (2000) regards generalised concerns for social justice issues such as poverty and oppression as the most mature form of empathy. It can help to break down biased stereotypes, foster tolerance, compassion and acceptance of difference and inclusive perspectives, all of which ought to be integral goals for educators. Allen (2011) has advised the need to focus educational provision on the promotion of children's social and emotional capacity and resilience to empower them to reach their full potential. Affective teaching can help us to do that.

Summary points

- To ensure successful learning, educators need to engage the affective dimensions of pupils' minds.
- Affective teaching endorses an ethic of care and develops nurturing and attachment-like relationships with pupils which enhance academic learning.
- Affective teaching involves emotion coaching which helps children to self-regulate and improves their behaviour and capacity for learning.
- Affective teaching contributes to social justice and promotes positive citizenship.
- Children's well-being is as important as academic knowledge and skills.

Questions for discussion

- What might be the qualities of an affective teacher?
- Reflect on your own school's behaviour management policy. Can you recognise any elements of an affective approach?
- Think about your own meta-emotion philosophy. How do you think this might affect how you view the process of supporting behaviour in schools?

Recommended reading

Immordino-Yang, M. and Damasio, A. (2007) We Feel, Therefore We Learn: The relevance of affective and social neuroscience to education. *Mind, Brain and Education Journal* 1(1): 3–10.
This article provides a useful overview of neuroscientific research which highlights the relationship between emotions and cognition and the implications of this for education.

Bergin, C. and Bergin, D. (2009) Attachment in the Classroom. *Educational Psychology Review* 21: 141–70.
The significance of attachment for pupils' learning and progress is outlined in this article; it offers a clear rationale for the importance of attachment-like relationships in the classroom.

Shechtman, Z. and Leichtentritt, J. (2004) Affective Teaching: A method to enhance classroom management. *European Journal of Teacher Education* 27(3): 323–33.
This study from Israel provides a perspective on affective teaching and how it can improve behaviour and enhance learning in schools.

Gottman, J. and Declaire, J. (1997) *Raising an Emotionally Intelligent Child: The heart of parenting*. New York: Fireside.

This is an easy introduction to the strategies of emotion coaching and how they can support emotional intelligence and well-being.

References

Allen, G. (2011) *Early Intervention: The next steps; an independent report to Her Majesty's Government*. London: The Cabinet Office.

Bergin, C. and Bergin, D. (2009) Attachment in the Classroom. *Educational Psychology Review* 21: 141–70.

Blakemore, S-J. and Frith, U. (2005) *The Learning Brain: Lessons for education*. Oxford: Blackwell Publishing.

Bowlby, J. (1969) *Attachment and Loss*. Harmondsworth: Penguin.

Bronfenbrenner, U. (1979) *An Ecology of Human Development*. Cambridge, MA: Harvard University Press.

Brooker, L. (2010) Constructing the Triangle of Care: Power and professionalism in practitioner/parent relationships. *British Journal of Educational Studies* 58(2): 181–96.

DfE (2012) *Ensuring Good Behaviour in Schools: A summary for heads, governing bodies, teachers, parents and pupils*. London: DfE.

DfES (2004) *Every Child Matters: Change for children*. London: DfES.

Ecclestone, K. and Hayes, D. (2009) Changing the Subject: The educational implications of developing emotional well-being. *Oxford Review of Education* 35(3): 371–89.

Ellis, S. and Tod, J. (2009) *Behaviour for Learning: Proactive approaches to behaviour management*. Abingdon: Routledge.

Goleman, D. (1995) *Emotional Intelligence: Why it can matter more than IQ*. New York: Bantam Books.

Goswami. U. (2011) Cognitive Neuroscience and Learning and Development. In: J. Moyles, J. Georgeson and J. Payler (eds) *Beginning Teaching Beginning Learning in Early Years and Primary Education*. Maidenhead: Open University Press.

Gottman, J. and Declaire, J. (1997) *Raising an Emotionally Intelligent Child: The heart of parenting*. New York: Fireside.

Gottman, J., Katz, L. and Hooven, C. (1997) *Meta-Emotion – How families communicate emotionally*. Mahwah, NJ: Lawrence Erlbaum.

Grootenboer, P. (2010) Affective Development in University Education. *Higher Education Research and Development* 29(6): 723–37.

Hoffman, L.W. (2000) Maternal Employment: Effects of social context. In: R.D. Taylor and M.C. Wang (eds) *Resilience across Contexts*. Mahwah, NJ: Lawrence Erlbaum.

Immordino-Yang, M. and Damasio, A. (2007) We Feel, Therefore We Learn: The relevance of affective and social neuroscience to education. *Mind, Brain and Education Journal* 1(1): 3–10.

Jones, E. and Schoon, I. (2008) Child Behaviour and Cognitive Development. In: K. Hansen and H. Joshi (eds) *Millennium Cohort Study*. London: Centre for Longitudinal Studies.

Kumpfer, K.L., Whiteside, H.O., Ahearn Greene, J. and Allen, K.C. (2010) Effectiveness Outcomes of 4 Age Versions of the Strengthening Families Program in State-wide Field Sites. *Theory, Research and Practice* 14(3): 211–29.

MacKay, T., Reynolds, S. and Kearney, M. (2010) From Attachment to Attainment: The impact of nurture groups on academic achievement. *Educational and Child Psychology* 27(3): 100–10.

McNess, E., Broadfoot, P. and Osborn, M. (2003) Is the Effective Compromising the Affective? *British Educational Research Journal* 29(2): 243–57.

Noddings, N. (1992) *The Challenge to Care in Schools*. New York: Teachers College Press.

Olson, C.O. and Wyett, J.L. (2000) Teachers Need Affective Competencies. *Education* 120(4): 741–62.

Robson, S. (2011) Attachment and Relationships. In: J. Moyles, J. Georgeson and J. Payler (eds) *Beginning Teaching Beginning Learning in Early Years and Primary Education*. Maidenhead: Open University Press.

Salovey, P. and Mayer, J.D. (1990) Emotional Intelligence. *Imagination, Cognition and Personality* 9: 185–211.

Shechtman, Z. and Leichtentritt, J. (2004) Affective Teaching: A method to enhance classroom management. *European Journal of Teacher Education* 27(3): 323–33.

Siraj-Blatchford, I. (2007) Diversity, Inclusion and Learning in the Early Years. In: J. Moyles (ed.) *Early Years Foundations: Meeting the challenge.* Maidenhead: Open University Press.

Swick, K.J. (2007) Insights on Caring for Early Childhood Professionals and Families. *Early Childhood Education Journal* 35(2): 97–102.

Underdown, A. (2007) *Young Children's Health and Well-being.* Maidenhead: Open University Press.

UNICEF (2011) *Child Well-being, Poverty and Overlapping Deprivation Analysis in Rich Countries.* Report card 10. Florence: UNICEF Innocenti Research Centre.

Weare, K. and Gray, G. (2003) *What Works in Developing Children's Emotional and Social Competence and Wellbeing?* Nottingham: DfES.

Chapter 19

Arriving in a new place

The ecology of learning

Miriam Hutchings

Introduction

This chapter examines ways of understanding influences on people's experiences of learning. It is designed as a tool for you to reflect on what influences learning and to understand how personal experience and choice interact with the place we are learning in and with the wider world. It is based on the assumption that all learning stems from our histories as learners, how we are connected to others in our learning and how immediate and wider environments shape our responses to learning. Some frameworks for observing, analysing and ways of thinking about learning for education studies are introduced.

Influences on learning

Learning is an intensely personal activity influenced by life experiences, views and approaches. Yet at the same time it seldom happens in isolation and is influenced by whom we learn with and the places where we learn. Illeris (2003, 2009) suggests that it is possible to construct an overview of the field of learning through life founded on two assumptions. The first is to appreciate that learning requires the integration of two processes: 'an external interaction process between the learner and his or her social, cultural or material environment, and an internal psychological process of acquisition and elaboration' (Illeris, 2003: 398).

The second is that learning includes three dimensions:

> [T]he content dimension of knowledge, skills, attitudes, ways of behavior – everything that can be learned – the incentive dimension, mainly dealing with emotions, feelings, volitions and motivations, and the interaction dimension, comprising communication, cooperation and community – all of which are embedded in a societally-situated context.
>
> (Illeris, 2009: 46)

Most theories of learning depict these processes separately giving a partial view of the field. For example, psychological perspectives on thinking tend to focus on the procedures within the mind, the internal processes of cognition such as recognising, understanding, storing information and monitoring performance. For educationalists this translates into an emphasis on thinking skills such as planning, reasoning and remembering within problem solving as a way to support learners in becoming more aware of and able to improve their learning. Similar limitations constrain social learning theories which concentrate on external processes of social interaction, influences and power relationships. For example, from the perspective of situated learning (Lave and Wenger, 1991), learning happens through participation within a community and cannot be separated from the place, social experiences, learning activities and available tools. Perkins (1993) describes 'the person plus': how individuals and communities of learners make use of 'tools' or the immediate physical and social resources (such as people, technology or pictures) to learn. This includes the idea that intelligence does not reside only within the individual but also within the resources used to accomplish learning. Within the classroom this might be viewed as thinking of all the people in the classroom (pupils, teachers, support assistants) working as a community, plus the physical support systems of pens, books and multimedia stories.

Illeris (2003) points out that this tendency towards separating cognitive, emotional and environmental aspects does not mean that these theories are worthless; it is simply that they do not cover the 'whole field of learning' (ibid.: 398). He also suggests that transformative learning is an example of a point in time when all three dimensions (cognitive, emotional and social) undergo dramatic restructuring as new challenges make change necessary in order to progress. What is required to aid us studying learning are frameworks that afford an overview of the landscape of learning. From this perspective it is possible to see how themes from a variety of theories and concepts about learning run in parallel, each contributing differing but significant understandings of what is going on as we look at learning in specific places. Transitions, such as moving countries, starting school or university, are times in our lives when we are most likely to experience changes or transformation.

Arriving in a new place – Laila's story

Laila has spent the first six years of her life in Norway. She grew up speaking Arabic with her father and Norwegian with her mother and in kindergarten. On her first day in a primary school in England she is nervous about the changes in her life, but confident about coping, as she has always been encouraged to join in everything at kindergarten and had good friends in Norway. The children in her new class know the morning routine and start reading with a partner. Laila's teacher has put her with a partner, who smiles and begins to read her book to her. Laila is puzzled. In her kindergarten in Norway no one had a reading book. She listens carefully to her partner who is reading aloud slowly, struggling to work out the words on the page. As Laila looks around the class everyone has a reading book. She was quiet that day, immersing herself in this new environment, watching, listening but getting quite cross. She had never felt that she couldn't do at least the same as everyone else. That evening she went home, determined to teach herself to read. She collected together all her books, asked her parents to help and by the next week was immersed in the reading partners game, determined to be a participant in her new environment.

Laila has what might be called 'a feel for the game' in the field of education. So, despite meeting new practices in the classroom, she has the cultural capital to understand, interpret and act in this new social world (Bourdieu and Waquant, 1992). She uses the practical social competencies learned in Norwegian education to make a choice about how and what she will do in this situation. Laila's choice is to accept the new values and immerse herself in what is required, to take ownership of her learning by learning to read. In order to do this she has to overcome her initial emotions of impatience, frustration and anxiety, to organise her cognitive resources, reflect on what she has to do and, with the support of strong learning relationships within the home, takes the first step in belonging in this new learning environment. This description emphasises the external and internal factors in Laila's transformation as a reader, which might have remained hidden had concentration been on a single dimension. In this example Illeris's (2003) three dimensions of learning – cognitive, emotional (internal) and environment (external) – interact.

Ecological systems

Bronfenbrenner's (2005) bio-ecological model of development suggests that personal, physical and social contexts of learning are interconnected within ecosystems which constantly interact and influence each other; they cannot be understood in isolation. The individual learner lives in microsystems which are connected with meso-systems, embedded within exo-systems. All of these are nested within macro-systems. These interactive systems are fluid and change over time – the chrono-system. Another way of understanding Laila's experiences would be to consider how the different systems she inhabits shift as she moves from Norway to England. The microsystems of kindergarten in Norway and school in England are different. These educational microsystems are influenced by macro-systems of political and policy factors such as differences in the age that children begin formal schooling.

As you read the following outlines of the ecological systems, consider how you might explore the shifts and changes which influence Laila's experiences.

At the core is an individual (the bio), living within 'microsystems' consisting of all the environments a learner inhabits, together with the face-to-face interactions within those environments. Examples include the home, the family and relationships with parents, grandparents, siblings and language/s used. Children inhabit more than one microsystem of places, relationships and languages such as home, education setting, play/social environments, both within school and the neighbourhood.

The 'meso-systems' consist of all the interactions and relationships which influence the learner directly within microsystems. Examples include: how family members relate to each other; how and whether an education setting values and builds positive home/school relationships; how language/s used at home are valued and used within education settings. Another example is parents' perceptions of the safety of their local area and whether there are safe play/social environments where children can meet their friends. Relationships between microsystems are reciprocal – parents and teachers influence each other and this in turn affects the child. When systems work collaboratively rather than in tension, the child's experiences and learning are more likely to be positive.

'Exo-systems' refer to the environments and relationships which the child does not experience first hand, but which have an indirect influence on them. Examples are: employment in the locality; parents' working hours and levels of stress within a workplace influencing home life; whether the education setting actively pursues multilingual policies; whether the organisation of safe play/social environments for young people was a local community and political priority. Although the exo-system is experienced second hand, its influence on the individual can be strong.

The broadest context is the macro-system in which all the other systems are embedded. Every person is a part of a wider political, economic, social and cultural setting which influences the world of individual learners. Economic decisions about relocating a manufacturing industry to another part of the world can change employment opportunities in a locality and have an impact on the embedded systems. Changing government policies affect individuals' experiences of education. Examples are the different Foundation Stage curriculum in England, Wales and Scotland, how community languages and knowledge are marginalised or absent from mainstream English schools and the priority for Welsh and Welsh medium education in Wales.

The chrono-system relates to changes in all the systems over time. Some changes relate to everyday events and transitions within an individual's life story such as transition through an education system for example moving from nursery to school. Other changes connect to critical events such as serious illness, divorce of parents or living in a war zone. Wider social and political shifts in national or global contexts ripple through the systems and affect the life and education of a child. For example, different policies and priorities for education arrive with a new government. Economic recession is likely to bring job losses, financial constraints and cuts to the provision of services such as health and education.

An ecological system suggests ways of understanding the interactions between a range of influences on learning and life. The ecology of learning within a setting becomes not just about how the learner changes, but also about the climate for learning: what kinds of learning relationships it is that educators value; how resourceful settings and individual educators are in drawing on languages, literacies and knowledge within their local environment. Although at first an ecological systems approach appears complicated, the concept of nested systems opens up opportunities for analysing connections across (lateral) systems and through time (temporal). As a child develops so associated systems change; as political, economic and social worlds change so does the experience of the individual.

So far two different frameworks for understanding influences on learners have been reviewed. Illeris's (2003) three dimensions suggest ways of understanding learners and learning within specific places such as classrooms. It offers potential for understanding why individuals learn something different from the same lesson, or the way a learner feels about a lesson, subject or teacher can affect learning. Bronfenbrenner's ecological system suggests that learning is embedded in a web of influences where changes within one of the systems can have a profound effect on learners and learning. The framework offers understanding of questions such as how transition from home into school or from kindergarten in one country to school in another, or from school to university, changes learners.

Transformations in learning

Transformations in learning focus on experience, critical reflection and personal change. The process of transformation begins from experience, moves through critical reflection and discourse to changes in a person's actions within the world (Mezirow, 1998). While transformational learning is most commonly connected with adult learning, Laila's story illustrates how these ideas may also relate to childhood.

Arriving in a new place: Faith's story

Faith's ambition was to be a teacher and a degree in education studies was her starting point. She was 22 and had worked since leaving school. She said:

> I'm the first person in my family to go to university so I didn't know what I was doing really but, umm, it turns out now that ... my family don't speak to me because I go to university.

Faith's early experiences within education studies were varied. A critical point at the beginning of the second year was not getting first year written work returned:

> [I]t just gets a bit annoying because we need to know where we're going wrong or where I need to improve so that's quite tricky ... I don't feel there's any encouragement if you're not getting work back.

Trying to cope on her own in an unsupportive environment had resulted in anxiety, anger, fear and failure in some assignments. Her aspirations wavered:

> I'm finding it really hard and I'm not sure whether I can be a teacher.

Faith was seeking ways of overcoming her prior negative educational experiences and her new identity as a learner with dyslexia. The wide choice of modules and broad scope of content was appealing but her experiences varied:

> [S]ome tutors really motivate you and get you to think and feel passionate about a subject, others just read slides and add nothing to it.

Active participatory learning, in some modules, helped her reflect on and evaluate her prior negative experiences and appreciate ways of teaching that might have helped her and would benefit all children. It is important to connect her experience to learning in education studies:

> [T]he compulsory module – that's really hard – but the SEN module because I'm interested in special needs I focus a lot more on what I'm doing.

In her final year Faith continued to find relevance through module and assignment choices linked to SEN. But it is experiences beyond education studies that trigger the most significant changes in surviving academic work. Sustained support from a support tutor, funded by Disability Support Allowance (DSA), was finally in place and she was finally gaining control over aspects of studying that she had found so difficult. What has shifted is her knowledge of her cognitive processes (meta-cognitive monitoring) and regulation of these processes (meta-cognitive regulation) especially in reading, writing and organising study for the course.

Faith says what is most important is

having people support you.

Most important was support in her personal life from her partner and his family:

> *I've now sort of got a family as such, like with my boyfriend they've kind of like adopted me into their family, so now I've got like a home if I ever need to go back to one. So yeah lots of relationships have got a lot stronger over the last year.*

It is more than just social relationships that shift. Faith is becoming became part of a professional family familiar with academic worlds and dyslexia. Her partner's sister is a successful professional who manages her dyslexia and offers her insight into what is possible. Faith's view of the world is shifting and the possibility of gaining a degree is becoming a reality.

While social relationships and growing control over her studies have changed. Faith's relationship with education studies shifts less dramatically. Although she still values how relevant it is to her experiences and aspirations, and reflects on what supports her learning, she continues to have experiences that dishearten and puzzle her, such as receiving a low mark for an assignment that she felt had been completed according to a tutor's guidance.

As Faith progresses through the degree her mark profile shifts and in the final year she achieved some 2.1s and graduated with a 2.2 degree.

> *I keep thinking to myself, if I had the help in the second year and I didn't have all these family things going on, I probably would be 2:1 It's about recognising where your dyslexia kicks in and just managing it. It's all about managing dyslexia; it's not that people are stupid. It's just they need to find other ways. Because they're intelligent people, just in different ways I think.*

As you read the following discussion on learning from experience, critical reflection and epistemological transformations consider how Faith changes as she progresses through her education studies degree.

Learning from experience

Throughout our lives we are immersed in experiences that shape our assumptions about ourselves and our worlds. Jarvis (2006, 2007) argues that we spend much of our lives in situations that are taken for granted and over time develop categories and classifications that provide a framework for making sense of and acting in our worlds. It is only at points where tacit ways of thinking are disturbed (disjuncture) that individuals become more consciously aware of the need to act to in order to reconstruct or to retain harmony in their lives. How we respond to critical events and disjuncture depends on the degree to which a tacit harmony with the world is challenged, and the level of learning required to re-establish harmony.

Critical reflection

Reflection is the act of looking back on experiences or looking forward to plan from them. In education it also refers to questioning an experience (Jarvis, 2006). The importance of reflection has a long tradition in education. Critical reflection on experience is a key concept underpinning transformative learning processes. Mezirow (1981) suggests that 'premise reflection' involves exploring the deeply rooted assumptions, beliefs and values socially constructed through our lives and is central to transformative learning. The change could be a radical new view of ourselves and the world we inhabit, or a deeper understanding of existing beliefs and values in how we view the world. Other kinds of reflection contribute to the process. First 'content reflection': thinking about an experience, such as understanding the ideas in this chapter. Second 'process reflection': thinking about the strategies for managing the experience or problem-solving around ideas that are new or difficult to understand. Transformational learning is about: 'dramatic, fundamental change in the way we see ourselves and the world in which we live' (Merriam *et al.*, 2006: 130).

Epistemological transformations: Ways of knowing

Epistemological transformation is the way that students make meaning from or interpret their experiences of a university education based on changes in their assumptions about the nature, limits and certainty of knowledge. It is concerned with questions such as what we know, how we know and how far we can say something is true. Changes in ways of knowing are a central part of how education studies expects students to think critically:

> The fully developed capacity to think critically relies on an understanding of knowledge as constructed and related to its context (relativistic) and it is not possible if knowledge is viewed only in an absolute manner (i.e. knowledge as a series of facts).
>
> (Moon, 2005: 12)

Baxter Magolda's (2004) framework is one perspective on how our relations with knowledge construction may change as a result of a university education. A version of the four stages, written to support first-year students in questioning their ways of knowing, is set out briefly below.

1. Absolute knowing

Knowledge is absolute if I learn the RIGHT answers. If I acquire the knowledge teachers give me all will be well.

2. Transitional knowing

Some knowledge is uncertain; what about other ideas and different opinions? Researchers seem to disagree with each other or don't know. All will be well if I just try and understand and not just acquire information.

3. Independent knowing

Knowledge is uncertain, differences simply represent the range of possible ideas in an uncertain world. I recognise myself as a participant who has to find a voice and make decisions in an uncertain world.

4. Contextual knowing

Knowledge comes from integrating the ideas of others with one's own, some truth claims are better than others; I recognise how to judge evidence supporting claims to truth and build them into my thinking and views. I can see that I will be tracing this whole journey over and over – but, I hope, more wisely each time.

Shifts in epistemological beliefs and thinking do not occur in a vacuum; they are related to pedagogy in the subject and peer/teacher interactions. As Faith indicates, differing experiences of modules, teachers and peer interaction promote or restrain possibilities for reflection and change within education studies.

A narrative turn

The case stories presented here have been used to explore frameworks for thinking about learning. Narrative is one way of analysing social realities as a basis for understanding social and inner worlds (Gubrium and Holstein, 2009). Laila's social world has been explored through bio-ecological systems theory and Faith's story offers a window on her inner world through the lens of transformations in learning. Prominent in ways of thinking about narrative is how stories are a way of thinking, through which humans make sense of self, their lives and worlds (Biesta *et al.*, 2008; Brunner, 2002). However, stories are never neutral, they are constructed, told to someone and have consequences. For example if you are asked 'why don't you tell me about yourself?' How you respond will be influenced by the social setting (a job interview, first date, research interview) and who is asking (friend, potential boss, teacher, social worker). The environments of story mediate what we choose to tell, how we tell and the meaning of accounts (Gubrium and Holstein, 2009).

Bruner (1990) considers how human experience is constructed through narrative and suggests that narrative frames our worlds and ways of thinking:

> Narrative provides a means of constructing a world, characterising its flow, of segmenting its events within that world, and so on. If we were not able to do such framing, we would be lost in a murk of chaotic experience and would probably not have survived as a species.
>
> (Bruner, 1990: 56)

At the same time Bruner (1996) argues that while we are competent habitual storytellers it is difficult to achieve consciousness of something we do so automatically. The solution, he suggests, lies in:

- Contrast: how two observers see the same thing happening and come away with different stories; or how differing accounts of a phenomenon can 'see' the world in different ways. How the two stories in this chapter open different possibilities for analysis.
- Confrontation: finding your narrative construction of reality conflicts with reality claims of others.

Both can be sources for acknowledging relativity in the construction of knowledge through:

- Critical reflection: thinking about how we know what we know and a reasoned basis for understanding.

I have suggested that through critical reflection on narrative we can contrast and confront our taken-for-granted views of the world. This can involve a personal journey of seeking out writings and research about young people's views of their experience.

Conclusion

This chapter has introduced some frameworks for theorising about what influences learning at different times and places. The frameworks have potential for exploring how individuals' educational careers are linked to wider contexts. The two stories were selected to demonstrate three interwoven strands:

- individuals: their personal stories of learning;
- contexts: influences from the immediate place of learner, and wider exo- and macro-systems;
- journeys: stories of how individuals negotiate their way through.

Together they suggest the importance of understanding how learning is connected to histories of experience and across structures that frame our learning. Much of what happens in education settings operates in a murky world of hidden practices and is based on collectively assumed values. At the same time the places and the policies of education are increasingly influenced by external forces locally, nationally and globally. These frameworks suggest that theory should engage with dilemmas, tensions, contradictions and the partiality of current western research on learning. A fully comprehensive theory of learning is probably not achievable. However, it is possible and practical to work with multiple perspectives to inform our thinking. To have schools and universities suitable for the education of diverse learners and capable of including vulnerable learners, we need tools to trigger reflection on what it means to be a learner in this place and at this time.

Summary points

- Learning is a complex interaction between external influences and internal processes.
- The frameworks introduced are 'tools' for reflecting on influences in learning. As such they suggest some starting points for theorising the contexts and processes of learning.
- Laila's and Faith's stories illustrate how learning is connected to individuals, contexts and their journey over time.
- Narrative is one way of analysing social realities and a basis for understanding of inner and outer social worlds.
- Multiple perspectives offer opportunities to view different theories and concepts as part of or contributing to a wider picture.

Questions for discussion

- How do these frameworks help you identify the influences on Laila's and Faith's learning?

- Where and when might you use these frameworks to observe, analyse and reflect on learning?
- When and how are you expected to write about your learning story and critically reflect on your learning and relations with the construction of knowledge?
- How do these frameworks connect to other perspectives on learning?

Recommended reading

Many organisations and charitable foundations conduct research in which young people and their views are central. The following three examples introduce UK and international studies:

Bold, C. (2012) *Using Narrative in Research*. London, SAGE.
An introduction to the use of narrative in research in social settings. It uses a range of examples many from foundation degree and education studies students.

Johnson, V. and Nurick, R. (2006) *Gaining Respect: The voices of the children in conflict with the law.* London: Save the Children. Available online at http://www.savethechildren.org.uk/sites/default/files/docs/gainingrespect_1.pdf (accessed 6 May 2012).

Knight, A. (2011) *What Have I Done? The experiences of children and families in UK immigration detention: Lessons to learn.* London: The Children's Society. Available online at http://www.childrenssociety.org.uk/what-we-do/research/research-publications (accessed 6 May 2012).

Wallace, W. (2005) *Life in an Inner City Primary School.* London Routledge.
A portrait of a year in an inner city primary school is a good starting point for contrast, confrontation and critical reflection on your experiences of school.

References

Baxter Magolda, M.B. (2004) *Making Their Own Way: Narratives for transforming higher education to promote self-development.* Sterling, VA: Stylus Publishing.

Biesta, G. Goodson, I., Tedder, M. and Adair, N. (2008) *Learning from Life: The role of narrative.* (Learning Lives. Summative Working Paper 2). London: Teaching and Learning Research Programme. Available online at http://www.learninglives.org/ (accessed 6 May 2012).

Bourdieu, P. and Wacquant, L.J.D. (1992) *An Invitation to Reflexive Sociology.* Cambridge: Polity Press.

Bronfenbrenner, U. (2005) *Making Human Beings Human: Bioecological perspectives on human development.* Thousand Oaks, CA: London: Sage.

Bruner, J. (1990) *Acts of Meaning.* London: Harvard University Press.

Bruner, J. (1996) *The Culture of Education.* London: Harvard University Press.

Bruner, J. (2002) *Making stories, law, literature, life.* Massachusetts: Harvard University Press.

Gubrium, J.F. and Holstein, J.A. (2009) *Analyzing Narrative Reality.* Los Angeles, CA, London: Sage.

Illeris, K. (2003) Towards a Contemporary and Comprehensive Theory of Learning. *International Journal of Lifelong Learning* 22(4): 396–406.

Illeris, K. (2009) A Comprehensive Understanding of Human Learning. *International Journal of Continuing Education and Lifelong Learning* 2(1): 45–63.

Jarvis, P. (2006) *Towards a Comprehensive Theory of Human Learning.* London: Routledge.

Jarvis, P. (2007) *Globalisation, Lifelong Learning and the Learning Society: Sociological perspectives.* London: Routledge.

Lave, J. and Wenger, E. (1991) *Situated Learning: Legitimate peripheral participation.* Cambridge: Cambridge University Press.

Merriam, S.B. Caffarella, R. and Baumgartner, L. (2006) *Learning in Adulthood: A comprehensive guide* (3rd edn). San Francisco, CA, Chichester: Jossey-Bass.

Mezirow, J. (1981) A Critical Theory of Adult Education and Learning *Adult Education Quarterly* 32(1): 3–24.

Mezirow, J. (1998) On Critical Reflection. *Adult Education Quarterly* 48(3): 185–98.

Moon, J. (2005) *We Seek it Here... A New Perspective on the Elusive Activity of Critical Thinking: A theoretical and practical approach.* (Discussions in Education Series no. 1) Bristol: ESCalate. Available online at http://escalate.ac.uk/2041 (accessed 6 December 2012).

Perkins, D.N. (1993) Person-plus distributed view of thinking and learning. In: Salomon, G. (ed.) *Distributed Cognitions: Psychological and practical considerations.* Cambridge: Cambridge University Press.

Chapter 20

Culture, creativity and learning
Arts education for a changing world

June Bianchi

Introduction

While academic achievement is of paramount concern within a contemporary curriculum, children's and young people's holistic potential to participate, contribute and understand their role as citizens in a diverse and changing society must also be a key educational aspiration. Rapid political, economic and cultural shifts taking place globally mean that children are being educated to contribute to societal contexts which are in transition. Alongside core skills of numeracy and literacy, creativity and cultural awareness must also be central tenets if the twenty-first century curriculum is to address the needs of lifelong learners across a range of changing sociocultural and educational settings.

Cultural and creative learning are essential attributes in equipping young people with the broad-ranging knowledge and skills for a world of increasingly pluralist values and complexity. While creativity and cultural learning can take place across the entire curriculum, this chapter advocates the significance of arts education. Current curriculum changes threaten this vital aspect of education policy and practice, risking impoverishment of young people's life experiences, and restrictions to their aspirations and potential.

Societal and political changes inform curricular philosophies and practice; this chapter will engage with current issues, debates and theories in an overview of relevant policies promoting the significance of the arts in education over more than 50 years. It discusses recent policy and practice in promoting creative and cultural learning through arts education, exploring the following:

- perspectives on cultural and creative learning;
- a historical overview of key educational policies and agendas on creative and cultural education;
- implementing creative and cultural strategies through arts education.

Perspectives on cultural and creative learning: a background to theoretical approaches

The significance of creative approaches across all domains of the curriculum is outlined by Craft (2005): '[C]reativity is situated in knowledge, both conceptual and procedural … creative action and thought are possible in any area of knowledge on the basis that at its heart is "possibility thinking"' (Craft, 2005: 41). Correlating the development of creativity with raising cultural awareness, Robinson (2001) recommends a partnership of creative practitioners and educators in addressing both individual and societal needs. Creativity, like culture, is presented as acculturated rather than an individualist phenomenon: 'Creativity can be inspired or stifled by cultural conditions. Understanding the culture of creativity is essential to being able to promote it in organizations and in nations' (Robinson, 2001: 167).

A hierarchy privileging subjects conventionally regarded as 'academic' is prevalent throughout the western world, but this paradigm has been widely challenged. Recognition of domains of experience other than the cognitive is well established, with approaches such as Gardner's (2011) theory of multiple intelligences which regards intelligence as multi-perspectival, rather than entirely logical–deductive. Gardner's model incorporates traditional spectrums of intelligence such as mathematical and linguistic, as well as modes of engagement with the arts: visual and spatial, musical and kinaesthetic; with human consciousness: interpersonal, intrapersonal, spiritual and existential; and with the phenomenological world – naturalist. While Gardner's premise is widely respected as an influential theory, demanding acknowledgement of both intelligence orientation and pedagogy on learners, it has had no effect on the traditional hierarchical curriculum. The more quantifiable modes of intelligence remain dominant within mainstream education internationally.

The privileging of cognitive intelligences in western culture and education reflects a society where achievement in these spheres garners respect, status and success. Gardner proposes a wider perspective, valuing cultures predicated on skills other than the mathematical–linguistic. For example a tribal society relying on shared enterprise, spatial skills and physical stamina fosters contrasting modes of intelligence in its urban western counterpart. Yet there is still reluctance to offer 'non-academic' areas of the curriculum equal importance to the traditionally academic spheres. Such preferences reflect the underlying ethos of a society, indicative of its dominant ideologies, values and aspirations. As Mihaly Csikszentmihalyi (2002: 218) observes, 'every human culture, by definition, contains meaning systems that can serve as the encompassing purpose by which individuals can order their goals'.

Such meaning systems are disseminated implicitly and explicitly throughout a society's entire cultural milieu; as Raymond Williams comments, 'culture is ordinary'; it takes place in 'the whole of life' as well as in domains we associate with the notion of culture: 'in institutions, and in arts and learning' (Williams cited in Higgins, 2001: 11). Cultural institutions such as galleries, theatres and concert halls bestow value on artists' production, establishing and reinforcing stratification of value by their patronage and support. Yet cultural theorists such as Williams have criticised this hierarchical approach to culture, its social divisiveness and perpetuation of unequal access and opportunity. Challenges to colonialism, class and patriarchy, from feminism, queer theory, post-colonialism and anti-globalisation activists, also challenge cultural supremacy, while postmodernism proposes the notion of parallel or competing narratives countering traditional paradigmatic structures.

Pluralist discourses present a breakdown of adherence to past judgements on what constitutes quality and value. As sociologist Bourdieu (1984) contends, the ability to operate across the spectrum of levels of cultural production, demonstrating a grasp of nuances of meaning and function, amounts to a valuable commodity which he calls 'cultural capital'. While ownership of cultural capital may not convey monetary wealth, it does give 'symbolic profit' (ibid.: 230), the acquisition of cultural knowledge and the corresponding level of social confidence and esteem.

Within this arena of cultural synthesis, educationalists acknowledge diversity of experiences and perspectives within the pluralist society encompassing British life. The National Curriculum has championed respect and understanding of cultural diversity, yet tension still exists in balancing the needs of antithetical cultural traditions. Nevertheless the curriculum has attempted to reflect the melange of sociocultural experiences constituting British life and to recognise the diversity of expression and experience in a heterogeneous society. The National Curriculum review, in process since the Coalition Government was formed in 2010, has promoted an English Baccalaureate (EBac) (see Chapter 1). Yet EBac appears retrograde with its emphasis on traditional 'academic' subjects, omitting arts subjects: visual art, drama, music, media studies from the 14–16 core curriculum (DfE, 2012) alongside citizenship and religious education. The cross-party Education Select Committee's (2011) report on the EBac raised concerns, advocating further consultation and recommending that plans for certification should be shelved. The report warned that it could engender 'a negative impact on the most vulnerable or disadvantaged young people', stating that 'all young people, regardless of background, must continue to have opportunities to study the subjects in which they are likely to be most successful, and which pupils, parents and schools think will serve them best'.

Ideally, a reformed National Curriculum would develop creative and cultural strategies to stimulate appreciation and respect in celebrating our diverse traditions, beliefs, values and cultural idioms, alongside fostering academic achievement. Provision is currently made through cross-curricular dimensions, as well as through designated subjects, particularly the arts and humanities. Creative and cultural learning can encompass a broad spectrum of issues impacting upon young people's well-being, including identity, cultural diversity, health, sustainability, critical thinking and citizenship. Such holistic approaches address aspects of students' experiences as individuals, as well as engaging them as citizens contributing to a changing society.

Learning through culture and creativity: An overview of key education policies

Statistics gathered and published invariably emphasise the centrality of core skills within the curriculum. Levels of numeracy and literacy are routinely monitored, compared and evaluated across local, national and international settings (see Chapter 10). UNESCO's Global Education Digest compares educational attainment across the world as 'a measure of the skills and competencies of a country's population and, thus, an indicator of the quantitative and qualitative aspects of the stock of human capital'. While levels of literacy are regarded as key to furthering educational capacity and 'human capital, which is one of the main determinants of economic growth' (UNESCO, 2011: 30), UNESCO also analyses international curricula in relation to their inclusion of wider knowledge bases focusing on science, humanities, arts and physical education. The need for a broad spectrum of learning experiences within a balanced curriculum has long been recognised and can be charted in education policy over the last half century. This section examines the advocacy of creative and cultural aspects of education encapsulated through the arts, highlighting a range of key policy documents within the United Kingdom (UK) spanning over half a century. Concerns repeatedly expressed over this period are equally relevant in addressing both societal and curricular change today.

The 1967 Plowden Report set out to provide a comprehensive review of primary education and secondary transition at a time of significant educational change. Under a Labour Government led by Harold Wilson, the move towards egalitarianism included replacement of the grammar school system with comprehensive education; group streaming was superseded by a focus on children's individual needs. Espousing a liberal view of child-centred learning, informed by Piaget's theories of development, Plowden argued for more equable, inclusive provision across a wide spectrum of socio-economic need. It regarded learning through the arts as an essential curriculum component, not only for the developing child, but also for a healthy society:

> Art is both a form of communication and a means of expression of feelings which ought to permeate the whole curriculum and the whole life of the school. A society which neglects or despises it is dangerously sick. It affects, or should affect, all aspects of our life from the design of the commonplace articles of everyday life to the highest forms of individual expression.
>
> (Plowden, 1967: 246)

Some 20 years later, following the 1988 Education Reform Act, the Conservative Government led by Margaret Thatcher established the National Curriculum, to ensure commonality of provision across the state sector. Schools within both primary and secondary phases were required to provide a core curriculum of subjects. Both art and design and music were identified as single subject areas while drama and dance were part of the English and physical education subject orders respectively. This curriculum provision remained in place, for state-funded schools in the UK, during the New Labour Government, although the 2010 Coalition Government's National Curriculum review presents a threat to the position of the arts. *The Arts in Schools Report* (Robinson, 1989) focused specifically on the role of the arts within the curriculum, reiterating the Plowden Report's emphasis on their relevance. Its agenda, over 40 years after its publication, is as pertinent as ever. The following societal conditions were cited by Robinson (1989: 3) as key factors in raising the profile of the arts within education:

a. the profound and long-term changes in the patterns of employment and of unemployment, especially among young people;
b. the changing relationships between education and society as a whole which must result from this;
c. the rate of cultural change in Britain.

Addressing these three core considerations, editor Sir Ken Robinson suggests that the challenges present in 1989 should be countered by an education system that does not merely address current employment needs, but also generates 'intuition, creativity, sensibility and practical skills' (Robinson, 1989: 5). These are prerequisites for enabling learners to generate new employment opportunities and adapt to societal change. The report advocates a curriculum balanced between logical deductive skills and expressive capacities, arguing that cultural and creative qualities engendered through the arts develop flexibility and understanding, and the ability to grasp pluralist perspectives and values. Such heterogeneity of thinking enables citizens to respond positively to the benefits and challenges of living within an increasingly culturally diverse world and to contributing effectively to it. Robinson identifies both our immediate society and the wider world as a cornucopia of differences to be understood, celebrated and assimilated: 'a rich mixture of regional, racial and class differences — differences in language, values, religion, political and cultural interests' (Robinson, 1989: 37); such factors provide a continuing agenda for contemporary education.

Throughout the 1997–2010 period of the New Labour Government, the National Curriculum purported to acknowledge the importance of learning beyond the boundaries of core subject knowledge. Nevertheless, in 1998, a narrowing of the curriculum was caused by the National Literacy and Numeracy Strategies (see Chapter 16), with limitations in provision for young people's creative and cultural development. This resulted in the formation of the National Advisory Committee on Creative and Cultural Education (NACCCE). Again chaired by Sir Ken Robinson, NACCCE investigated provision and made recommendations to the Secretary of State for Education and Employment and the Secretary of State for Culture, Media and Sport (DCMS). Its report, *All Our Futures: Creativity, Culture and Education* (1999), placed creativity and cultural education as interrelated key components within an education system that could enable young people to foster skills, knowledge and understanding to respond to a changing society. Defining creativity as 'imaginative activity fashioned so as to produce outcomes that are both original and of value' (NACCCE, 1999: 30), the report presented a democratic perception of creative engagement, regarding it as attainable by everyone across the full spectrum of subject disciplines. It construed cultural learning, in its most democratic sense, as taking place across 'shared values and patterns of behaviour that characterise different social groups and communities' (ibid.: 47).

The NACCCE Report demanded government support for creative and cultural education and for training to enable teachers to 'facilitate development of young people's creative abilities and cultural understanding' (ibid.: 12). A direct response was the establishment of the *Creative Partnerships* initiative by the DCMS in 2002, managed by the Arts Council of England. It provided opportunities for young people aged 5–18 years in deprived areas to develop their creativity and experience, working collaboratively with a range of partners. The initiative fostered partnerships between multidisciplinary agencies: schools, arts practitioners, creative organisations and businesses. Its mission statement pronounced the potential of the arts to extend and stimulate: 'creativity is not simply about doing the arts – it is about questioning, making connections, inventing and reinventing, about flexing the imaginative muscles' (Creative Partnerships, 2012).

Based in 36 areas of England, *Creative Partnerships* involved children in approximately one third of schools across the educational sector. Despite their wide-ranging projects incorporating *Cultural Hubs* and *Schools of Creativity* initiatives, *Creative Partnerships* was not sustained by the Coalition Government; its funding ceased after the final round of 2011 projects. Aiming not only to inspire young people to be innovative, risk-taking, adventurous and cooperative members of society, but also to rejuvenate teachers through productive and regenerative connections between educationalists, arts professionals and institutions, *Creative Partnerships* leaves a lasting legacy. It is hoped that its aims for promoting cultural activities among young people, fostering sustainable networks between schools and cultural sector organisations, while providing professional development provision for staff in the educational sector, will continue through alternative funding.

The processes of crossing disciplinary boundaries to foster creative collaborations have been widely celebrated through dissemination of partner projects, still viewable on the Creative Partnership website. The Cultural Learning Alliance (CLA) document, *Imagine Nation: The Case for Cultural Learning* (2011) presents a persuasive rationale for maintaining creativity and cultural education within a revised curriculum. It presents evidence for improved cognitive abilities, attainment, social participation and employability. Vigorously supporting the significance of creative and cultural learning across all aspects of human experience and endeavour, CLA advocates the place of arts subjects within the curriculum for 'depth, rigour and an established canon of knowledge. They are of equal weight, status, value and importance within the curriculum as other subjects, and require equal resource and provision' (CLA, 2011: 16).

As part of their curriculum reform process the 2010 Coalition Government asked Classic FM Managing Director, Darren Henley, to produce an independent review, *Cultural Education in England* (2012) for the DCMS and for the Department for Education (DfE). Henley, who undertook a review of music education in 2011, argued for universal access to cultural and creative educational opportunities across statutory education. His vision for cultural education included 'ensuring that all children and young people in England, no matter what their background, circumstances or location, receive the highest quality Cultural Education both in school and out of school, in formal and in informal settings' (Henley, 2012:.4). Henley advocates a rethinking of EBac's 'academic' emphasis:

> If we are to create a generation of fully rounded individuals, then the government should consider whether an education in at least one cultural subject (aside from English literature and history) to at least GCSE level should be mandatory... This would include Cultural Education subjects such as art and design, dance, drama, design technology, film studies and music.
>
> (Henley 2012: 41)

Henley's plea for increased access to the arts, creativity and culture within a well-rounded contemporary educational system provides a welcome addition to the 50 years of policy documents and reviews calling for the same. It is hoped that the Cultural Review will lend weight in determining the focus of the revised National Curriculum and provide incentives for the inclusion of the arts.

Creative and cultural strategies: Transformation through arts education

The curriculum from the foundation phase through to completion of GCSE examinations at Key Stage 4 and post-16 is constantly under review. The current curriculum review takes place against a backdrop of wider educational change informed by a neoliberal agenda informed by the political rhetoric of individual choice, implemented through rapid decentralisation (see Chapter 1). Newly constituted academies and free schools, such as the established network of private schools, are not required to implement a government-determined curriculum. Nevertheless a new curriculum is in process, which will hopefully incorporate established good practice, with continued commitment to addressing wider societal and cultural issues extending beyond narrow academic achievement.

The *Every Child Matters* (ECM) legislation established by the New Labour Government (DfES, 2004) placed pressure on educational institutions to support young people's spiritual, moral, social and cultural needs (SMSC), along with their physical, emotional and intellectual personal development. Schools were required to demonstrate the extent to which the curriculum contributed to meeting the five ECM outcomes, addressing children and young people's health, safety, achievement and enjoyment, their ability to contribute to society and their economic well-being (see Chapter 2). These are laudable aims, but are less easily measured than the statistical data of external examinations and standard assessment tests (SATs) results published in school league tables. While Ofsted does acknowledge wider aspects of a school's provision such as SMSC, the challenge lies with the government to more fully redress the balance in priorities set for schools' achievement, ensuring that support is provided for schools to fulfil their social as well as their academic duty to pupils.

Economic and sociocultural factors can place additional pressure on schools in meeting both academic and ECM outcomes. Schools in socially deprived environments, attempting to meet extensive social needs alongside academic targets and league tables, risk being demoralised by a curriculum that does not fully support their holistic aims. Reduction of the status of arts subjects which contribute to wider creative and cultural learning, to developing future economic growth, as well as providing fulfilling leisure activities for young people, is detrimental to the economic and social needs of its future citizens, particularly those vulnerable to unemployment and cultural exclusion. CLA's research suggests that immersion in the arts widens creative engagement and cultural understanding, encouraging students' aspirations and addressing priority social, political and economic agendas.

Partnership is a unifying factor within all of the policies and reviews discussed here; it is widely regarded as essential that inclusive creative and cultural education should challenge the limitations and prejudice that destroy students' potential. Henley regards cultural education as 'driven by partnership, with government departments, non-departmental government bodies, the National Lottery, local authorities, schools, cultural organisations, voluntary organisations, the creative and cultural industries, conservation practitioners, business sponsors, charities and philanthropists all contributing' (Henley, 2012: 8). Partnership-based creative and cultural projects build individuals' self-esteem, promoting human rights and extending understanding and appreciation of diversity. Such values are pivotal within the Centre for Research in Arts Education (CRAE) based at Bath Spa University, where educational and arts professionals initiate innovative, pluralist arts projects across age, ability and need, with local, national and international educational and cultural partners. CRAE's partnership projects foster arts participation alongside educational foci related to global development, citizenship, personal, social, health and economic (PSHE) education, and SMSC. Building international partnerships with Europe, India and Africa (Bianchi, 2009, 2011), CRAE's local participants are drawn from primary, secondary, arts specialist, tertiary and special school settings. Projects incorporate interdisciplinary arts strategies featuring events and workshops instigated by arts professionals leading to performances, exhibitions, sculpture trails and creative writing outcomes, linking diverse learners in collaborative endeavour.

CRAE's partners include arts organisations affiliated to the research centre such as *5x5x5=creativity* and *My Future My Choice (MFMC)*. South-west England's arts-based action research organisation, *5x5x5=creativity* initially engaged five schools in partnership

with an artist and cultural centre. Now based in over 55 schools, it applies an investiga-
tive, process-based approach, informed by the *Reggio Emilia* system of education. Research
Director Penny Hay affirms that *5x5x5* addresses all five ECM outcomes, and identifies
four key creative elements instrumental within the research process: values, relationships,
environments, behaviours and dispositions. Artistic outcomes are process-focused,
emerging from exploratory child-centred methodologies which support learners 'as independent, creative and reflective thinkers involved in rich and authentic learning' (Bancroft
et al., 2008: 4).

Operating on both cognitive and affective levels of learning, the arts engender personal
and social change in a powerful and direct form. MFMC's Director, Hugh Thomas,
describes the process as 'embodied learning', empirical insights applying culture and
creativity in practice. Working with industry, cultural and educational partners, MFMC
aims to raise participants' aspirations and esteem, widening their perspectives and access
to opportunities, and fostering 'the self-belief that they can achieve and be successful in
whatever they chose to do' (MFMC, 2012). MFMC deploys local expertise from multimedia, culture and other industries, engaging learning communities nationally through
collaborative projects and learning resources. Partnership projects frequently focus on
widening the cultural access of students from socio-economically disadvantaged areas,
introducing them to cultural venues, professional contexts and learning partners beyond
their immediate environment.

Establishing creative and cultural partnerships, providing space for experimentation and
innovation, and generating interdisciplinary links within and beyond institutions
are central strategies in the practice described here. Ofsted's (2012) *Making a Mark* report
on art, craft and design education also advocates curricular links: 'sustained partnerships
with art galleries and creative practitioners' and supporting 'subject leaders in articulating
and evaluating their specific contribution to the creative and cultural development of
all pupils' (Ofsted, 2012: 4). Recommendations require continued investment in future
curricula and further extension of EBac's syllabus.

Conclusion

Practitioners and theorists share commitment to the arts as transformational tools, engaging learners in creative and cultural activities which facilitate extrinsic and intrinsic
benefits to themselves and their community. The challenge to government is to recognise
the potential of creative and cultural strategies in evolving educational policy. Current
educational paradigms are predicated on notions of western society as post-industrial and
systems-based; yet evidence suggests that global societies are in flux, struggling to respond
to economic, environmental and cultural challenges. New possibilities demand acknowledgement through educational legislation and change. While publication of cultural
policy and reviews signals awareness of issues impacting upon education, teachers
arguably need strategies beyond the provision of further reading matter in order to address
the challenge of a wider educational agenda. If creative and cultural education is to be
more than a theoretical paradigm, teachers need to develop their own skills in order
to meet the needs of learners in their care. Craft (2005: 49) contends 'teaching for creativity and fostering creative learning all involve a high level of pedagogical sensitivity
and skilfulness', and creative teachers need inspiration and resources to enable them to
meet the challenge.

Summary points

- Creative and cultural theorists challenge narrow subject hierarchies, advocating pluralist educational perspectives to foster diverse intelligences and learning.
- An overview of policy documents expounds the need for creative and cultural education to be recognised as pivotal in children's development.
- Cultural and creative partnerships develop key knowledge and skills, equipping learners for twenty-first century life.
- Arts education incorporates strategies to address wider holistic educational agendas.

Questions for discussion

- Identify holistic skills enhanced through creative and cultural engagement discussed in key policy documents.
- How can creative and cultural strategies contribute to wider learning across the curriculum?
- How can cultural and educational institutions foster creative and cultural education locally, nationally and internationally?
- Could partnerships between educational and cultural institutions extend provision for creative and cultural education in your locality?

Recommended reading

Banaji, S. and Burn, A. with Buckingham, D. (2010) *The Rhetorics of Creativity: A literature review* (2nd edn). Newcastle Upon Tyne: Creativity, Culture and Education. Available online at http://www.creativitycultureeducation.org/wp-content/uploads/rhetorics-of-creativity-2nd-edition-87.pdf (accessed 12 May 2012).
An overview of key literature on creativity, outlining perspectives such as democratic, political, social, cognitive, economic.

Fleming, M. (2011) *The Arts in Education: An introduction to aesthetics, theory and pedagogy.* London: David Fulton.
Analysis of current debates within arts education in relation to policy, theory and practice.

Meager, N. (2011) *Creativity and Culture: Art projects for primary schools.* London: Collins Educational Press.
Inspirational strategies for developing creative and cultural art projects addressing wider learning.

References

Bancroft, S., Fawcett, M. and Hay, P. (2008) *Researching Children Researching the World: 5X5X5=creativity,* Stoke on Trent: Trentham Books.

Bianchi, J. (2009) *Myth meaning and spectacle: Understanding Indian arts and culture.* Corsham, Wiltshire: NSEAD.

Bianchi, J. (2011) Life Stories: An intercultural collaborative arts project. *AD* Issue 3. Corsham, Wiltshire: NSEAD.

Bourdieu, P. (1984) *Distinction: A social critique of the judgement of taste,* London: Routledge and Kegan Paul.

Craft, A. (2005) *Creativity in Schools: Tensions and dilemmas.* Abingdon: Routledge.

Creative Partnerships (2012) Available online at http://www.creative-partnerships.com/about/about-cp/ (accessed 3 May 2012).

Csikszentmihalyi, M. (2002) *Flow: The classic work on how to achieve happiness.* London: Rider.

Cultural Learning Alliance (2011) *Imagine Nation: The case for cultural learning.* Available online at http://www.culturallearningalliance.org.uk/userfiles/files/FINAL_ImagineNation_The_Case_for_Cultural_Learning.pdf (accessed 3 May 2012).

DfE (2010) *The English Baccalaureate* London: DfE. Available online at http://www.education.gov.uk/schools/teachingandlearning/qualifications/englishbac/a0075975/theenglishbaccalaureate (accessed 3 May 2012).

DfE (2012) *English Baccalaureate.* London: DfE. Available online at http://www.education.gov.uk/schools/teachingandlearning/qualifications/englishbac (accessed 14 September 2012).

DfES (2004) *Every Child Matters: Change for children in schools.* London: DfES.

Education Committee (2011) *Fifth Report English Baccalaureate.* Available online at http://www.publications.parliament.uk/pa/cm201012/cmselect/cmeduc/851/85102.htm (accessed 3 May 2012).

Gardner, H. (2011) *Frames of Mind: The theory of multiple intelligences* (3rd edn). New York: Basic Books.

Henley, D. (2012) *Cultural Education in England: An independent review by Darren Henley.* London: DCMS.

Higgins, J. (ed.) *The Raymond Williams Reader.* Oxford: Blackwell.

My Future My Choice (MFMC) (2012) Available online at http://www.myfuturemychoice.co.uk/ (accessed 3 May 2012).

National Advisory Committee on Creative and Cultural Education (NACCCE) (1999) *All Our Futures: Creativity, culture and education.* London: DfES. Available online at http://tna.europarchive.org/20050302191834/http://www.dfes.gov.uk/naccce/naccce.pdf (accessed May 2012).

Ofsted (2012) *Making a Mark: Art, craft and design education 2008/11.* London: Ofsted.

Plowden, B. (1967) *Children and their Primary Schools: A Report of the Central Advisory Council for Education.* London: HMSO.

Robinson, K. (1989) *The Arts in Schools: Principles, practice and provision.* London: Calouste Gulbenkian Foundation.

Robinson, K. (2001) *Out of Our Minds: Learning to be creative.* Oxford: Capstone Publishing.

UNESCO (2011) *Global Education Digest: Comparing statistics across the globe.* Paris: UNESCO Institute for Statistics. Available online at http://www.uis.unesco.org/Library/Documents/global_education_digest_2011_en.pdf (accessed 3 May 2012).

Williams, R. (2001) Culture is Ordinary. In: J. Higgins (ed.) *The Raymond Williams Reader.* Oxford: Blackwell.

Chapter 21

Educational research

So what?

Dan Davies

Introduction

Through this chapter you should gain:

- an appreciation of the importance of educational research for effective classroom practice;
- an awareness of the role of research in the life of a university department of education;
- an understanding of the continuity between undergraduate student research and that being undertaken by schools, postgraduate students and university tutors.

Research and the teacher

We live in a research-saturated culture. It seems that every day the media report on 'research' emanating from some university or other, often appearing to confirm the blindingly obvious, or find a link between a hitherto benign foodstuff and cancer. Market research is used to develop and sell us new products, while a writer might claim to be 'researching my new novel'. The word 'research' appears to have a multiplicity of meanings in the political, commercial and academic worlds – some of them trivial, some respected, some even sinister. It is perhaps not surprising that many teachers are cynical about research in general and educational research in particular. Research can be seen as the opposite of action: finding more out about a situation rather than doing anything about it. But perhaps this is an unfair characterization. We need to look again at research in general, and at educational research in particular, to ascertain whether it has any value to the development of teaching and learning.

The arguably tarnished image of research and its misuse as a term by advertisers can obscure its essential purpose and meaning. Cohen *et al.* (2006) characterize three ways of finding out about the world: reasoning, experience and research, the latter differing from the informal, *ad hoc* nature of the first two in that it is 'systematic, controlled, empirical and self-correcting' (ibid.: 5). Research *should* be able to produce reliable, valid and tested knowledge that will be of as much (or even greater) use to practitioners than their own reasoning and experience, which will necessarily be limited and subjective. Perhaps the most powerful argument that can be made for the importance of educational research, however, is for that undertaken by teachers themselves:

> We believe that lasting improvement in education can come about only through the
> work of individual teachers and school staffs as they seek, through inquiry into their

own practice, to provide optimal learning conditions for the particular students in their care.

(Wells, 2001: 2)

Comparisons between the medical and teaching professions (e.g. Hargreaves, 1996) might lead us to question why teaching is not more 'research-led' or 'evidence-based'. A surgeon from the nineteenth century transplanted into a twenty-first century operating theatre would be completely lost. He or she would not recognize the technology employed, would be unfamiliar with the vast majority of drugs used and treatments pre-scribed. In short, medical research has advanced practice in that profession to such an extent that it bears almost no resemblance to the work of physicians 100 years ago. By contrast, while the nineteenth-century teacher might be baffled by interactive white-boards and computers, he or she would almost certainly recognize most of the curriculum and the majority of the teaching methods. We might argue that teaching is a social science rather than a physical (or biological) one, dealing with human interactions which are less likely to change than the scientific interventions of drugs, so we might not expect such a radical change; but the lack of apparent 'progress' or sense of engagement with educational research by most teachers is still striking. It is important, however, not to overestimate medical research as a model for education. Pring (2000) warns that:

[C]aution is required even about this rather selective view of medical research, let alone about the connection between such research and professional practice. The Cochrane Centre in Oxford was established precisely because the connection between such research and professional practice was tenuous indeed.

(ibid.: 157)

Criticisms of educational research

One of the reasons for the lack of impact of educational research on practice might be a widespread mistrust of its quality or relevance on the part of teachers and other educa-tional commentators. Educational research has received widespread criticism, rising to a crescendo in the late 1990s. The main thrust of this criticism is summarized in the fol-lowing quote from a speech given by David Hargreaves to the Teacher Training Agency annual conference: 'educational research is poor value in terms of improving the quality of education in schools' (Hargreaves, 1996: 1).

This criticism implies either that the 'problems' worked on by educational researchers do not match well with the concerns of teachers, or that the results of such research are too poorly disseminated to inform and improve practice. The notion of 'value for money' relates to public funding for such research, either directly from government departments or from research councils, and suggests that the time has come for the beneficiaries of expenditure (by implication universities) to be called to account. The implied lack of engagement with the 'real world' of classrooms is echoed in the words of the then chief inspector of schools, who described educational research as 'irrelevance and distraction' (Woodhead, 1998). Its location in university departments of education led the then Secretary of State for Education to describe it as 'ivory-towerism' (Blunkett, 2000), taking place in privileged academic communities divorced from the realities of classroom life.

The quality of educational research also came under criticism at this time, being described as 'sloppy' (Tooley and Darby, 1998), i.e. not fulfilling many of the character-istics of research proposed by Cohen *et al.* (2007 – see above): systematic, controlled, empirical and self-correcting. In a study of the criticisms levelled at educational research in the late 1990s, Oancea (2005) found a litany of reported shortcomings in research methodology:

> Educational research was deemed non-reliable and inconclusive. Much of this was charged to flaws of empirical research, especially qualitative – lack of triangulation, sampling bias, purposeful distortion, ideological bias, etc; but also to flaws of non-empirical research, such as, contentiousness, superficial literature review, logical incoherence, excessive reliance upon secondary sources, adulation of great thinkers.
>
> (Oancea, 2005: 167)

As well as being an amplification of the charge of 'sloppiness', the list implies that educational research was mistrusted because of suspicions of ideological bias. This charge has come particularly from official and government sources, perhaps because the research concerned had been critical of government initiatives. Generally governments tend only to be interested in educational research that supports the policies they wish to intro-duce; hence the emphasis on the 'research-basis' for the Rose Review of approaches to the teaching of reading (2007). The small sample size and lack of corroboration for the single study used to justify the exclusive prescription of systematic synthetic phonics for five-year-old children have received little attention from government critics of research, despite the characteristics of 'sloppiness' highlighted above.

One of the solutions to the perceived ills of educational research has been to propose a 'new orthodoxy' in the approach adopted by future studies, drawn from the methodology of the physical and social sciences and already prevalent in much American educational research (large sample sizes, quantitative methods, controlled experiments). The likelihood of this approach producing more reliable, useful findings for teachers has been contrasted with the 'inconclusive' interpretative approach adopted by much current educational research:

> Two main possible patterns are largely distinguishable: one characterized by the emphasis on *cumulativeness/convergence/rationality/teleology* (the so-called 'new ortho-doxy'); the other by *discontinuity/divergence/non-rationality/non-teleology* in various degrees and combinations.
>
> (Oancea, 2005: 175, emphasis)

In this definition of the 'new orthodoxy', cumulativeness refers to the idea of each research study building on the findings of previous ones, so that they converge towards an agreed message. Rationality implies a belief that there is a 'truth' out there to be discovered by such research, and that researchers can be objective, disinterested observers. Teleology is the extent to which the research deals with issues central to educational practice – applied research, as opposed to that dealing with philosophical or political issues. Many educa-tional researchers are wary of this model and agree with Pring's (2000) argument that, since educational research deals with the complexity of 'social reality' it can never really be scientific. Yet perhaps they should also heed his warning that questioning 'the relevance of notions such as "truth", "knowledge", "objectivity", "reality", "causality" ... (has) caused much harm, playing into the hands of those who wish them ill' (Pring, 2000: 159).

While the 'new orthodoxy' has yet to direct the progress of much educational research in the UK, it has had the effect of concentrating the minds of educational researchers on the usefulness of their findings to practitioners. For example, the process by which university research is judged – the Research Excellence Framework (REF) – will from 2014 include a requirement to demonstrate *impact* on users (teachers, pupils, education policy). The Department for Education (DfE) publishes *Schools Research News* online, a digest of recent research findings for potential classroom implementation. These represent a purposeful attempt to move away from what Wellington (2000) describes as the 'osmosis' model of research informing practice: 'This is the idea that educational research somehow permeates or percolates into the discourse, thinking and practice of teachers over a long period, often unnoticed' (ibid.: 178). There has also been a new emphasis on gathering the results of research studies together to accumulate a weight of evidence on particular topics, as in the Evidence for Policy and Practice Information (EPPI) Centre research reviews (see Chapter 15).

This idea that educational research should be both 'use-inspired' and 'basic' implies that it should produce both practical and theoretical knowledge. The people in the best place to ensure that the knowledge generated is practical are teachers themselves. There is a long tradition of teachers as researchers; Dewey (1929) advocated that they should enquire into their own practice as a means of improving it. Perhaps the golden age of teacher research was the 1970s and 1980s, inspired by the action research movement. The rationale for practitioner action research was clearly articulated by Lawrence Stenhouse:

> [E]ffective curriculum development of the highest quality depends upon the capacity of teachers to take a research stance to their own teaching. By a research stance I mean a disposition to examine one's own practice critically and systematically.
>
> (Stenhouse, 1975: 156)

However, while teachers' enquiry into their own teaching will clearly generate practical knowledge, to produce 'basic' theoretical insights, such enquiry might need to be undertaken as part of a wider research community, including academics who are more theoretically orientated and who can help practitioners theorize their work. This is why many teachers undertake research into their own practice in collaboration with a university department of education, perhaps as part of a higher degree. Access to knowledge and expertise from a wide range of sources; a stimulating atmosphere of discussion and debate; opportunities to be part of larger collaborative projects all contribute to what we might call a 'research culture'. This is a concept that is explored in the next section.

A research culture

Schools can themselves become research cultures, with staffroom discussion becoming dominated by discussion of strategies to improve the learning experiences of pupils. However, in practice this is difficult to maintain because of the many domestic and administrative necessities of the school day. Most schools are too 'full on' to enable teachers to stand back and analyse their practice. While university departments of education might be criticized for being detached from the realities of the classroom, they do at least offer the opportunity for reflection and exchange of ideas. If not too exhausted after a day's work, teachers can find this atmosphere stimulating and refreshing. Tutors in the university need this interchange of views with teachers every bit as much as the teachers do. At one level, they require good relationships with schools in order to gain access for their own research, but the idea of academics doing the research for the teachers to implement is both out of date and deeply flawed; as Wellington argues, 'this metaphor, of one group providing a "commodity" to another (who may take it or leave it) is clearly unacceptable as a future model' (Wellington, 2000: 174).

Academics need to undertake their research with teachers as co-researchers, ensuring that it is 'use inspired' and involves the perspective of the user. Some research projects such as the *Listening to Children* project in Kingswood, Bristol (Barratt and Barratt Hacking, 2007) have involved children as researchers within their own schools. This effectively closes the loop between the originators of research and its ultimate beneficiaries, if we suppose that the ultimate aim of educational research is to improve children's lives.

But there is still a missing group here in our research culture. Most university schools of education exist to teach students, perhaps in the academic study of education as a subject, but also usually in training them to become teachers. Even though these students are often required to undertake some small-scale research as part of their qualification, they are often overlooked when it comes to thinking about the department's research culture. Not only is this missing an opportunity to benefit from the findings of some excellent student projects, but it is neglecting an important part of their induction into the professional life of the teacher. Education Studies is, as the name suggests, the study (i.e. research) of education. Therefore, undergraduate students of education need to be included in the research life of the department as much as possible from an early stage. They then become both the audience for research undertaken by tutors and schools, and later the presenters of the outcomes of their own research to these groups. This is equally true for trainee teachers, particularly those undertaking Master's level PGCE courses which require engagement with educational issues at an academic level.

Figure 21.1 is an attempt to represent diagrammatically the overlapping research interests and activities of students, teachers and academics in a university department of education research culture. The boxes round the edge represent the various activities undertaken within the department of education which sustain this culture. For example, research seminars could be undertaken as part of an undergraduate module; as a staff-only activity to discuss a colleague's project; as a partnership event to which local schools are invited; or as an evening of sharing ideas between teachers on a higher degree programme. But why not combine some of these contexts and audiences? Undergraduate students can present at the same seminar as PhD students, teachers and tutors, so that there is a building sense of continuity in research at all levels. Similarly, conferences could be combined to mix professional and academic purposes. Instead of mounting a series of events – one aimed at partnership schools, another at students, a third at teacher researchers or academics from other universities – a single event can have multiple strands. Often we assume that 'research' is only of interest to one type of audience.

A website is essential to keep members of the research culture up to date with current projects, events and opportunities for collaboration and funding. There might be a regular email newsletter to let everyone know what is going on and to remind or encourage them to get involved. Research groups or centres are another way to break down the

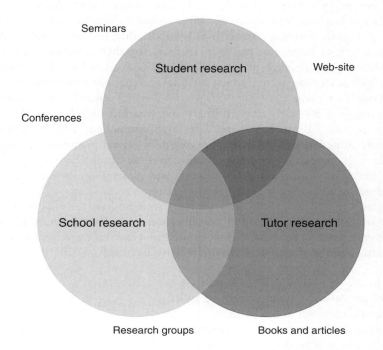

Seminars

Student research

Web-site

Conferences

School research

Tutor research

Research groups

Books and articles

Figure 21.1 Diagrammatic representation of a university school of education research culture

isolation often experienced by the educational researcher. Finding other people interested in the same topics or methodologies can save a lot of time in fruitless searches for relevant literature, and can also offer new researchers an apprenticeship by becoming involved in larger collaborative projects led by experienced staff. Such groups should certainly involve tutors, teachers and students with similar research interests working together – perhaps in formal, supervisory relationships but preferably more as equals. Books and articles constitute both the outputs of research activity within the culture (an in-house online journal can also be a useful form of dissemination) but also as resources for sustaining the intellectual life of the department. We all need to keep on learning, so the sharing of published literature in seminars or research groups can help stimulate new ideas or approaches to our work. We can also support each other by writing collaboratively or acting as 'readers' for each other's drafts before submitting them to the *Dragons' Den* of academic publishing. Often the most vital component of a vibrant research culture, however, is that which occurs naturally on an informal basis. Discussions over coffee or in the corridor often spark an idea or move a research project forward just as much as a more formal meeting or seminar.

Collaborative research within a university research culture

Students, schools and tutors need to learn to research together to enable a practice-based research culture to emerge. This is particularly important in the context of an increasingly fragmented state education sector, such as that in England where newly created academies, free schools and teaching schools are all being invited to pursue their own paths to success (DfE, 2010). By forming partnerships with the diversity of school models, a university department of education can help to draw together common strands of concern and establish shared research priorities. Bath Spa University has a large undergraduate Education Studies programme, which includes a compulsory first year research module and two other opportunities to undertake school-based research. The School of Education also trains over 500 early years, primary and secondary teachers on Masters level PGCE courses, each of which includes a research component. The Professional Masters Programme, aimed at practising teachers, includes several practitioner research modules, together with research methodology leading to dissertation. There is a growing interest amongst tutors in joining research groupings and undertaking research in collaboration with their own students and partnership schools.

On the undergraduate Education Studies programme, students have the opportunity to undertake research commissioned by, or in collaboration with, local primary schools. They often work with teachers to an agenda set by a current interest the school has with an aspect of teaching and learning. Recent examples have included:

- children's choice of play activities in reception;
- multiple intelligences and children's learning styles;
- children's use of computers in the home;
- gender differences in behaviour management strategies;
- quality of provision in extended schools.

A research conference at the end of each year enables students to present their findings to peers, tutors and the schools in which they have conducted the research. There is also the opportunity to write for publication in collaboration with staff, or to present at the annual British Education Studies Association (BESA) conference. Often the dissemination of such research can be the weakest element of an emerging research culture. Tutors, teachers and students alike can feel abashed at the prospect of sharing their work with a wider public, so few potential users benefit from the knowledge generated. Students in particular

> have limited possibilities or outlets to publish their findings, thus much of their work exists only as university assignment. However, when they are encouraged to describe their learning and their new understandings, the response from others (peers, experienced teachers and teacher educators) can be very positive.
>
> (Loughran, 2006: 144)

Starting out as an education researcher

Having, I hope, established the relevance and importance of research to students on an Education Studies programme, it remains nevertheless a daunting prospect to undertake a research project. A list of anxious questions may arise:

- What can I research into?
- What if it's a topic someone else has already done?

- What research methods should I use?
- How big should the study be? (how many schools/classrooms/children?)
- Do I have to produce new findings no-one else has come up with before?
- How do I write it up?
- Does my report have to include graphs and statistics?

Many of these queries can be addressed by referring to a good general guide to educational research. There are many of these on the market; one that we recommend for the research-based modules on the Education Studies programme at Bath Spa University is *Research Methods for Education* by Peter Newby (2010). This includes advice on selecting a research issue and framing a question; preparing a proposal; selecting either qualitative, quantitative or mixed methods; collecting and analysing data; using literature to discuss findings and writing up. There is a companion website for students and Newby helpfully demystifies the research process by acknowledging that it is inherently 'messy' because:

- The real world is not as clearly defined as research templates require.
- You will rarely have the luxury of an abundance of resources to draw on, so you will have to make real choices and compromises.
- The transition from fact to opinion is not always clear cut, especially when the research is on attitudes and beliefs.

(Newby, 2010: 28)

These should be words of comfort to an undergraduate dissertation student wrestling with a mountain of data which appear to bear little relation to the original research question. In my experience, research almost always yields too much data rather than too little; the skill is to select the data of most relevance to the issue being studied and not to worry about either not collecting enough or discarding that which is irrelevant.

The best student research projects are those which are very tightly focused and limited in scope. It is unrealistic for a single student undertaking an empirical study over a few weeks to answer a question such as 'is there a relationship between class size and educational attainment?' As well as being ill-defined (What age group(s)? Attainment in what area of the curriculum? How measured?) this question is simply too big and needs to be left for major national or international research projects to address. Equally, questions which attempt to link specific classroom approaches to 'improvements' in learning tend to be problematic because of the difficulties of measuring learning and establishing any kind of causal link, since there could be many other reasons why a particular child's attainment has improved.

Empirical research studies at undergraduate level tend to be successful in addressing their research questions if they are attempting to describe practice in a case-study setting (for example a single school's policy on X, or two teachers' contrasting approaches to Y); or to elicit school leaders', teachers', parents' or pupils' views of or attitudes towards an educational issue. Small-scale observational studies or surveys of attitudes employing semi-structured interviews or focus groups tend to be the most common approaches adopted, simply because they are achievable within the resources available and can say something meaningful in relation to the issue being researched. This is not to say that other more innovative methodologies – or indeed philosophical or policy-based enquiries – are not possible or potentially successful. It is just that case-study approaches (Stake, 1995) enable us to research a specific instance of a wider issue in depth and so lend themselves well to undergraduate projects. Whether the 'specific instance' is representative of the 'wider issue' is open to question, but most case-study researchers would rather claim that their work is 'illuminative' to others working in similar circumstances. While action inquiry may be the best approach for the practising teacher to research his or her own practice, for the undergraduate education studies student standing outside that professional role, the in-depth description of a particular situation achievable through case study is an attractive option.

However, if research can become a collaborative activity between students, their supervisors and teachers, this could increase the scope of what is possible within undergraduate projects. If a dissertation is part of a wider study being undertaken by a research group within the university in partnership with a number of schools, the student can be assigned a specific part of the project (e.g. classroom observations in different settings), capturing comparative data on a larger scale than is usually possible for the lone researcher. Involving student research more fully in the departmental research culture in this way could free it from the restrictions of case-study methodology and potentially produce findings of wider applicability, which would then be worthy of wider dissemination.

Summary points

- Discussion of the role, value and relevance of educational research for teachers and schools, examining some of the criticisms levelled at educational research during the 1990s and some of the responses of government and the research community in making the findings more applicable to classroom practice and readily accessible to users.
- Teachers should themselves be researchers of their own practice, along the lines suggested by the action research movement.
- University departments of education can play a key role in supporting such research and working alongside schools to identify priorities for developing evidence-based practice.
- Students in the university, whether undergraduate, postgraduate trainee teachers or practitioners taking higher degrees, all have an important part to play in this process, together contributing to a research culture.
- A research culture, located within the university–school partnership and supported by seminars, conferences, web-based dialogue and publication, can involve students, staff and schools researching and learning together.

Questions for discussion

- How would you defend the government funding spent every year on educational research?
- Do you feel part of a research culture in your university department? If not, what could be done to involve students more in the research of the department?
- What aspects of current educational policy or practice do you think merit further research?

Recommended reading

Cohen, L., Manion, L. and Morrison, K. (2007) *Research Methods in Education* (6th edn). Abingdon: Routledge.

This is the standard introductory text, now in its sixth edition. It provides a valuable overview of research paradigms, methodology and data collection methods.

Hitchcock, G. and Hughes, D. (1995) *Research and the Teacher: A qualitative introduction to school-based research* (2nd edn). London: RoutledgeFalmer.

This text is invaluable for teachers undertaking small-scale research projects in their own classrooms using ethnographic or action research methodologies. It takes an interpretative approach to the collection and analysis of qualitative data.

Newby, P. (2010) *Research Methods for Education*. Harlow: Longman.

This is an accessible yet thorough guide to educational research, covering a wide range of traditional and contemporary approaches to the collection and analysis of data.

References

Barratt, R. and Barratt Hacking, E. (2007) A Clash of Worlds: Children talking about their community experience in relation to the school curriculum. In: A. Reid, B.B. Jensen, J. Nikel and V. Simovska (eds) *Participation and Learning: Perspectives on education and the environment, health and sustainability,* Dordrecht: Springer.

Blunkett, D. (2000) Influence or Irrelevance: Can social science improve government? [Speech] made by David Blunkett, Secretary of State for Education and Employment, to a meeting convened by the Economic and Social Research Council, 2 February 2000, *Research Intelligence* 12–21.

Cohen, L., Manion, L. and Morrison, K. (2007) *Research Methods in Education* (6thedn). Abingdon: Routledge.

Department for Education (2010) T*he Importance of Teaching: The Schools White Paper.* London: Department for Education.

Dewey, J. (1929) *Experience and Nature.* New York: Dover.

Evidence for Policy and Practice Information (EPPI) (2007) *Eppi Centre.* Available online at http://eppi. ioe.ac.uk/cms/ (accessed 12 November 2007).

Hargreaves, D.H. (1996) *Teaching as a Research-based Profession: Possibilities and prospects. Teacher Training Agency Annual Lecture.* London: Teacher Training Agency.

Loughran, J. (2006) *Developing a Pedagogy of Teacher Education.* London: Routledge.

Newby, P. (2010) *Research Methods for Education.* Harlow: Longman.

Oancea, A. (2005) Criticisms of Educational Research: Key topics and levels of analysis. *British Educational Research Journal* 31(2): 157–84.

Pring, R. (2000) *Philosophy of Educational Research.* London: Continuum.

Stake, R.E. (1995) *The Art of Case Study Research.* Thousand Oaks, CA: Sage.

Stenhouse, L. (1975) *An Introduction to Curriculum Research and Development.* London: Heinemann.

Tooley, J. and Darby, D. (eds) (1998) *Educational Research: A critique. A survey of published educational research.* London: Ofsted.

Wellington, J. (2000) *Educational Research: Contemporary issues and practical approaches.* London: Continuum.

Wells, G. (2001) *Action, Talk and Text: Learning and teaching through inquiry.* New York: Teacher's College Press.

Woodhead, C. (1998) Foreword. In: J. Tooley and D. Darby (eds) *Educational Research: A critique. A survey of published educational research.* London: Ofsted.

Notes on contributors

All the authors are members, or former members, of staff of Bath Spa University where they have taught on the Education Studies programme. Stephanie Brown was a student on the undergraduate programme and Louise Gilbert a PhD student.

Viki Bennett is Principal Lecturer in Early Years Education and Programme Leader of the Education Studies Foundation Degrees. A former teacher, she became Early Years Adviser for Bristol City Council and has published reading guidance for early years teachers. She is currently researching the academic journey of teaching assistants who undertake the Foundation Degree.

June Bianchi is an artist, National Teaching Fellow and Senior Lecturer in Art Education. She manages and teaches courses in the arts across the spectrum of undergraduate, postgraduate and Masters programmes, as well as acting as Leader of the Centre for Research in Arts Education. June's research focuses on issues of identity within the arts and arts education, and she works in a collaborative way, exploring constructions of the self across an intercultural context, through exhibitions, video films and publications.

Stephanie Brown's main interests are the sociological issues associated with agency, discourse and the relationships between power and language. She has previously worked in the education and charity sectors, focusing on supporting children with disabilities and their families. She has presented a paper at the British Education Studies Association conference on global imaginaries, policy borrowing and political economy.

David Coulby is visiting Professor of Education, where he teaches the Masters module on Globalisation and Education. He has published widely, and occasionally deeply, in the fields of international education and interculturalism, most recently in an ongoing series of articles in *Intercultural Education*. His main research theme is the sociology and history of culture, though current interests include the political decline of Europe and the impact of climate change on curricular systems.

Denise Cush is Professor of Religion and Education and subject leader for Religions, Philosophies and Ethics. She has taught religious studies at school and university levels, and religious education in both primary and secondary teacher education. Her best known book is *Buddhism*, a textbook for A-level. Recent publications include several articles on teenage witches and young Pagans, co-editing an *Encyclopedia of Hinduism*, and articles on the place of religious education in state schools internationally. She is interested in experiential learning through fieldwork with religious/belief communities and has set up a website to facilitate such activities www.livingreligion. co.uk. She is Deputy Editor of the *British Journal of Religious Education*.

Dan Davies is Professor of Science and Technology Education and Head of Applied Research and Consultancy in the School of Education. His current research is in the fields of electronic assessment in science education, position-linked data-logging and creative learning. He has published widely in the fields of primary science and technology education, including *Design & Technology for the Future, Science 5–11: A guide for teachers* and in 2011, *Teaching Science Creatively*, all published by Routledge.

Graham Downes has a particular interest in the social and political aspects of education. He spent six years working as an advisory teacher, developing ICT projects and partnerships in inner city schools, for the Central Bristol Education Action Zone. He has an MSc in Education, Technology and Society and is currently undertaking a PhD examining free schools as political projects. He is a member of the Centre for Globalisation Education and Societies research group based at Bristol University. His teaching has a particular focus on multiliteracies, creativity and the sociology of education.

Christine Eden is Assistant Dean of the School of Education with an interest in using her background in sociology to explore education systems and access to educational opportunities. In recent years she has undertaken evaluation research into the interface between education and the needs of the labour market. Her research interest is in educational inequalities with a particular focus on gender.

Howard Gibson leads the full-time Masters in Education. He lectures and writes on issues concerned with literacy, links between language with power, Citizenship Education and the assumptions underpinning current models of Economics Education in England.

Louise Gilbert is Senior Lecturer in Early Years at Gloucestershire University. Her background is in health and education and her research interests are in holistic approaches to health and the promotion of sustainable futures. She is currently co-leading a research project focusing upon active participation and transformational learning, and is a lead researcher in a project promoting children and young people's resilience via the adoption of emotion coaching into practice. Her doctoral thesis is related to emotion coaching and the promotion of sustainable futures.

Nicki Henderson is Programme Leader for the Primary and Early Years PGCE. She is a passionate advocate of the potential and capabilities of young children and promotes a respectful and autonomous environment that allows for children's self-initiated activities. She is a keen advocate of the philosophies and practices of the Reggio Emilia Approach to Early Years Education and her research is linked to this.

David Hicks is Visiting Professor and internationally recognised for his work on the need for a global and futures dimension in the curriculum. He is now a freelance educator with a particular interest in how schools can help to create a more sustainable future. His most recent books are: *Sustainable Schools, Sustainable Futures* (WWF, 2012) and *Teaching the Global Dimension* (Routledge, 2007).

Alan Howe is co-subject leader for Education Studies. He has published in the areas of science and technology education, early years education and Education Studies. His research interest is in creativity in education.

Miriam Hutchings' main specialist teaching area is social and educational inclusion. Her research interests are the learning experiences of undergraduate students in Education

Studies and dyslexia and multilingualism. Her previous lives have included teaching in schools (nursery through to secondary) and universities, working as an Adviser for Special Educational Needs and within Ethnic Minority Support Services.

Elaine Lam is Research Fellow and formerly led the International Education degree programme prior to relocating to Canada. She has extensive experience consulting on education policy and programmes in both the UK and Ontario, Canada. Her PhD covered the role of multilateralism in shaping education policies in the Caribbean. Elaine is currently the Director for Business Development and Strategic Planning at The Chang School of Continuing Education at Ryerson University in Toronto and a Visiting Scholar at the Ontario Institute for Studies in Education (OISE) at the University of Toronto.

Tilly Mortimore joined Bath Spa from Southampton University in 2007 as Senior Lecturer in Education Studies and Inclusion and has developed a successful Masters programme in Specific Learning Difficulties (SpLD)/dyslexia. She currently researches dyslexia, inclusion and vulnerable learners and heads the research team in the Big Lottery funded project Dyslexia and Multilingualism, in partnership with the British Dyslexia Association. She has taught and lectured in a range of international educational and training contexts including South Africa. Her recent publications include a second edition of *Dyslexia and Learning Style* and, with Jane Dupree, *Supporting Learners with SpLD/dyslexia in the Secondary Classroom*.

Richard Riddell is Senior Lecturer in the School of Education. He teaches undergraduates predominantly, but also a changing group of postgraduates. Before coming to Bath Spa University, Richard had taught in comprehensive schools, had been a local authority officer for 22 years, including seven at Bristol as their Director of Education, had undertaken Education Consultancy for local authorities and learning and skills councils and been joint Head of Education for Amnesty International. His publications and research for the past 15 years or so have been concerned with disadvantage and how it affects students and their schools. His books are about urban schooling and the social basis of aspiration.

Janet Rose is Senior Lecturer and the Award Leader for Early Childhood. She has recently co-written a book on *The Role of the Adult in Early Years Settings* and is currently leading a research project on developing a community-wide, cross-disciplinary approach to promoting children and young people's resilience via the adoption of emotion coaching into practice.

Robin Shields is Senior Lecturer in Education Studies and leads the BA in International Education. His teaching and research focus on international development education and the globalisation of education. He has also worked in the international development sector, mainly in Nepal.

Catherine A. Simon is Senior Lecturer in Education and Childhood Studies. She has a particular research interest in Education policy which is the focus of her doctoral dissertation. Catherine has published work on Every Child Matters, schools and parent policy, multi-agency working and extended schools, including, with Stephen Ward, *Does Every Child Matter: Understanding New Labour's social reforms* (Routledge, 2010).

Hilary Smith is Senior Lecturer in Education with particular expertise in learning behaviour and early years. She is a recognised national school leader in behaviour and attendance (NPSLBA) and her research profile reflects a special interest in key aspects of social and emotional learning and development.

Stephen Ward is Emeritus Professor of Education and was Dean of the School of Education until August 2012. He was formerly the subject leader for Education Studies. A founder member of the British Education Studies Association, he was Chair in 2006–07. He has published books on the primary curriculum, primary music teaching and education studies. His research interests are education policy and university knowledge.

Index